EXPERIENCING BROADWAY MUSIC

The Listener's Companion
Gregg Akkerman, Series Editor

Titles in **The Listener's Companion** provide readers with a deeper understanding of key musical genres and the work of major artists and composers. Aimed at nonspecialists, each volume explains in clear and accessible language how to *listen* to works from particular artists, composers, and genres. Looking at both the context in which the music first appeared and has since been heard, authors explore with readers the environments in which key musical works were written and performed.

Experiencing Beethoven: A Listener's Companion, by Geoffrey Block
Experiencing Billy Joel: A Listener's Companion, by Thomas MacFarlane
Experiencing Broadway Music: A Listener's Companion, by Kat Sherrell
Experiencing David Bowie: A Listener's Companion, by Ian Chapman
Experiencing Jazz: A Listener's Companion, by Michael Stephans
Experiencing Led Zeppelin: A Listener's Companion, by Gregg Akkerman
Experiencing Leonard Bernstein: A Listener's Companion, by Kenneth LaFave
Experiencing Mozart: A Listener's Companion, by David Schroeder
Experiencing Peter Gabriel: A Listener's Companion, by Durrell Bowman
Experiencing the Rolling Stones: A Listener's Companion, by David Malvinni
Experiencing Rush: A Listener's Companion, by Durrell Bowman
Experiencing Schumann: A Listener's Companion, by Donald Sanders
Experiencing Stravinsky: A Listener's Companion, by Robin Maconie
Experiencing Tchaikovsky: A Listener's Companion, by David Schroeder
Experiencing Verdi: A Listener's Companion, by Donald Sanders
Experiencing the Violin Concerto: A Listener's Companion, by Franco Sciannameo

EXPERIENCING BROADWAY MUSIC

A Listener's Companion

Kat Sherrell

ROWMAN & LITTLEFIELD
Lanham • Boulder • New York • London

Published by Rowman & Littlefield
A wholly owned subsidiary of The Rowman & Littlefield Publishing Group,
Inc.
4501 Forbes Boulevard, Suite 200, Lanham, Maryland 20706
www.rowman.com

Unit A, Whitacre Mews, 26-34 Stannary Street, London SE11 4AB

British Library Cataloguing in Publication Information Available

Library of Congress Cataloging-in-Publication Data

Names: Sherrell, Kat, author.
Title: Experiencing Broadway music : a listener's companion / Kat Sherrell.
Description: Lanham, Maryland : Rowman & Littlefield, [2016] | Series: Listener's companion |
Includes bibliographical references and index.
Identifiers: LCCN 2016009832 (print) | LCCN 2016011285 (ebook) | ISBN 9780810889002
(cloth : alk. paper) | ISBN 9780810889019 (electronic)
Subjects: LCSH: Musicals–United States–Analysis, appreciation.
Classification: LCC MT95 .S55 2016 (print) | LCC MT95 (ebook) | DDC 782.1/4097471–dc23 LC
record available at http://lccn.loc.gov/2016009832

Printed in the United States of America

For Marie Roberts, with love:
this one's for Grandma,
my first piano teacher,
lifelong musician

CONTENTS

Series Editor's Foreword   ix

Acknowledgments: (or, Curtain Speech)   xi

Timeline   xiii

Introduction: (or, Overture)   xix

 1 A Great Big Broadway Show: *Wicked*   1

 2 The Roots of American Musical Theater: *The Great Ziegfeld*   21

 3 The Beginnings of Integration: *Very Good Eddie*, *Shuffle
        Along*, and *Show Boat*   41

 4 The Great Depression and the Great American Songbook:
        Anything Goes and *Porgy and Bess*   65

 5 A Golden Age of Broadway: Rodgers and Hammerstein   83

 6 Rock on Broadway: *Hair*   107

 7 Concept Musicals: *Sondheim! The Birthday Concert* and *A
        Chorus Line*   127

 8 Megamusicals: *Andrew Lloyd Webber: Gold Album* and *Les
        Misérables*   147

 9 Musicals for the MTV Generation: *Rent* and *Spring
        Awakening*   167

10 Diversity and Integration: *Hamilton*   187

Glossary   209

Selected Reading   217

Selected Listening   221
Index   225
About the Author   235

SERIES EDITOR'S FOREWORD

The goal of the Listener's Companion series is to give readers a deeper understanding of pivotal musical genres and the creative work of its iconic composers and performers. This is accomplished in an inclusive manner that does not necessitate extensive music training or elitist shoulder rubbing. Authors of the series place the reader in specific listening experiences in which the music is examined in its historical context with regard to both compositional and societal parameters. By positioning the reader in the real or supposed environment of the music's creation, the author provides for a deeper enjoyment and appreciation of the art form. Series authors, often drawing on their own expertise as both performers and scholars, deliver to readers a broad understanding of major musical genres and the achievements of artists within those genres as lived listening experiences.

The music of Broadway has furrowed its way into nearly every corner of American culture. Movies become musical shows (*The Producers*), musical shows become movies (*Les Misérables*), Broadway soundtracks sell millions of copies (*Cats*), million-selling albums become Broadway smash hits (*Tommy*), Broadway singers become movie icons (John Travolta), pop stars seek acceptance on Broadway (Elton John), Broadway shows find new audiences in special television productions (*Grease* in 2016), while classic television is reimagined for the Broadway stage (*Addams Family*). What a fabulous time period we live in where such dizzying and delicious cross-pollinations occur. But for those seeking to unwind the line of history Broadway music has followed, context is desperately needed. How can we know more about what we are *hearing* in the music coming from the stage? Is there a style of music simply called "Broadway"? Do we still call it "Broadway" music when it increasingly sounds just like what we hear on TV's *Glee* or classic radio or urban hip-hop neighborhoods? The Listener's Companion series is an ideal forum to address those questions for the contemporary enthusiast of Broadway music, and author Kathryn Sherrell (if you ever meet her, call her Kat) is ideally qualified to do just that by combining her astute writing style with her experience as a working pianist on Broadway shows in New York City. With recent credits that include *The Book of Mormon*, *In the Heights*, and television's *Smash* (a show about Broadway musicals), Ms. Sherrell is uniquely placed in the industry to guide you through listening to the groundbreaking *Show Boat* (1927) all the way to the current hit *Hamilton* (2015).

Gregg Akkerman

ACKNOWLEDGMENTS

(or, Curtain Speech)

In a theatrical production, there are many behind the scenes who make the show happen, and it is customary in a preshow curtain speech to thank those people and institutions. As in theater, so in writing: firstly, to series editor Gregg Akkerman, a heartfelt thank-you for the opportunity, and for the encouragement and guidance along the way; likewise to Bennett Graff, the senior music editor when the book was contracted, and to Monica Savaglia and Natalie Mandziuk at Rowman & Littlefield.

I owe a debt of gratitude to the Broadway professionals and other experts who took the time to talk or correspond with me about their areas of expertise and/or shows they worked on: Sharon Bookwalter, John Bronston, Kingsley Day, Matt Doebler, Oscar Andrew Hammerstein, Christopher Jahnke, Christine Toy Johnson, Alex Lacamoire, Telly Leung, Rori Nogee, Guy Olivieri, Chris Ranney, Trav S. D., and Ann van der Merwe. I am also so fortunate as to have many smart and opinionated colleagues, family, and friends, a number of whom generously agreed to read segments or drafts along the way. The insight and feedback of Gilbert Bailey III, Bill Berry, John Callahan, Michael Cassara, Kurt Crowley, Albert Evans, Erik Holden, Isaiah Johnson, Victor Legrá, Jesús Martínez, Velvet Ross, Anne Sherrell (a.k.a. Mom and most trusted grammar consultant), Ken Sherrell, Mona Sherrell, Tamara Sherrell, and Kwapi Vengesayi has been invaluable; certainly any remaining inaccuracy or lack of clarity is mine alone. To my multitalent-ed friend Cherie B. Tay, thank you for standing in Times Square traffic with me one August dusk to get photographs of my favorite Broadway views.

I am inspired every day by my talented and hardworking colleagues at the 5th Avenue Theatre in Seattle; by the personal and artistic integ-rity of executives David Armstrong, Bill Berry, and Bernadine Griffin; by the kindness and general musical genius of my boss, music supervis-or Ian Eisendrath; by the professional excellence and humor of my "Clubhouse" officemates Dane Andersen, Lauren Smith, Trisha Hein, and Kelsey Thorgalsen. I am fueled by Julia's homemade treats and Mo's candy jar, by conversations with Albert and Orlando, and most of all by being a part of a supportive professional creative community. It's a blessing to have colleagues I want to spend time with even after long hours of work, and who leave me with energy and inspiration to write about the same subject in the time left over.

Thanks to my dear friend and creative partner in crime Natalie Wil-son for her wisdom and support; to my besties Sarah Smith and Erin Lecocq and my sister Tamara for sanity-preserving conversations and care packages; and to Ruth Landstrom and Nathan Palmer, who helped me develop the mental game to complete a long-term project in a new medium. At the risk of never having a boyfriend again, I will throw in a shout-out to my cat, Diesel, who provides me with reliably amiable company so long as I keep his food dish topped up. Last but not least, to my parents, Anne and Paul, who are themselves avid musicians and scholars, and who kept any apprehensive grimaces to themselves when I chose to pursue a career in the arts: thank you, Mom and Dad, for your support and encouragement.

TIMELINE

1735   *Flora*, an English ballad opera (opera using existing popular songs, equivalent to modern-day jukebox musical) in Charleston, South Carolina, marks first performance of an opera in the English colonies of what is now the United States

c. 1830   Thomas "Daddy" Rice, a white traveling actor, popularizes his blackface act as a African American stereotype character, Jim Crow

1843   First organized minstrel troupe show, with the Virginia Minstrels in New York

1860s   First transcontinental telegraph and railroad revolutionize long-distance communication and travel in United States, laying foundation for vaudeville circuits that will span the nation by the 1890s

1865   First well-known African American minstrel troupe, Brooker and Clayton's Georgia minstrels, formed

1866   *The Black Crook*, widely considered the first modern musical for its use of songs and dances interspersed in a play, premieres on Broadway and runs a record-breaking 474 performances

1877   Phonograph invented by Thomas Edison

1879   Gilbert and Sullivan's hit comedic operetta *HMS Pinafore* establishes them across the English-speaking world; because of lax international copyright law, their works are cheaply produced and widely used in parody because of their widespread familiarity

1881   Tony Pastor pioneers family-friendly, all-variety entertainment format that becomes known as vaudeville

c. 1890 Music publishers centralized in block of Manhattan nicknamed Tin Pan Alley for the clamor of popular song demonstrations happening in their offices

1891   Charles K. Harris sentimental ballad "After the Ball" published.

1893   Chicago World's Fair

1900   Publication of L. Frank Baum's children's novel, *The Wonderful Wizard of Oz*

1903   Victor Herbert's first major hit operetta, *Babes in Toyland*

1904   George M. Cohan has first Broadway hit with *Little Johnny Jones*, which includes the song "Give My Regards to Broadway"

1907   First edition of the *Ziegfeld Follies*; the popular annual revue will run every year but one until 1931

1907   Viennese composer Franz Lehar's hit operetta, *The Merry Widow*, arrives on Broadway

1911   Irving Berlin's breakthrough international hit song "Alexander's Ragtime Band"

1915   Jerome Kern, Guy Bolton, and Schuyler Greene write the first two musicals for the tiny Princess Theatre; Kern and Bolton are later joined P.G. Wodehouse as a writing team

1917   First jazz recordings released by the Original Dixieland Jass Band

1921   *Shuffle Along* is a hit on Broadway, rekindling popularity of African American musical comedies

1927   *Show Boat* premieres at the Ziegfeld Theatre; first musical to combine black and white ensembles; step forward in integrating songs with plot

1931   *Of Thee I Sing* becomes first musical to win the Pulitzer Prize; awarded to Ira Gershwin, Morrie Ryskind, and George S. Kaufman but omits composer George Gershwin because the prize only applied to text

1934   *Anything Goes* opens on Broadway

1935   *Porgy and Bess* opens on Broadway

1938   *Hellzapoppin*, longest-running Depression-era musical, opens on Broadway

1943   Rodgers and Hammerstein's first collaboration, *Oklahoma!*, opens to great commercial success, which spurs a golden age of about two decades during which many classic shows will be written by them and their contemporaries

1947   First year of annual Antoinette Perry Awards for Excellence in Theatre (better known as the Tony Awards)

1954   Early rock hits "Shake, Rattle and Roll" and "Rock around the Clock" released

1957   Stephen Sondheim debuts as a lyricist with his work alongside Leonard Bernstein, Arthur Laurents, and Jerome Robbins in *West Side Story*

1960   Musical comedy *Bye Bye Birdie* uses rock to satirize pop culture

1962   Sondheim makes his Broadway debut as a composer-lyricist with *A Funny Thing Happened on the Way to the Forum*

1965   Original release of *The Sound of Music* musical film starring Julie Andrews

1967   Joseph Papp, founder of the New York Shakespeare Festival, inaugurates the Public Theater, his new indoor performance complex in the East Village, with the new musical *Hair*

1968   *Hair* opens on Broadway

1970– Concept musicals *Company* and *Follies* open on Broadway,
1971   beginning a long collaboration between Sondheim and
            director Harold Prince

1971   *Jesus Christ Superstar*, Andrew Lloyd Webber's first musical
            on Broadway

1975   *A Chorus Line*, developed at the Public, opens on Broadway

1975   *The Wiz* opens on Broadway, first African American cast
            musical to win Tony for Best Musical

1979   *Evita* opens; Andrew Lloyd Webber has had at least one
            show, often more, running on Broadway ever since

1979   "Rapper's Delight," Sugar Hill Gang's breakthrough hip-hop
            single, released

1980   *Les Misérables* French concept album recorded

1981   MTV launched

1982   Lloyd Webber's *Cats* begins its Broadway run, which will last
            eighteen years (on the long side for the life span of a cat)

1987   *Les Misérables* opens on Broadway

1988   Lloyd Webber's *The Phantom of the Opera* begins Broadway
            run; still open as of this writing

1994   Disney opens *Beauty and the Beast*, first Broadway stage
            adaptation of one of its animated features

1996   *Rent* transfers from short sold-out Off-Broadway run at the
            New York Theatre Workshop to a become a hit on Broadway

2001   *Mamma Mia* launches modern popularity of jukebox
            musicals with its ABBA hits

2003   *Wicked* opens on Broadway

2007   *Spring Awakening* opens on Broadway with score by pop
            songwriter Duncan Sheik

2008   Lin-Manuel Miranda uses rap as storytelling tool in musical
            In The Heights

2010   Sondheim's eightieth birthday celebrated at Lincoln Center
            with *Sondheim! The Birthday Concert*

2015 *Fun Home* librettist Lisa Kron and composer Jeanine Tesori win Tony for Best Score, first female writing team to win the award in that category

2015 *Hamilton* opens on Broadway after a sold-out Off-Broadway run at the Public

2015–2016 Season characterized by diversity: racially diverse casts and stories including *Allegiance*, *The Color Purple*, *Hamilton*, *On Your Feet*, *Shuffle Along*; Deaf West revival of *Spring Awakening* features actors performing sign language alongside singing counterparts. Also features major revivals of *Fiddler on the Roof* and *She Loves Me*, and new musicals by Andrew Lloyd Webber and Duncan Sheik

INTRODUCTION

(or, Overture)

Bright lights! Sparkly costumes! Jazz hands! Broadway musicals are everywhere, not just in theaters across the United States and around the world, but in a plethora of musical episodes on popular television shows, in shows like *Glee* that revolve around musical theater, in the recent resurgence of classic musicals broadcast live on major networks, on airwaves in the form of show tunes that have become popular, and occasionally even sampled in the track of a hip-hop song.

Why should we care about musicals? They are dismissed by some as an inferior hybrid art form, or as simply too commercial to have any artistic merit. But it is their very reach, and their use of commonly understood musical symbolism, that gives musicals their power to communicate. Shows can be cathartic, or can at least offer perspective on our problems; the ancient Greeks sought answers to their deepest existential questions in their theater. Even the lightest, most seemingly inconsequential comedies are opportunities to make memories with loved ones or decompress after a stressful day. Musicals have become an international language, and a fragment of lyric or song can become a touchstone for people who otherwise have nothing in common. They deal with enduring, universal themes of the human experience, and they are often at the forefront of cultural and political conversations. Understanding more about musicals and the sounds they use to illuminate a story can offer insight into deep questions in our lives, or at the very least enhance our enjoyment of a ubiquitous form of entertainment.

Broadway is, to employ a terrible pun, a broad topic, and there were several obvious options in determining repertoire for this listener's companion. Rather than cramming every show worth a mention into these pages with very little exploration of any of them, or focusing on shows within a narrow time period I deem the "most Broadway" of Broadway music, I have chosen to create a "sampler platter" of approximately one century of American musical theater. I introduce the basic tenets of theatrical music with *Wicked*, a high-profile contemporary frame of reference, then take the listener back to the roots of American musical theater and explore chronologically through the 2015 blockbuster *Hamilton*, covering approximately a decade per chapter, making an exception to the American circumscription for the European musicals that dominated the 1980s. The decade-by-decade approximation is very loose, because trends in musical theater do not obligingly sort themselves into neat time periods, and because I fit several decades' worth of nineteenth- and early twentieth-century background information into chapter 2. As with any sampler platter at a restaurant, this book will inevitably be missing a favorite morsel, or contain a weird item you never would have thought to try à la carte. My aim is to provide a framework for understanding the language of theatrical music that will pique the reader's curiosity about the musicals mentioned in these pages as well as the ones that didn't fit.

In the course of my research, I discovered to my surprise a far greater number of women working throughout Broadway history than I had expected to find. For any number of entrenched societal reasons that should continue to be analyzed in places other than this book, the genre-defining figures of the type to end up in an anthology such as this one are rarely women. And, with each shake of the historical sieve, only the biggest monoliths make it to the next generation's anthology, leading to the assumptions that women have just begun to work in creative or leadership positions and that they can only become better represented going forward, when in fact neither of those statements is necessarily true. It is far from my intention to write a feminist history masquerading as a Broadway sampler platter, but while only one of the recordings explored has a female composer, lyricist, or librettist, I do feel compelled as a female author and musical theater professional to ensure that women receive recognition for their contributions to the music of the shows in question, including but not limited to the ones visible onstage. In the same way, it was also my aim to show the ways in which racial diversity has evolved on Broadway, from the largely segregated shows and audiences of the early twentieth century, to the recent prevalence of shows with diverse casts intended for diverse audiences. Race is a prominent topic in this supposedly fluffy genre, and my hope is to fairly represent the discussion on race in and about many of the shows covered in this book.

I have made an effort to minimize technical musical terminology, and when the use of musical or theatrical jargon is unavoidable, terms appear in bold type and are also included in a short glossary at the back of the book.

Each chapter contains one or more dramatized listening experiences, as is the conceit of the Listener's Companion series. These "vignettes" include a variety of hypothetical settings, professional, amateur, and educational, showing how Broadway musicals are woven into many aspects of our culture. Most of the listening experiences explore a specific audio or video recording. There are a great many Broadway cast albums among them, but in the interest of variety, and also to highlight certain aspects of repertoire and composers, I have included other formats as well. In an effort to show bygone performance styles while considering availability of recordings, chapters 2, 3, and 4 include two 1936 films and a 1954 live television broadcast, respectively. Chapter 4 pays special attention to the unit of the song, focusing on the golden era of the Great American Songbook and illustrating how the relationship between song and show evolved over the course of the twentieth century. The works of Stephen Sondheim and Andrew Lloyd Webber are explored in chapters 7 and 8, an overview and opportunity for comparison of their styles provided by a birthday concert celebrating the former and a greatest hits album of the latter. All the recordings explored in the chapters are widely available at present, easy to find online or through major retailers, and are listed in the Selected Listening section at the end of the book. The Selected Reading list contains some of the books I found to be most enlightening during the course of my research; as indicated in the descriptions, some are friendly to the lay reader, while others contain advanced musical analysis.

One more thing before the house lights are dimmed and the curtain goes up: Broadway is a very self-referential form, and as such, the reader will probably get the most out of reading this book in order, picking up terminology and tradition along the way. However, when referencing a subject discussed in a different chapter, I often parenthetically point the reader to that source, so the musicals in the book can also be explored in a sort of connect-the-dots manner. Either way, it is my aim that both a Broadway novice and a seasoned theater geek can find something new to add to their inside-joke vocabulary.

1

A GREAT BIG BROADWAY SHOW

Wicked

It's Wednesday evening, and around seven or eight o'clock in theaters across the United States, lights will go up on the performance of a musical. The show might be a familiar classic or an edgy new work, and it might be performed in a historic regional theater, in a performance space that hosts Broadway tours, or in one of the several dozen theaters that are clustered along *the* Broadway in New York City, the thoroughfare from which the most prestigious live theater in the United States takes its name. Technically, a Broadway theater is a professional theater with more than five hundred seats located in Manhattan's theater district, but for many people, the word "Broadway" is simply synonymous with musicals.

Performances are well into their first act by 9:00 p.m. in New York, while across the country in downtown Seattle at six o'clock, restaurants are starting to fill up with pretheater patrons who have tickets to a seven-thirty show. This particular Wednesday hums with anticipation of the first night of the national tour of *Wicked*, which will play for several weeks at the nearby Paramount Theatre. Ninety minutes before showtime, the Paramount bustles with preparations for the evening's show. Audio technicians test dozens of microphones as well as keyboards and sound equipment, while the rest of the crew makes sure every costume, prop, and set piece is in its proper place.

Musicians start trickling into the pit to warm up and practice difficult passages in the music. The orchestra for *Wicked* combines rhythm section elements of a rock band (bass, drums, guitar, keyboard) with instruments of a symphony orchestra to capture the epic sound and wide range of musical styles the score requires. Like most Broadway tours, *Wicked* travels with a conductor and several musicians, hiring local musicians in each city to fill out the rest of the parts. There are only a few hours of rehearsal to put all the music together in each new stop on the tour, so local musicians have to be well prepared in advance.

The actors are busy warming up their bodies and voices and getting into costumes and makeup with the help of dressers and makeup artists. At seven o'clock on the dot, the stage manager's voice comes over the loudspeaker, giving the company a half-hour call. At this point, all the actors must be present and accounted for. Preparations continue backstage, with the stage manager calling fifteen minutes, five minutes, and finally, places for the top of the show. What the audience sees onstage at *Wicked* is just the tip of the iceberg. Musical theater is a fundamentally collaborative art form, involving many people whose work is invisible except to those on the inside.

As to a musical's script, some are written entirely by one person, but more often they are written by a team of two or more people who share the responsibility of writing the text and music. The theater-specific term for the person who writes the dialogue and other nonsung text is **book writer**, or librettist. The lyrics might be written by the book writer, by the composer, or by a lyricist who specializes in writing words that are to be expressed musically. The music and lyrics to *Wicked* were written by veteran Broadway composer Stephen Schwartz, whose other hit shows include *Godspell* (Off-Broadway 1971) and *Pippin* (Broadway 1972). He draws from diverse artistic palettes, having studied piano and composition at Juilliard and drama at Carnegie Mellon. He gained professional experience with popular music before *Godspell* became a hit when he was twenty-three. *Wicked*'s book is by Winnie Holzman, who is known for her Emmy-winning television writing on *My So-Called Life*.

Once they have a script drafted, the authors assemble a creative team: a director, music director, and choreographer, who instruct performers (who are usually hired with the help of a casting director) on interpreting the script according to the authors' vision. In addition to working with costume, set, and lighting designers to create a look for the show, the director often provides valuable feedback to the authors during the process of creating a musical. The adage "Writing is rewriting" is nowhere more true than in a Broadway musical. Even getting to the point of bringing in actors, directors, and designers takes a lot of work, and then musicals go through a developmental process of workshops, pre-Broadway productions, and Broadway previews during which many changes are made before the big opening night.

Like many musicals, *Wicked* is an adaptation of another art form, in this case Gregory Maguire's 1995 novel *Wicked: The Life and Times of the Wicked Witch of the West*. The Wicked Witch's name in the novel and musical is Elphaba, which Maguire derived from the name L. Frank Baum (El—F—Ba), the author of the widely read 1900 children's novel *The Wonderful Wizard of Oz*. The story of Kansas farm girl Dorothy's cyclone-caused trip to Oz and her plight to escape the Wicked Witch has been adapted many times, most notably in the 1939 classic film *The Wizard of Oz* starring Judy Garland, and in the musical *The Wiz* (1975), an African American urban retelling of the story. The adaptations tell how Dorothy's quest to get back home is impeded by the Wicked Witch of the West and helped by Glinda the Good. *Wicked* offers an alternate version of the tale: Elphaba's backstory and her perspective on the event.

Wicked the musical makes several significant changes from *Wicked* the novel, and streamlines the novel's epic story to focus on the relationship between Elphaba and Glinda. Since its opening on Broadway in 2003, the musical has played all over the world, and has been seen by tens of millions of people on Broadway, on tour, or in one of numerous international productions. It's a quintessential **integrated book musical**, and a great jumping-off point for understanding. . .

HOW MUSIC WORKS IN A BROADWAY SHOW

What is music's job in an integrated book musical? First of all, what is an integrated book musical? In a nutshell, it is a musical in which the songs, dance, lighting, costumes, et cetera—all the elements of the production, are woven seamlessly into the plot (this might seem like a given, but we will see in the couple of chapters after this that it was not always the case). Theater is essentially a complex set of symbols, and theatrical music is full of sounds that have strong associations with good (harp **glissando**) and evil (trombones and timpani: dun-dun-DUNNN!!!). Theater music works in tandem with all the other parts of the show to make the audience understand and feel something about the characters and the story, through songs that advance the plot and help us understand the characters.

The most concrete way music conveys information is through the actors' voices. Lyrics, melodies, and styles of singing show us a great deal about the characters onstage, what they're going through, and how we the audience should feel about it. We identify with the main characters during their solos, and come to understand their community through the ensemble numbers; duets and other small-group numbers give us insight into important relationships.

Music's basic building blocks—rhythm, melody, and harmony, as Aaron Copland defines them in his classic treatise *What to Listen For in Music*—are also storytelling building blocks. Theater music draws from well-known genres of music, whose distinctive rhythmic styles have emotional significance: a driving rock groove, an orchestral **fanfare** (a musical flourish), or a seductive tango enhance the meaning of the lyrics—or reveal things the lyrics do not.

And what would a musical be without a tune to hum on the way out of the theater? A good melody can capture the spirit of a show and linger long after the final curtain has fallen. A melody, or sometimes a short musical idea called a **motive** or **leitmotif**, is often used to represent a character or theme in the story. Schwartz uses this technique throughout the score of *Wicked*, making it not just a collection of show tunes, but a unified score. Harmony also creates mood and conveys information. Notes that clash inform the listener of conflict or danger, and groups of pitches in chords and scales can sound cheerful or melancholy together. The former mood is usually associated with **major** chords and keys, and the latter with **minor**.

Rhythm, harmony, and melody can lead to a sense of finality, or can leave the listener yearning for a resolution. One important way of creating an emotional arc in a show is by controlling when the audience is allowed to applaud. Many songs have a **button**, a last "bump" at the end, like a punctuation mark. Buttons can be large (!) or small (.), and they signal a definite end to a song, allowing emotional release and applause. However, if the story calls for the emotion built up by the song to be carried into the next scene, the composer will create an ending, sans button, that seems to trail off like this . . .

See, you didn't clap, did you? It may sound ridiculous, but to button or not to button is a big part of creating the emotional experience of a show.

The size of the **pit orchestra** and the instruments chosen for it have a huge impact on the atmosphere created by the music. The composer may write the orchestrations but more often will work with an orchestrator. The degree to which a composer will specify his or her wishes to the orchestrator varies, but it is generally a very close collaboration. The orchestrator is instrumental (pun intended) in determining the size and makeup of the orchestra, and decides which instrument should play which musical lines, down to the last detail of texture and mood. The **timbre**, or tone quality, of instruments accompanying a song or scene can define a moment—imagine a melody played by a flute versus an electric guitar.

Last but definitely not least: the sound department. All the sounds in modern shows—voices, music, sound effects—are run through speakers. The sound department is responsible for mixing all the input from dozens of microphones in such a way that the show sounds good, and the most important things (like the lead vocal) are distinguishable, and the unimportant things (like an actor changing costumes or going to the bathroom) are not heard. Getting a good balance can be particularly challenging in theaters that were built before advanced sound technology existed. In addition to amplifying and mixing the sounds the actors and orchestra produce, they also add their share of atmosphere to make the show compelling and believable: reverb, surround sound, and other such effects are the milieu of the sound department.

WICKED **PERFORMANCE, NATIONAL TOUR**

Warning: spoilers ahead! This section deals with a hypothetical performance, and includes discussion of a couple of plot points that are not obvious on the Broadway cast recording.

Excitement fills the air of the theater as you settle into your seat and read the short artists' biographies in the program. Many of the actors are just starting their careers; if they do well on tour, it can spell future work, maybe in *Wicked*'s Broadway company or on other shows with the same writers or creative team. The lights dim, and the preshow announcement acknowledges local sponsors and reminds you to silence your phone, which you double-check to make sure it won't ring during the show.

Schwartz starts *Wicked* with a doomsday crash and exciting offbeat accents—a figure that clearly represents the Wicked Witch. This "wicked theme" will recur in various guises as the story progresses. William David Brohn's orchestrations paint the vivid colors of another world: a frenetic repeated figure in the woodwinds and percussion accompanies monkeys like the ones you remember from *The Wizard of Oz*. After the music is transformed into something magical by the harp and chime tree, the trombones, horns, and bass oboe play a prominent melody whose warm tones and sweeping rise and fall create a sense of openness and anticipation. You will hear this melody many times later, often attached to the lyric "unlimited." You have in fact heard this melody before, though you don't recognize it because the rhythm has been changed: in homage to one of Harold Arlen's best-loved songs from *The Wizard of Oz*, Schwartz borrowed the first seven notes of "Over the Rainbow," altering the rhythm to create this "unlimited" motive.

The **opening number** of a musical sets the tone for the rest of the show and gives the audience an idea what to expect of the story. A buoyant fanfare heralds the citizens of Oz, but you can't quite tell if the Ozians are happy or angry: they proclaim "good news," but the bottom note played by the low instruments of the orchestra gives an ominous effect to the bright chord the chorus is singing. The good guys from the movie have become a threatening mob, in the first of many twists on familiar characters in this alternate history.

Schwartz gives Glinda the first solo on her grand entrance, musically designating her as a leader. She comes across as a bit of a charlatan, singing made-up words like "rejoicify" in a light soprano tone. The crowd is in no mood to rejoicify, crying with a mob mentality, "No one mourns the wicked." This is not pretty choral singing with sweet little solos; it is guttural, primal use of the voice, giving sound to text that expresses fear and hatred. Schwartz emphasizes the word "wicked" by putting "wick-" on a strong beat and a slightly dissonant note. He will similarly bring out other important words throughout the score—good, bad, wonderful, truth, deserve. Such recurring words illuminate the themes of the story.

One of the challenges of writing a show, and another task of the opening number, is to give the audience enough background information, or **exposition**, for the show to make sense. The challenge lies in conveying that information through characters' conversations with each other in a natural way, without having them explain things that would be common knowledge among the characters in the story. *Wicked* accomplishes this by having Glinda, pressed by the crowd for details on the Wicked Witch's death, rationalize the Witch's wickedness by explaining her childhood. Nothing brings back memories like the sounds of yesteryear, and Glinda's narration is accompanied first by a waltz, then a light swing tune, as we learn that the Wicked Witch's mother had an affair with a traveling salesman while her husband was away on business. To add insult to cuckoldry, the salesman steals the melody the husband used to say good-bye. We infer that the salesman with his seductive "green elixir" is the father when the baby is born green.

With a dissonant chord on the word "green," the music shows us that the Wicked Witch was rejected from the moment she was born, but the Ozian crowd doesn't want to hear any rationalization. Whose side is Glinda on, anyway? Her echoes in the final chorus are revealing. She echoes only "Goodness knows," avoiding the Ozians' vocal condemnation of the Wicked Witch. When the chorus intones that "the wicked" (impersonal, rhetorical) "die alone," Glinda responds, "*She died alone*"—not a despised hypothetical symbol but a personal, specific *she*. Yet Glinda seems to enjoy the adulation of the crowd at the end of the number, proclaiming the "good news" and joining in the last shrill statements of "wicked!"

Where does rhetoric end and Glinda begin? The music and lyrics of the opening number raise more questions than they answer. We can't know it yet, but the question marks and layers themselves *are* the answer. The opening number has done its job, getting us ready for the story we're about to see. The opening declares that this show will be full of spectacle—and beware: it may cause you to reconsider what is good, what is bad, and what is wicked.

How else to tell an alternate history than with a flashback, starting with the familiar ending of the Wicked Witch's death, then going back in time to reexamine the facts? Now that the foundation has been laid, it's high time to introduce the Wicked Witch. Holzman's dialogue and Schwartz's music work in perfect synchronicity to transition from the mob scene to the flashback that will make up the rest of the show. The setting is an exclusive boarding school, implied by a four-part chorale of the type sung at churches and private schools. "Dear Old Shiz" is a paean to privilege and respectability, but the music is subversive: the sustained "zzz" at the end of the chorale reminds us not to take any institution too seriously.

It's a rough first day at school for Elphaba. Her classmates recoil at her verdant appearance; her father makes clear by his words and by a gift of jeweled shoes that her sister Nessarose (who is not green skinned but is in a wheelchair) is the favored daughter; and the headmistress, Madame Morrible, assigns her the annoying, self-important Galinda as a roommate (Galinda will later change her name to Glinda). The final straw is when Mme. Morrible starts to take Nessarose away. The "unlimited" theme, with one note modified to creepy effect, plays as Elphaba unwittingly unleashes her magical powers on the crowd.

It turns out that Mme. Morrible has spent years searching for someone with raw sorcery talent like Elphaba's. A majestic chorale plays as Mme. Morrible begins to speak-sing about the opportunities that might lie ahead should Elphaba "make good." When first Elphaba sings, she has to borrow Mme. Morrible's melody, because she has no melody of her own for these thoughts; this is the first time she has ever allowed herself to dream. "The Wizard and I" is a type of song known in musicals as an **"I-want song."** The audience has to identify with the **protagonist**, or main character, enough to care what happens to him or her in the story, and an I-want song usually occurs early in the show to get the audience on board right away. Elphaba's desires are universal; she craves acceptance. If the Wizard accepts her for who she is, so will her father, her sister, and all of Oz. The music and Elphaba's dreams grow wilder with every verse, until the music opens up under her vision of a future that is unlimited. It's the first time we've heard words to the "unlimited" theme—fitting, since it's probably the first time Elphaba has said those words herself. Elphaba has found something to yearn for, and the song gets the audience on her side.

To make things more interesting, Galinda wants to learn sorcery, too, but Mme. Morrible has rebuffed her attempts to get into the sorcery seminar, adding to Galinda's annoyance at having to room with Elphaba. "What Is This Feeling," a duet between the two roommates, begins with them both writing a letter home. Their words to their parents are a character study: Galinda, adept at euphemisms, has a long, frilly list of adverbs to capture Elphaba's . . . indescribability, while Elphaba flatly calls a spade a spade (or, in this case, a blonde a blonde). This is the first time Elphaba and Galinda relate to each other in song, and their **unison** melody indicates that they may be more alike than they'd care to admit. The song is also a send-up of a love song; if each instance of the word "loathe" were replaced with "love," it would mean something totally different, but the lyrics would still make sense. Through this song, the battle lines are drawn, and, as the chorus shows us by singing with Galinda, it's Elphaba against the world.

At least Elphaba finds a kindred spirit in one of her professors. Dr. Dillamond is also an outsider; he is a goat and the only animal on the faculty at Shiz. In the duet "Something Bad," Dillamond shares with Elphaba the rumors he has heard about his fellow animals losing their powers of speech. The rumors are given weight when he loses control of his own voice and bleats like a sheep, "Something ba-a-a-a—." The anxiety of this song is heightened by a murky, flowing triplet accompaniment reminiscent of the film music that **underscores** the "lions and tigers and bears" scene of *The Wizard of Oz*. The flowing figure is broken up and passed among different instruments, as if the orchestra were gossiping among itself; it is punctuated by splashes of sound from the violins, mandolin, and other instruments. The effect is a musical manifestation of the unknown, of shadows, of things about which it is not safe to speak openly. This music will recur later in the show, highlighting moments of political oppression. The plight of the animals gives Elphaba a stronger sense of purpose in meeting the Wizard, and the unresolved ending leaves the audience without the emotional release of applause at the end of the song.

Instead of finishing with a button, the music transitions seamlessly into the swaggering entrance of that standard fixture in almost every musical: the love interest. The newcomer is a prince named Fiyero, we are treated to his manifesto of sorts, which builds into a number with considerable plot-thickening properties. Fiyero's rock-star status is made clear by the use of the acoustic guitar (you can imagine Fiyero traveling across Oz with a six-string strapped across his back), and his casual delivery of his carefree, careless philosophy of "Dancing through Life." He enunciates the lyrics just enough to make the words understood, and frequently scoops or falls off notes. Fiyero's charisma takes hold of Galinda and the other students at Shiz (except Elphaba), and they join him to party at the Ozdust Ballroom.

Several important things happen as a result of this party. Galinda, her sights set on Fiyero, rids herself of her unappealing Munchkin suitor Boq by convincing Boq to ask Nessarose to the dance. Enamored of Galinda, Boq obliges, freeing Galinda and Fiyero to start their romance. Next, Galinda regifts an unfashionable tall, pointy black hat to Elphaba. The short dialogue sequences are underscored with music, and interspersed with choruses of "Dancing through Life," which take on a slightly different meaning each time.

Most importantly, Elphaba and Galinda become friends. Seeing her sister's happiness at being invited to the dance, and having no fashion sense, Elphaba decides to trust Galinda's good deeds, and repays her "kindness" with a real favor: convincing Mme. Morrible to allow Galinda to take the sorcery seminar. Consequently, Galinda feels terrible when the Ozdust Ballroom falls silent upon Elphaba's arrival in the awful black hat. The silence is deafening, more effective than any music could be, and underscores the contrast between Elphaba and her peers. Fiyero and the others use dancing as a way to ignore their problems or keep up appearances. For example, when Boq says, "Let's dance," it covers a lie to Nessarose that sets their destiny in motion. Elphaba, on the other hand, uses her humiliating moment in the center of the dance floor to confront Galinda's treatment of her in all its pettiness. Galinda, having a change of heart, turns her back on her popular friends to join Elphaba. The music starts, tentatively at first, combining the "dancing through life" theme with the "unlimited" theme, and growing to include the whole group as Elphaba and Galinda's friendship is born.

If "Dancing through Life" is Fiyero's manifesto, then the next song is Galinda's. "Popular" has all the characteristics of a comedy song: it starts the old-fashioned way, on a punch line and a **bell tone** that gives Galinda her note, and the light, perky accompaniment imitates Galinda's "flirt and flounce," as she milks every word to great comedic effect. It's interesting to note Galinda's facility with words in her lyrics and dialogue throughout the show. Among the clever rhymes and alliteration in this song, there are none of the malapropisms or "ditzy blonde" techniques that she employs in other parts of the show. Don't be fooled by her perky melody or cartoon character voices: the intelligent words she chooses in the privacy of her own dorm room leave us in no doubt about Galinda's ambitious, calculating brand of intelligence. Galinda fails to turn Elphaba's plain frock into a ball gown, because as Mme. Morrible could have told you, she's no good at casting spells. But as she has just been singing, it's not about "brains or knowledge"—it's about appearances, and Galinda is nailing that aspect of the game.

When Galinda sticks to her strengths, she succeeds, and when she puts a flower in Elphaba's hair, a delicate accompaniment pattern that contrasts with the rest of the song shows Elphaba believing in her own outer beauty for the first time. This hint of music is soon brought back as the accompaniment to Elphaba's solo, "I'm Not That Girl." Elphaba has a lot on her mind in this moment—Dr. Dillamond has been fired, and his replacement teacher brought a lion cub in a cage, which caused Elphaba to lose her temper and unleash her powers—but it is Fiyero and the burning moment of connection when they freed the lion cub that is foremost in Elphaba's mind. As Elphaba admits to romantic desires, the accompaniment confesses along with her, in a rhythm that imitates "Dancing through Life." She allows herself to dream "ev'ry so often," and the music follows her into a distant key and a romantic waltz-like rhythm, but she concludes with her plaintive repeated note melody from before, describing Galinda as "that girl" Fiyero would want.

Before Elphaba sinks into the depths of despair, Mme. Morrible brings glad tidings: the Wizard wants to meet Elphaba! A short reprise of "The Wizard and I" rekindles Elphaba's excitement and reveals that Mme. Morrible's specialty is casting weather spells. Galinda is preoccupied with boy problems when she comes to see Elphaba off; she changes her name to Glinda in a desperate ploy to get attention from Fiyero, who seems to be gravitating toward Elphaba. Seeing her friend despondent, Elphaba invites Galinda-now-Glinda to come with her to the Emerald City to meet the Wizard.

A trip to the big city is just the thing to snap them out of their blues. Their "One Short Day" of sightseeing begins with the hushed excitement of a metropolis in the morning. The ensemble sings in unison, a syncopated "one short day" as the scenery shifts to reveal the fantastical denizens of the Emerald City going about their business. Glinda and

Elphaba go to a show, *Wiz-O-Mania,* on Oz's equivalent of Broadway. The show-within-the-show is an old-fashioned Broadway number with the chorus singing the praises of the Wizard. Things could not be better for Elphaba: she is finally in a place where everyone is green like her, Glinda said they were best friends, and she's about to meet the Wizard!

. . . who is not at all like Elphaba expected. The booming voice is just the effect of a machine, and the man who steps out from behind it declares himself just "A Sentimental Man," whose one wish is to be a father. The melody is masterfully written, but the Wizard speak-sings it in a way that fails to inspire confidence. His vocal interpretation tells us he's a milquetoast, a people pleaser. How did he ever get to be such a great leader? Still, in one of his more sweeping phrases, he declares that "ev'ryone deserves a chance to fly," and Elphaba is still hopeful and willing to prove herself to the Wizard.

And prove herself she must. This is a turning point for Elphaba: she is at the precipice of realizing her dreams with the Wizard, and her next few actions will determine her future. Music plays almost continuously under the scene, weaving in themes from earlier in the show to add dimension to the momentous events onstage. Mme. Morrible, who has risen to the position of the Wizard's press secretary, brings Elphaba the Grimmerie, the ancient book of spells. Elphaba's test is to cast a levitation spell on the Wizard's monkey servant, Chistery. She instinctively intones a spell from the Grimmerie, and the Wizard and Mme. Morrible rejoice as the bevy of flying monkeys indicate that Elphaba is even more powerful than they'd hoped. Elphaba, in a deadly moment of silence, intuits that the Wizard and Mme. Morrible are behind the oppression of the animals and that the Wizard has no real power and needs her powers to continue his reign. The Wizard, Mme. Morrible, and even Glinda see this as a win-win situation, but the music sides with Elphaba: the accompaniment pattern for "Something Bad" plays, as if in slow motion, as she realizes her dreams are built on a lie.

The moment Elphaba chooses to flee rather than be a government dupe, she ceases to be the Wizard's protégée and becomes a fugitive. As Elphaba runs, electric guitar (an instrument with a rebel connotation) plays the "no one mourns the wicked" melody—the first statement we've heard of anything "wicked" since before the flashback. It presages the smear campaign that is the logical next step for Press Secretary Morrible.

The chase is on, and Glinda runs after Elphaba to convince her to make things right with the Wizard. In "Defying Gravity," we once again find our two witches **belting** identical melodies in each other's faces. Glinda entreats Elphaba with the tune from Elphaba's own I-want song, reminding her musically as well as lyrically what she has yearned and worked for. But Elphaba, her nascent dreams in tatters, takes the melody to a different end than she did in "The Wizard and I," illustrating her fateful change of mind: having found her faith in the Wizard to be built on a lie, she will put her faith in herself instead. Familiar music plays as Elphaba gives Glinda the chance to join her, telling her that together they can be unlimited. For two glorious phrases, they sing together, but Glinda is not quite convinced. The lyrics from the beginning of the song have a different meaning when they are sung now, as the two best friends sincerely wish each other happiness before going their separate ways. Glinda stays grounded while Elphaba defies gravity vocally and literally. Her determination growing, Elphaba sings a thrilling high riff as she tells the public to look for her in the western sky. She sarcastically borrows the Wizard's line about "a chance to fly," and all of Oz points at her and sings of her wickedness as she rides out act 1 on a broomstick and her newfound confidence.

INTERMISSION

Act 1 has ended with a perfect cliff-hanger. What will happen to Elphaba and Glinda? There is a long line at the merchandise table where people can buy souvenirs, including the original cast album, which features Idina Menzel and Kristin Chenoweth, the original Elphaba and Glinda. As you make your way through the crowd, you think about the way Elphaba and Glinda sing, and how it reflects their personalities. Glinda sounds alternately like an opera singer or a Valley girl: everything she does is highly trained and stylized, for public presentation. When she's upset or thinks no one is listening, she uses a more natural voice. Elphaba's vocals are uncensored, and occasionally very powerful—just like Elphaba herself.

ACT 2

Act 2 of *Wicked* keeps the tension high by not showing Elphaba right away, instead paralleling act 1 by opening with the ensemble. The frenetic monkey music is now added to the accompaniment, implying the constant undercurrent of stress the Ozians feel as they sing the familiar tune of their terror of the Wicked Witch. The scope of their fear can be heard clearly, in the range between the ringing, dissonant chord as they sing of her alleged lies, to the unison almost whisper, "Where will she strike next?" The unknown is ever so much more terrifying than that which is known, and rumors grow.

As in act 1, Glinda soon enters to make a public speech, this time flanked by Mme. Morrible and Fiyero. Glinda's announcement is made in a quintuple **time signature**, five quick beats in groups of three plus two making a cheerfully lopsided lilt: "*Oh* what a *cel-e-bra*-tion we'll *have* to-*day!*" The celebration concerns Fiyero, who is introduced as the man in charge of the Wicked Witch hunt, and as Glinda's fiancé—the latter of which Fiyero learns at the same time as the crowd. As Glinda give the details of their engagement, her voice is as steady and perky as ever, but the rhythm of the music betrays her. The lilting quintuple **meter** is still there, but it is interrupted by other rhythms—Glinda is literally losing her groove. As the rumors continue to fly among the Ozians, the lilting rhythm turns driving, reminding you of the anxious triplet accompaniment of "Something Bad." The music reaches a high point as the crowd grabs onto the idea of a possible solution, which they sing three times as their determination grows to "melt her!" At the end of the song, Glinda's voice expresses her complicated emotions. Her voice struggles to stay steady along with the rhythm, and she falters as the façade begins to crack, going so far as to admit that her happiness comes at a price—but then she takes a breath and belts through her internal conflict. She must choose between the integrity of her friendship with Elphaba and her love of popularity and power, and the music makes clear her choice: Glinda finishes her public speech in a strong voice, supported by the ensemble that sings her praises.

Elphaba finally surfaces at the unhappy home of Nessarose and Boq. When their father died, Nessarose became the governor of Munchkinland, and in an attempt to keep Boq with her, she has stripped Munch-

kins of most of their freedom. Elphaba tries to help her sister by en-
chanting Nessarose's sparkly shoes so that she can walk, turning them
ruby red in the process. Elphaba rejoices that something good has finally come of her powers, but the instrumental music underneath hints
that "something bad" will come of this, and sure enough, her good deed
quickly backfires. Boq, seeing that Nessarose can walk, uses the same
tune in which he lied to her in act 1 to tell her the truth: he lost his
heart to Glinda long ago, and wants to go to her engagement ball.
Nessarose botches a spell intended to make Boq lose his heart to her,
and Elphaba saves his life by turning him into a tin man with no need
for a heart. Finally realizing she and her self-loathing sister can't help
each other, Elphaba departs to the Emerald City to make things right
with the monkeys, leaving Nessarose to put the blame for Boq's heart-
less state on Elphaba.

The transition into the next scene works like a movie montage: much
is said in little time, with no words. As Nessarose exits, Fiyero and
Glinda dance in semidarkness to a sweeping waltz version of "No One
Mourns the Wicked," the music implying that Elphaba is on both their
minds in the midst of their engagement ball. There is a triumphant
fanfare as they pose center stage and then exit arm in arm: Glinda is
getting what she has always wanted. The "unlimited" theme announces
Elphaba's arrival to the Wizard's lair, and the music fades into a scene
between the two of them.

The dialogue in which the Wizard tries to convince Elphaba to join
him flows seamlessly into the introductory verse of "Wonderful," with
the Wizard rationalizing his almost accidental rise to power to a lightly
swung tune. The orchestration mocks him, using the banjo, slide whistle, and woodblock—not the dignified instruments of a statesman, but
rather ones that are associated with comedy acts that lampoon politi-
cians. In trying every rhetorical tactic to convince Elphaba to come over
to his side, the Wizard makes the most explicit statement of the theme
of the show: in a lyric that rivals the cleverest polysyllabic rhymes of the
Great American Songbook, Schwartz rhymes "few at ease" with "ambi-
guities" in explaining that what goes down as history is simply a version
of events that people agree on. This point echoes Glinda's pronounce-
ments in "Popular"; in fact, "Wonderful" illustrates a strong similarity
between the Wizard and Glinda. Lacking any real talent, they capitalize
on people's perception that they are wonderful, popular, or good.

Elphaba finally accedes to the Wizard's proposition, on the condition that he set the monkeys free, but she changes her mind and vows to fight him when she finds Dr. Dillamond, now cowering and speechless after being imprisoned. Fiyero saves the day: rushing in with guards to apprehend Elphaba, he instead uses his position to act as a sort of double agent, and runs away with her instead. The Wizard and Mme. Morrible fret over how to bring Elphaba into custody, and Glinda, betrayed by the two people she loves most, suggests they use Elphaba's sister as bait. Mme. Morrible takes the idea further than Glinda intended, conjuring a cyclone that will put Nessarose in real danger.

As Mme. Morrible works her magic, Glinda reprises a song from act 1. **Reprises**, or shorter reiterations of a previous song, are usually given to the character who first sang them, but this time the tables are turned, and it is Glinda who laments "I'm Not That Girl" whom Fiyero loves and chooses. We hear Glinda in a rare moment with nothing affected in her voice, nothing put on for public consumption, only the private devastation of losing her love to her best friend.

Glinda's reprise leads directly into Elphaba and Fiyero's love duet, "As Long as You're Mine." The introduction is the "wicked" theme, only this time it is not a bold statement by the full orchestra, but a gentle and plaintive one featuring the piano, flute, and clarinet. This song is in fact the seed of the pervasive "wicked" theme; it existed long before the rest of the score. It is a **trunk song** from 1971, so called because Schwartz wrote it for a rock musical called *The Survival of St. Joan*, for which he was the music director. The song didn't end up in the show, and it was relegated to a figurative (or possibly literal) trunk of songs cut from shows. Schwartz liked the song, but could never find a place for it in any of his shows until he was playing with musical ideas for *Wicked*. He realized if he played the intro "Rachmaninoff-style" (as it is described in Carol de Giere's *Defying Gravity: The Creative Career of Stephen Schwartz from* Godspell *to* Wicked), imitating the suspenseful chords of Rachmaninoff's Prelude in C-sharp Minor, he could use it as a theme for the Wicked Witch. In addition to the influence of the Russian romantic composer, the song bears some of the hallmarks of progressive rock, as altered tones are added to basic rock chords to invite us to join in on the cocktail of emotions Elphaba and Fiyero are experiencing. They are overjoyed to be together, yet painfully aware that their union may last "just for this moment." There is a poignant change from major to minor at the end of each chorus where they ache with the knowledge that their happiness is fleeting. The third time, singing together "until it is through . . .," they sustain each chord twice as long as in previous choruses, unwilling to let go of the moment. Their passion is subtle, befitting a show that is suitable for families, but the lyrics imply the sexual connection that is beautifully described in the novel. When at the end of the song Elphaba confesses to feeling wicked for the first time, it's open to interpretation whether she's believing her own bad press or referring to her amorous activities with Fiyero. Either way, the clear ending of the song gives everyone a chance to take a breath and applaud before the storm hits.

Morrible's cyclone brings us to the beginning of *The Wizard of Oz* narrative, and as in that story, Elphaba does not manage to save her sister or the ruby slippers that are all she has left of Nessarose. Fiyero arrives just in time to save Elphaba, sacrificing himself to the guards who take him out to a field as the "wicked" theme comes back with a vengeance. Glinda runs after them, her heart-wrenching cry of "Fiyero!!!" dovetailing with Elphaba's furious one as the latter rises through a trapdoor in the stage, full of rage and purpose.

In "No Good Deed," her last big solo, Elphaba searches desperately in the Grimmerie for a spell that will save Fiyero's life. Like in Glinda's "Thank Goodness," the wild variations in Elphaba's vocals illustrate the transformative nature of her actions: this is where she begins to sound like—to *become*—the Wicked Witch. As Elphaba intones spells, Schwartz gives her a narrow vocal range that widens as she becomes more frustrated. The orchestra's accompaniment becomes more agitated, its triplet figure quickening to faster sixteenth notes, as Elphaba awakens to the fact all her attempts to do good have instead turned into a "generous supply" of disasters. She draws the horrifying conclusion that "no good deed goes unpunished," spitting out the word "unpunished" like the bitter lesson it is. Elphaba becomes introspective, her voice soft, as she recalls the consequences of her good intentions toward Nessarose, Dr. Dillamond, Fiyero—she snaps back to the present at Fiyero's name, repeating it with such a cry that he must be able to hear it, wherever he is. The orchestra changes to a heavy, marchlike pulse as Elphaba puts herself on trial in the court of self-awareness. Once again, her voice begins in a narrow range as she questions her motives, widening to the final histrionic leaps as she vows never to do a good deed again.

A drumroll cuts through the applause, and the orchestra resumes the marchlike beat. The ensemble's lyrics clearly indicate they are on a witch hunt, but even a non-English speaker could understand the action from the militaristic style of music and the rising vocal interval that imitates a hunting horn. Elphaba's "no good deed" figure is now used by the chorus, but with opposing words—"wickedness must be punished"—as once again, Schwartz's music and lyrics draw the battle lines between Elphaba/Wicked Witch and the self-righteous crowd. A short underscored scene draws a parallel between Elphaba's narrative arc and Glinda's: her well-intentioned pursuit of goals hasn't turned out so well, either. She's gotten the powerful life she wanted, but now she's stuck in a lie.

In the next scene, Glinda tries to convince Elphaba to release Dorothy and give herself up. Elphaba gives in only after the monkey Chistery delivers a letter to her. Elphaba doesn't read the letter out loud, but the strains of "As Long as You're Mine" and Elphaba's stony face imply that the letter contains bad news about Fiyero.

Elphaba admits her shortcomings in a lyrical twist on the "unlimited" theme, and passes the torch (or rather, the Grimmerie) to Glinda, intoning as if it's a spell, "now it's up to you." Elphaba makes Glinda promise not to try to clear her name; Glinda will need to keep her political power to continue Elphaba's work. Alone, neither of them has any power, but together, they are unlimited. In the duet "For Good," they acknowledge the importance of their friendship, taking time to listen to each other at last. This is the surrender, the final farewell, and the tempo at the **bridge** ("and just to clear the air") increases with the urgency of them each asking for forgiveness before they part ways. The end of the song bears witness to the effect they've had on each other's lives in a melodic echo of the "two best friends" moment from "One Short Day," and they finish the song in unison. The music says, whatever our differences have been, they have been "for good."

Elphaba pulls a curtain across the stage and instructs Glinda to hide, and the ensemble sings in close harmony with no vibrato, giving a ghostly edge to the words "the wicked die alone." Glinda clutches the Grimmerie as she watches Elphaba's death at Dorothy's hand as if it were a shadow play. During Elphaba's watery demise, we hear a dissonant version of the "unlimited" theme, as if the orchestra is playing in two keys at once. Mournful woodwinds recall "For Good" while Glinda retrieves all that is left of Elphaba: that awful black hat, and a green bottle that belonged to Elphaba's mother.

Glinda recalls the only other place she's seen a bottle like that—when the Wizard offered her a drink from it. When Glinda confronts the Wizard, his own prerecorded voice sings his tune from the opening number, the sound of the memory of a certain dark-eyed beauty he once seduced when he was on the road. The Wizard makes the slow realization while reprising "A Sentimental Man," getting only as far as the word "father" before he breaks down: he has found and lost his daughter at the same time. Glinda banishes him from Oz, then has Mme. Morrible thrown into jail.

As the guards haul Mme. Morrible off, we come full circle with a fanfare and a proclamation of "good news" that is musically identical to the moment in the opening. This time, though, instead of leading directly into Glinda's speech, the music diminishes to a sparse instrumental fragment of the accompaniment to "No One Mourns the Wicked," as Elphaba's side of the story is resolved. The viola, its dark tone perfect for elegiac moments, is featured as the lights come up on the familiar brainless *Wizard of Oz* character, the Scarecrow. He knocks three times on the trapdoor, and applause ensues after Elphaba emerges, crying "Fiyero!" for the benefit of anyone who missed the foreshadowing of the multiple instances of words like "brainless" in Fiyero's lyrics. This musical isn't a tragedy, after all—Elphaba's desperate spell casting during "No Good Deed" at least managed to save Fiyero's life. The letter contained the news of his transfiguration, not his death, and so the plan was hatched for Elphaba to fake her death and escape with him.

There is joy in their reunion, but also solemnity, because they must now live in exile. The orchestra and ensemble resume "No One Mourns the Wicked," but all the anger present in the opening number has been taken out of the music, mirroring Glinda's stricken face and our new knowledge of the story. The singing and accompaniment are articulated softly instead of aggressively, the key is a step lower than the fever-pitched opening, and (among other the changes in the orchestration) the drums are silent this time around. Glinda's speech is also different: no more frilly cadenza, this time she uses her real voice to speak to the Ozians, accepting the mantle of leadership Elphaba placed upon her.

As the show draws to a close, the final phrases from "For Good" are woven into the tapestry of the **finale**. Glinda will follow Elphaba's wishes by continuing her work—which depends on her not clearing Elphaba's name. So, the ensemble gets the last word, with the verdict on Elphaba that will go down in history: "wicked."

Wicked's opening and finale function as bookends, and the development of musical themes we have experienced throughout the show give a satisfying depth to their return in the finale. And while the show is perfectly enjoyable to those who are not familiar with *The Wizard of Oz*, there is certainly a layer of added delight in understanding the references, large and small, that are peppered throughout the show. Theatergoers and composers love a good inside joke, and Broadway scores are filled with countless—one might say *unlimited*—references to music from songs and shows that have come before. In consideration of the value of knowing the backstory and getting the inside jokes, let's go on a flashback of our own, into Broadway history . . .

2

THE ROOTS OF AMERICAN MUSICAL THEATER

The Great Ziegfeld

A number one train pulls into the station, a few dozen feet below the hustle and bustle of Forty-Second Street and Broadway in New York City. The doors open, and, as the Stephen Sondheim song from the musical *Company* so aptly tells it, "Another Hundred People" get off the train. Although that song was written in 1970, the lyrics and the relentless motion of the music could be setting the scene any time after the subway system began running in 1904. New York is perpetually a city of transplants, and in the late 1800s and early 1900s, they arrived in record numbers. In particular, immigrants from Ireland, Germany, and Eastern Europe, and African Americans from the Southern states came to New York with the hope of building better lives than the ones they left behind. Many of those who stayed in the area took the subway to this crossroads for business or pleasure.

The business of this area, then called Longacre Square, was the carriage trade: horses and the attendant manure, peep shows, thievery. The theater scene had been born farther downtown in Manhattan, but had slowly been creeping northward for decades. Starting in the mid-1890s, impetuous impresarios such as Oscar Hammerstein I (whose namesake grandson we will encounter in later chapters) began constructing theaters north of the unofficial taboo line at Forty-Second Street. In 1904, the *New York Times* set up shop in the heart of the square. Its publisher convinced the mayor to make the intersection a hub for the city's new public transportation system, and the newly renamed Times Square was on its way to becoming a world-class landmark. The subway meant that the new, elegant theaters were accessible to more people than ever before; attendance increased, and more theaters were built in the area.

Their stages were filled with a wide range of music—the romantic waltzes of Viennese operetta, **up-tempo** ragtime songs that owed their catchy rhythm to African American music, European brass band marches, and more. Musicals themselves were a hodgepodge of unrelated songs, dances, and sketches. In fact, the first prototype of a modern Broadway musical, *The Black Crook* (1866), came about almost by accident when the members of a visiting Parisian dance troupe were given jobs in a drama after their performance venue burned down. The presence of the extra dancers turned what might otherwise have been a normal play with some music into a song-and-dance extravaganza. Much of the music and comedy of the time was based on ethnic stereotypes as varied as the passengers on the subway—Italian, Yiddish, Irish, German, Chinese, African American, and many more. Plots for musicals were frivolous, far fetched, and totally beside the point, a fact of which the makers of musicals were fully aware. For example, the program credit for the libretto of the 1914 musical comedy *Watch Your Step* reads, "Plot, if Any, by Harry B. Smith."

Perhaps the most exciting illustration of the unimportance of the story in a musical comedy was the opening night of *Stop! Look! Listen!* in 1915. John Philip Sousa and his band, who were doing a show nearby, made a surprise appearance during the act 3 finale. The show's star, irresistible French beauty Gaby Deslys, and the rest of the company of *Stop! Look! Listen!* finished the final song, "Everything in America Is Ragtime," with the additional complement of the most famous band in the country. The show's producer, Charles Dillingham, recounted the tale in the unpublished draft of his memoirs, remembering the surprise as a compliment typical of the nice things the popular bandleader would do. Something like that would never happen in the complex, story-driven machines that are modern Broadway shows!

BROADWAY'S ROOTS IN VARIETY—THE MINSTREL SHOW

The variety-based format grew out of the blackface **minstrel show**, a genre that was wildly popular, integral to the development of American entertainment—and deeply controversial. Race is a recurrent theme in American musical theater, reflecting the fundamentally interracial culture of the United States. In addition to the prominent influence of European and African performance traditions, American entertainment also reflects the effect on those traditions of life during formative times in America, particularly the oppression of African Americans through slavery and subsequent forms of racial discrimination. The minstrel tradition is thought to have begun in 1828 when white actor Thomas "Daddy" Rice developed an act as a character called Jim Crow, a caricature of a simpleminded slave (for whom laws discriminating against people of color were later named). Rice was widely imitated, and a genre developed, featuring songs and sketches that parodied many aspects of society at the time, and portrayed negative stereotypes of African Americans played by white actors in blackface makeup.

Minstrel shows featured racist archetypes such as Jim Crow and his urban counterpart, Zip Coon, who dressed sharply but spoke in malapropisms. Even the seemingly positive aspects of the portrayal of African Americans—that they were happy-go-lucky and naturally musical—had origins in something more sinister in real life. As Yuval Taylor and Jake Austen detail in the second chapter of their book, *Darkest America: Black Minstrelsy from Slavery to Hip-Hop*, happy-looking slaves reflected well on the master, so a slave might be obliged to dance or sing for the master and his friends, adding a tarnished dimension to blacks performing for a white audience. They write, "The more brutish the relationship, the less sophisticated the foolery—brutes have little capacity to appreciate subtlety or nuance. In America, where slavery was particularly brutish, slaves had to act particularly clownish." Furthermore, in the years leading up to the Civil War, the spurious rationalization that slaves benefited from slavery was reflected in songs such as "Dixie" (the de facto anthem of the Confederacy), in which the singer reminisces about a rose-tinted version of Southern plantation life. Minstrel shows were also a reflection of the attitudes toward women in a society in which white women were held up as objects whose purity must be guarded at all costs, and black women were viewed as objects who could be bought, sold, and either sexually exploited or desexualized. The difference in the way white and black women's sexuality is perceived in the public sphere plays out in how female roles throughout Broadway history have been written, typecast, and performed.

All this notwithstanding, the minstrel show became widespread family entertainment for black and white audiences alike by the 1850s, and remained the most popular form of mass entertainment until vaudeville began to supplant it in the late 1800s. In a culture where slavery was either reality or recent history, the fictionalized version of that world, racist stereotypes and all, captured aspects of American culture not to be found in entertainment imported from Europe. Minstrel songs were one of the first genres of American music to have roots in both black and white traditions. They became so widespread that many, like Stephen Foster's "Oh! Susanna," are well known over a century after the minstrel show gave way to other forms of entertainment. Ragtime, explored in more depth in chapter 3, is a descendant of the minstrel song, and its combination of **syncopated** (offbeat) melodies and on-the-beat accompaniment forms the basis for the classic, upbeat Broadway sound.

The structure of minstrel shows also influenced later forms of entertainment. By the 1840s, the shows were performed in three stylized segments by troupes such as the Virginia Minstrels. The first segment was a series of jokes and songs that featured a straight man–stooge relationship between the interlocutor (the only performer not in blackface) and two blackface comedians, Tambo and Bones. The latter two sat on either end of a semicircle of performers, playing the tambourine and a set of rib bones and lampooning the interlocutor's faux-upper-class speech. Next came the **olio**, which was the direct predecessor to the vaudeville shows that crisscrossed the nation for half a century. In the olio, a variety of novelty acts were performed, often culminating in a spoof of a political stump speech. The afterpiece, a one-act piece that was often a parody of a popular play or novel, formed the third part of the show.

African American performers had their own minstrel troupes by the 1850s, donning blackface and performing for both black and white audiences. Troupes like Brooker and Clayton's Georgia Minstrels were billed as "authentic" interpreters of minstrel material, a marketing advantage especially once spirituals—actual African American music, as opposed to minstrel songs largely penned by white songwriters—were added to the repertoire in the 1870s. Minstrel performance was the first major foot in the door for African Americans in show business, bringing with it the double-edged experience of having to weigh the benefits of individual success against the effects of portraying a stereotype.

Comedian Bert Williams (b. 1874) was one of the most prominent African American performers to get his start in black minstrel shows. With his comedy partner George Walker, he was on Broadway in *In Dahomey* (1903), the first full-length musical written by and cast with African Americans to play a major Broadway theater. Seven years later, he was the first African American to be a featured performer in an otherwise white cast Broadway show when he was hired to star in the *Ziegfeld Follies of 1910*. When several cast members threatened to quit over having to share the stage with Williams, producer Florenz Ziegfeld informed them that while they were replaceable, Williams was not. For Williams, who faced criticism for playing along with minstrelsy stereotypes, blackface performance was many contradictory things: an inconvenience, a liberating mask behind which it was easier to create a character, and an opportunity to subvert the racist status quo. In addition to being a way into the entertainment industry for black performers, post–Civil War minstrelsy brought about the juxtaposition of blackface performers with actual African American performers, which ultimately led to the end of blackface as a mainstream tradition. As vaudeville expert Trav S. D. explained in an e-mail interview, "The presence of actual African Americans in show business . . . is what eventually killed blackface. Seeing them side by side pointed up the unfairness and inaccuracy of the stereotype by direct example."

Viewed at a distance of more than a century, it is the element of overt racism in minstrel shows that stands out most starkly. What is harder to perceive at such a remove is that minstrel shows were in fact broader, parodying and making light of contemporary society as a whole, thus providing for audiences an escape from daily life. Blackface served as a mask from behind which taboo or controversial subjects— race, gender, class, sex, politics—could be discussed. In that sense, minstrel performers might be comparable to the faux journalists of the early 2000s, such as Jon Stewart or Stephen Colbert, whose words and satirical performance style may or may not make sense to the casual observer a century later.

To be sure, minstrel shows have had critics throughout their history, from abolitionist and statesman Frederick Douglass to filmmaker Spike Lee. Douglass wrote in an October 1848 issue of his antislavery paper, the *North Star*, describing blackface minstrel troops as "the filthy scum of white society, who have stolen from us a complexion denied to them by nature, in which to make money, and pander to corrupt taste of their white fellow citizens." The debate as to whether entertainment based on stereotypes is a harmless escape from reality or pernicious propaganda has persisted for well over a century as new entertainment genres have emerged, with arguments flaring up around hotspots like the mid-twentieth-century sitcom *Amos & Andy* and more recent blaxploitation films such as those by filmmaker-actor Tyler Perry.

And so, an introduction to the minstrel show tradition raises many questions that don't have easy answers. Does entertainment perpetuate societal problems, or merely reflect them? What are the advantages and disadvantages of archetypal characters in storytelling? What is the cost-benefit analysis of a performer achieving individual success portraying a negative stereotype? How will the politics of race, class, and gender evolve in the future, and how will that alter our perception of what is funny and what is offensive? Whatever arguments can be made in answer to those questions, the fact remains that the minstrel show, with its diverse origins, its eclectic format, and its stylized performance of race, can be seen and heard in almost every aspect of American entertainment, not least in Broadway musicals.

VARIETY AND VAUDEVILLE

The musical *Gypsy*, about a stage mother's determination that her daughters will make it big in **vaudeville**, captures the showbiz dreams and crowd-pleasing antics that were the trademark of the form. Audiences who saw *Gypsy* in its original 1959 Broadway production would have been familiar with actors who had performed in vaudeville, including its star, Ethel Merman. Vaudeville dominated American mass entertainment from the 1880s until the early 1930s, when the Great Depression finished off a business that had already been weakened by competition with the growing movie industry.

The business model that kick-started vaudeville is alive and well: good, clean fun for the whole family. In the mid-1800s, nightlife in New York centered around saloon shows that featured singing waiters, scantily clad dancing girls, and many other types of acts. Many saloons, and in fact many of the legitimate theaters of the day, had enclosed spots for trysts with illicit lovers or prostitutes. Shows were no place, in other words, for respectable women and children. Around 1865, performer turned impresario Tony Pastor realized he could increase his ticket sales by making his shows appealing to women and children as well as men. He stopped serving liquor, made a practice of kicking out rabble-rousers, and presented shows sans vulgarity. An evening at Pastor's resembled the latter two sections of a minstrel show: a variety show with song-and-dance acts, comedians, and the like, followed by a one-act spoof of a well-known play or opera. In 1881, Pastor dropped the afterpiece and kept the family-friendly variety format, in a move that came to be viewed as the birth of vaudeville.

A typical vaudeville bill featured a mix of large and small acts—magicians, comedy duos, dance troupes, singers, jugglers, and many more unusual acts. For example, Trav S. D. mentions a "regurgitation act" in his book *No Applause—Just Throw Money: The Book That Made Vaudeville Famous*. To keep the shows fast paced, large and small acts were alternated, so that a small act with no scenery would perform in one (a theatrical term meaning in front of the curtain), while behind the curtain the stage was set for the next big number. In the mid-1880s, vaudeville managers Benjamin Franklin Keith and Edward Franklin Albee pioneered the concept of continuous vaudeville, in which the program was repeated back to back from ten thirty in the morning until ten thirty at night. This format resulted in the convention of the final act of a vaudeville bill as a chaser—a dull or eccentric performance intended to "chase" the audience from the theater for quick turnaround.

In prevaudeville days, before telephones, transcontinental railroads, and large corporations, most theater managers were small businessmen who set their shows according to their own taste. The beginnings of vaudeville coincided with the construction of telephone and telegraph lines that made it possible to book shows long distance, and railroads that made it profitable to send performers on tour. Laws at the time were conducive to incorporation, creating the conditions for vaudeville to become big business, "showbiz" in the modern sense. Enterprising managers formed consolidated networks of theaters, called vaudeville circuits, which were some of America's first large corporations. Vestiges of vaudeville circuits can be seen in the names of some theaters, such as the many Orpheum theaters called for the Orpheum circuit, and the Pantages in Los Angeles, which is named after impresario Alexander Pantages.

As vaudeville grew into nationwide big business, different level circuits developed: small time, medium time, and big time. Those few who "made it to the big time" had better pay and travel conditions, fewer performances per week, and longer engagements in each town. For African American performers, there was also the Toby Time. TOBA, which stood for Theater Owners Booking Association (or, colloquially, "Tough on Black Artists"), was the circuit of theaters that sought African American acts and audiences. A who's who of great performers, including jazz pioneers Louis Armstrong, Duke Ellington, and Count Basie, played the Toby Time. Others, like singer-actress Ethel Waters and Bert Williams, made it in big-time white vaudeville. It was not unheard of for performers of color and white performers to be on the same vaudeville bill; managers only cared about the bottom line. Unfortunately, that also meant that managers often overlooked things like the fact that people of color were denied hotel accommodation and were otherwise harassed in many parts of the country.

With stiff competition and no unions to protect them, all vaudevillians were at the mercy of the managers. There were more aspiring performers than there were jobs, and most hopefuls came from the ranks of the first- or second-generation immigrant working class, for whom show business was an attractive alternative to manual labor. Since vaudeville acts weren't related to one another, one could easily be pulled and replaced at a moment's notice, for reasons like violating the stringent family-friendly code (Keith and Albee would fire you for saying "Hully gee!") or just being replaced by another act. The work and constant travel were grueling, and there was no guarantee of success; but unlike with other forms of manual labor, if you made it you could really *make it*, from rock bottom to Rockefeller—the American dream. In the absence of talent, a gimmick or sheer gall might suffice, as with the aforementioned regurgitation act. However, most vaudevillians who made it to the big time succeeded through hard work—"getting their act together" and dazzling audiences in their fifteen-minute slot.

GEORGE M. COHAN

Many vaudevillians were part of a family act. The Marx Brothers started out in vaudeville, as did comedian Bob Hope. Frances Ethel Gumm performed in a trio act with her sisters before she became known to the world as Judy Garland.

Irish American George M. Cohan (b. 1878) was a dyed-in-the-wool vaudevillian, traveling and performing with his parents and sister from the time he was an infant. Precocious Cohan took over managing the family's act as a teenager, and by the time they left vaudeville in 1899 over a dispute with Keith, The Four Cohans were the highest paid four-act in the business, thanks in large part to young George's assertiveness. His drive took them on to Broadway, where the family played in musical comedies expanded from sketches Cohan wrote while they were on the road. Speed and perpetual motion were Cohan's trademarks, and his lyrics were simple and vernacular. The melodies of his hit songs "You're a Grand Old Flag" and "Give My Regards to Broadway" are typical of his tunes in mimicking the cadence of natural speech. Cohan self-effacingly cited his own limitations in vocabulary and vocal technique as reasons for the relative simplicity of his songs. Though not a vocal technician or a critics' darling, he was a virtuoso at pleasing the crowd. Cohan's lifelong performing experience had ingrained in him the vaudeville creed: the audience is always right.

OPERETTA—THE EUROPEAN INFLUENCE

The patriotism in Cohan's musical comedies of the early 1900s reflected America's growing importance as an economic and military power. However, most Americans still looked to Europe as the standard bearer for the arts. **Operetta**, opera's lighthearted cousin, began to emerge in mid-nineteenth-century Europe as romantic opera became increasingly serious. While Wagner and Verdi were composing their weighty masterworks, French composer Jacques Offenbach was pioneering a lighter form of opera that incorporated dance hall music styles such as the cancan. Meanwhile in Austria, the so-called waltz king Johann Strauss made his mark on Viennese operetta. Austrian composer Franz Lehár's 1905 masterpiece *The Merry Widow* scored a smash hit first in Vienna, then London, then New York in 1907, rekindling the embers of the European operetta torch and leaving dozens of imported shows waltzing up and down Broadway in its wake. Operettas usually have fanciful narratives with a large cast of characters, often involving aristocracy, mistaken identity, and a great number of plot twists.

Operetta first took off in the United States in the 1870s with works by the English writing team W. S. Gilbert and Arthur Sullivan. Sullivan set Gilbert's clever rhymes to delightful melodies, and the stories were interesting, believable, and funny. Shows like *HMS Pinafore* and *The Pirates of Penzance* were hits in London, and they lost nothing in transatlantic translation. Not only were they already in English, but they also didn't have the pesky sexual content of their Continental counterparts, which had to be toned down for American audiences. As an added bonus, international copyright law hadn't yet been established. Thrifty impresarios swooped in, and Gilbert and Sullivan imports were freely produced, parodied, and pirated. Speaking of pirates, the afterpiece Tony Pastor eliminated in 1881 to create the vaudeville format was a Gilbert and Sullivan parody: *The Pie Rats of Pen Yan*.

VICTOR HERBERT

Irish-born and German-educated Victor Herbert was the most prominent composer of operetta in the United States around the turn of the twentieth century. Herbert came to New York in 1886 when his wife was hired to sing for the Metropolitan Opera; conductor Walter Damrosch found a spot for him as principal cellist in the opera's orchestra. A gregarious man with a strong work-hard, play-hard ethic, Herbert soon made inroads in the musical community. Between trips to the beer garden, he managed to perform in orchestras, lead a string quartet, direct a prominent brass band, conduct the Pittsburgh Symphony, and compose music in many genres. Herbert had the musical skill to do whatever he wanted, but the glamour of theater suited his outgoing personality, and he liked the income potential of working in popular entertainment. Herbert began writing operetta in the 1890s, and his first big hit on Broadway was *Babes in Toyland* (1903), whose hit song "March of the Toys" stayed popular for years.

Whereas George M. Cohan's melodies are speech-like and within the reach of average voices, Herbert's vocal writing grew from the classical tradition—wider range, longer phrases between breaths, complex melodies—and required highly skilled singers. He persuaded Fritzi Scheff from the Metropolitan Opera to stoop to the lowly Broadway stage to star in *Babette* (1903). A minor scandal ensued after a curtain call in which she planted a big smooch on the composer's lips. This moment is supposed to have inspired "Kiss Me Again," the most famous song from *Mlle. Modiste* (1905). It became Scheff's signature song, and she sang it throughout her career, even in an appearance on *The Ed Sullivan Show* on her seventy-fourth birthday in 1953. Herbert's understanding of a woman's voice is apparent in "Kiss Me Again," whose melody starts in the seductive low range, and soars on the repetition of the lyric "Kiss me again." Herbert's biggest success, *Naughty Marietta* (1910), remains his most familiar score among Broadway enthusiasts, through the interpolation of the songs "Ah, Sweet Mystery of Life" and "I'm Falling in Love with Someone" into the Jeanine Tesori–Dick Scanlan score of the 2002 musical comedy, *Thoroughly Modern Millie*.

A few pretentious classical critics aside, Herbert was lauded as one of America's greatest composers during his lifetime. He was a household name when he died in 1924, and so he remained for several decades, remembered best for his hits of the 1900s and 1910s. During the years of World War I, anti-German sentiment ran high, and operetta and other styles of music associated with Germany and Austria dipped in popularity: the waltz was out, and ragtime was in more than ever. In his later works for the stage, Herbert tried to conform to changing tastes by writing shorter songs and incorporating syncopated rhythms, but his strength lay in the more romantic, through-composed forms.

FLORENZ ZIEGFELD AND THE REVUE

The early twentieth century was the era of the star and the producer, and the producer who made the most stars and had the most lasting influence on Broadway was Florenz Ziegfeld Jr. His shows were lavish; an incorrigible spendthrift, he made and spent several fortunes in his lifetime. He is most closely identified with the *Ziegfeld Follies*, an annual **revue** that ran every year but one from 1907 until his death in 1931. A revue has many of the same trappings as a musical comedy—stars, hit songs, leggy chorus girls—but without even the pretense of a plot. Bearing a resemblance to shows from the fashionable French *Folies Bergère*, the evening would include topical sketches and songs—a review, or in the French spelling, *revue*, of the latest news and trends. A revue might feature vaudeville acts, but as a whole, most were (or tried to be) more sophisticated than vaudeville.

Ziegfeld was bad at following instructions and good at taking risks. When his German-born father, a prominent Chicago music teacher, sent him to Europe to find musicians for his Trocadero Club outside the 1893 Chicago World's Fair, Florenz Jr. came back with a strongman named Eugen Sandow instead. It was clear that the younger Ziegfeld couldn't be trusted to book high-class entertainment. But when he got his first big break by allowing high-society ladies to pay to stroke Sandow's muscles, it also became clear that the budding impresario had an eye for talent, and a flair for classing up sex (or is it sexing up class?) that would define his contribution to the American stage. Ziegfeld also had a knack for publicity, and for giving the public what they wanted before they even knew they wanted it. In addition to performances from the era's greatest stars, the *Ziegfeld Follies* became known for its large choruses of beautiful girls in revealing costumes and dazzling headdresses. In claiming to "glorify the American girl," Ziegfeld landed on an idea and a catchphrase that appealed to an audience brimming with patriotism and eager to move on from the squeaky-clean Victorian era of vaudeville.

Though Ziegfeld is remembered most for visual spectacle, he worked with many musical greats, including Victor Herbert, Irving Berlin, and Jerome Kern. His over-the-top aesthetic shaped Broadway musicals for decades, on both stage and screen. He was the kind of producer willing to try something new and different, keeping Broadway fresh for each generation.

THE GREAT ZIEGFELD, 1936 FILM

Ziegfeld is immortalized in the Academy Award–winning 1936 film *The Great Ziegfeld*, which was overseen by his second wife, actress Billie Burke (who is best known for her portrayal of Glinda the Good Witch in *The Wizard of Oz*). As you settle in front of your screen to watch *The Great Ziegfeld*, the five-minute **overture** transports you to a time and place of grandeur. Bright lights spell out the names of the stars: William Powell as "the Great Glorifier" himself, Luise Rainer as Anna Held, and Myrna Loy as Billie Burke. The credit sequence finishes with a frame explaining that William Anthony McGuire's screenplay is "suggested by romances and incidents" in Ziegfeld's life. As implied by the word "suggested," the semifictionalized story blurs timelines, downplays the more illicit of Ziegfeld's romances and incidents, and changes some details in favor of a good drama (for instance, Ziegfeld died quietly in California, not overlooking his brightly lit theater on Broadway). But most of the broad strokes are correct, and more importantly, the *essence* of Ziegfeld's outsize life rings true, in his relationships with fellow producers, his treatment of the women in his life, and his charm and stubbornness, brilliantly rendered by Powell. He created constellations' worth of entertainment stars, some of whom appear in the film as themselves, played by other actors, or as equivalents or composites of the real-life versions. Ziegfeld's love of opulence and grandeur and the ups and downs that resulted from the risks he took to fulfill his vision are captured in this film that premiered less than four years after his death.

The first section of the film deals with Sandow (played with aplomb and twitching biceps by Nat Pendleton) and his rise to stardom. The music underscoring these scenes includes many popular pieces from the era: Sousa's march, the *"Washington Post"*; "After the Ball," a 1891 ballad written by Charles K. Harris; and "The Streets of Cairo." The latter is a minor-mode melody that came to signify exotica associated with the Middle East (belly dancing, snake charming, etc.) through its wide use in mass entertainment from the time of the 1893 Chicago World's Fair. It is often credited to Sol Bloom, the entertainment director of the World's Fair, where it was used as the accompaniment for a belly dancer performing under the name of Little Egypt. Tracing the origin of melodies is difficult in an era in which copyright laws were relatively new and lax; fragments of the melody can be traced, via

France and Algeria, to an Arabic folk song. A popular 1895 version of the tune was published by James Thornton, and it has appeared frequently ever since as "The Hootchy-Kootchy Dance," "the snake-charmer song," and under many other names. As a pop song, the tune retains about as much authenticity as most of the supposedly educational exhibitions of Asian, African, and Native American cultures at the World's Fair: commercial entertainment intended first and foremost for profit, having the double-edged effect of incompletely or inaccurately representing these cultures, and providing many European Americans who lacked the means to travel with their first exposure to non-European cultures.

The first musical production number of *The Great Ziegfeld* occurs around the half-hour mark, when Ziegfeld first discovers Anna Held in London. The charming Polish-born French actress who will become Ziegfeld's first wife is performing "I Wish You'd Come and Play with Me" by Alfred Plumpton. The number has a small vocal range and a speech-like melody. Held had a pleasant enough voice, but was the type of pop star who was famous for her overall charisma rather than her vocal fireworks. The music from the number is echoed in the film score under the following scene, as Ziegfeld cleverly convinces Anna to come to the United States with him. After she fails to make a splash with American audiences, she rehearses "It's Delightful to Be Married," with music by Vincent Scotto and lyrics by the real-life Anna Held. The rich and privileged are not exempt from stereotyping, and Anna's coach and pianist has an even thicker French accent than she. In any case, the dialect and vocal coaching is a red herring; Ziegfeld's real strategy to ensure Anna's stardom is a publicity stunt, based on actual events, involving the delivery of large quantities of milk that Anna purportedly uses for baths. This segment ends with Anna reaching musical comedy stardom, fronting eight chorus girls to sing "It's Delightful to Be Married." Music directors will empathize with Held's pianist, who cringes visibly when Held persists in singing *"jolie"* instead of "jolly" after repeated corrections.

Having succeeded in making Anna a star, Ziegfeld moves on to his next big idea, the *Ziegfeld Follies*, an idea that was at least partly Anna Held's in reality, not a cause for her hysteria as in the film. The film refers to how Ziegfeld convinced producers Klaw and Erlanger, who were notoriously stingy vaudeville managers, to finance the first *Follies* in 1907. Historical facts and timelines are blurred as stars and songs from all over the *Follies* timeline are lumped together in this sequence, but the film succeeds at capturing the opulence of a *Ziegfeld Follies*. Audiences clamor to see such luminaries as Eddie Cantor (played in the film by Buddy Doyle), who starred in the *Ziegfeld Follies* several times between 1917 and 1927. "If You Knew Susie," a 1925 song by Buddy DeSylva and Joseph Meyer, was one of Cantor's signature songs. It contains very mild sexual innuendo, some of which is excised in the choice of alternate lyrics. Suggestive songs like these were usually done under the cover of blackface, vestiges of the minstrel show in the early years of the twentieth century. By the same token, African American men were typically confined to performing comedic songs such as these, and were not cast as the romantic hero like the one in the next production number.

That number is the finale, which comes after a series of scenes that show the controlled chaos backstage of any big production. It involves hundreds of people—both onstage and those offstage who made it possible to film this sequence in two extended shots. The song, Irving Berlin's "A Pretty Girl Is Like a Melody," was written for the *Ziegfeld Follies of 1919*; it became the theme song for the *Follies* thereafter. One of a genre of "girl" numbers that feature a romantic male soloist surrounded by a chorus of beautiful girls, it starts with soloist Dennis Morgan (singing dubbed by Allan Jones) alone in one (in front of the curtain), his rich vibrato and the rise and fall of the melody emphasizing the simile in the lyrics. The curtain is drawn back to reveal the chorus, as "haunting refrains" of well-known opera arias and concert pieces are alternated seamlessly with phrases of Berlin's song. The first selection is Antonín Dvořák's "Humoresque," a lilting violin melody that in the 1919 *Follies* was set with comical lyrics about the singer's conquests, as were several other well-known classical tunes. Instead of comedy, *The Great Ziegfeld* here goes for sheer spectacle, using climactic musical excerpts to match the grandiose sets and costumes. The choice of George Gershwin's 1924 piece, *Rhapsody in Blue*, adds modern pizzazz to the medley, not to mention an excuse for the male dance ensemble to play "air piano." The final refrains of the song include the shimmery sound of large singing choruses and orchestrations thick with romantic strings and brassy fanfare. The tiered set looks like a wedding cake, and the sounds are equally rich.

The next few musical numbers occur at a midnight rooftop show after an unspecified period of time has passed. Ziegfeld's knack for spotting talent is shown by the rise to stardom of an ambitious and talented stagehand played by Ray Bolger, a star best remembered as the Scarecrow in *The Wizard of Oz*. In the opening number of the midnight show, scantily clad chorines sing "You Gotta Pull Strings," a metaphor whimsically made literal by the use of strings attached to balloons, which the audience pulls to reveal Bolger perched among another cluster of chorus girls. Bolger's number, "She's a Follies Girl," is a send-up of romantic tenor-and-chorines numbers like the one we just saw. His comedic dance routine shows the incredible degree of skill it took to make it in big-time vaudeville and beyond.

Walter Donaldson and Harold Adamson, who are credited with writing additional lyrics and music for the film, wrote all the songs in the midnight show segment. In a Hollywood studio project the size of *The Great Ziegfeld*, they would have been assisted by a large team of mostly uncredited arrangers, orchestrators, and copyists, who were responsible for creating the parts for each musician—at a time when orchestras were large and everything was written out by hand! The next song, "You," appears frequently throughout the film, a choice that lends unity to the film score and was also likely more economical than paying to reuse a hit song by someone like Berlin or Kern. The song's romantic refrain, with its sustained "you" and sinuous melody, is performed by a singing chorus of amorous couples, who are followed by a dancing chorus of single ladies. As the vocal part of the song idealizes conventional romance, so the dance music celebrates the fancy-free single life, with comedic percussion hits accenting the steps of the single girls mixing cocktails for themselves. The extended dance break runs the gamut from orchestral grandeur to muted trumpet rhythms idiomatic of 1930s swing: the arrangers and orchestrators pulled out all the stops to glorify the American girl.

The music resumes after applause, and the most glorious single girl of all appears, flanked by an ensemble of suitors who tell her "You've Never Looked So Beautiful Before." The up-and-coming chorus girl is Audrey Dane (Virginia Bruce), Ziegfeld's latest protégée and conquest—a barely disguised version of Lillian Lorraine, who was one of the great loves of Ziegfeld's life. As was the case with Anna Held, the glorified girl's solo voice is pleasant but not virtuosic. The melody is intended for an average voice, with the virtuosity instead found in the lush instrumental accompaniment created to match the sparkly visual glorification of the "ordinary" girl.

Ziegfeld's next discovery is Fanny Brice (who plays herself in the film), an ordinary girl with extraordinary stage presence and a gift for both comedy and pathos. The daughter of Jewish immigrants from Central Europe, Brice grew up in Manhattan's Lower East Side, and was performing in **burlesque** when Ziegfeld discovered her. Burlesque became synonymous with striptease in later years, but in the early 1900s, it simply referred to a spoof of refined entertainment. The Yiddish stereotype on which Brice built her career can be heard in "Yiddle on His Fiddle." She then switches to a faux-operatic tone and a posh accent replete with rolled *R*s to introduce the chorus number "Queen of the Jungle." The "gorgeous girls" of the chorus introduce themselves with nasal tone, blurry **diction**, and vernacular lyrics. Every part of their performance is a subversion of glorified American girlhood. Brice reenters after a quick costume change, just in time to confirm the cringe-worthy caricature implied by the costume's grass skirt. The "native style" of the "cannibal isles" is a stereotype typical of the time period. It mocks one of the few socioeconomic groups more oppressed than the working-class "Tenth Avenue" people in the burlesque audience, while simultaneously parodying the preferred entertainment of the well-heeled "Fifth Avenue" crowd. Brice is later shown singing "My Man," which would become her signature song, in a rehearsal scene that shows Ziegfeld's determination to capitalize on the exact thing Brice had hoped to escape by getting into the *Follies*: her underdog status. Though her road to fame is vastly simplified here, it was indeed Brice's accessibility—not obscured by glorification—that helped her elicit the cathartic audience response that made her a star.

In the 1920s, Ziegfeld went on to produce musical comedies that had at least nominal plots, such as *Sally* (1920). The rags-to-riches show was a star vehicle for Marilyn Miller, fictionalized in *The Great Ziegfeld* under the convenient name of Sally Manners (Rosina Lawrence). *Sally*'s hit song was Jerome Kern's "Look for the Silver Lining," which appears in a cameo in which the composer (played by an uncredited actor) demonstrates the song for Ziegfeld and his business team. The straitlaced businessmen join in singing the song as they hear it for the first time, implying their ability to spot a hit and snag it for their production.

Though Ziegfeld did turn to producing musical comedies, the *Follies* revue format remained strong over the years, as shown in one last big production number, a circus number inspired by a request from Ziegfeld's young daughter (another accurate detail: Ziegfeld really did have a menagerie at home, including an elephant named Ziggy). The circus number begins with an 1897 march entitled "Entrance of the Gladiators" by Czech composer Julius Fučík that has become inextricably associated with the circus through its use as a "screamer march," or piece intended to excite the audience while an act was being introduced. Dressed as archetypical circus performers, Ziegfeld's male chorus members announce their various roles in "the greatest show on earth." As impressive as they are, they are ousted from the stage by a chorus of identically dressed, uniformly beautiful women, whose entrance music is a slow, romantic version of the descending chromatic "Gladiators" melody, and who tell the men in no uncertain terms that "A Circus Must Be Different in a Ziegfeld Show." The moral of the story: the *Ziegfeld Follies* will always be about the glorified girls and the star in front of them. This time, the star is ballerina Harriet Hoctor as herself, dancing to music by Con Conrad that includes quotes of the "Gladiator" melody and slight tempo changes to accommodate the timing of her jumps.

The next scene transition mimics the pacing of a live musical, as applause from the circus number segues into portentous music that adds drama to a montage of newspaper headlines about Ziegfeld's financial difficulties. Two more montages bookend Ziegfeld's final fortunes. He makes a comeback in the late 1920s with four hit Broadway shows, and the brightly lit marquees of *Rio Rita*, *Whoopee*, *The Three Musketeers*, and *Show Boat* are shown with a medley of hit songs from those shows. Then, after Ziegfeld and many others lose everything in the stock market crash of 1929, the marquees are shown going dark one by one.

In the final scene, Ziegfeld expresses regret that he is leaving nothing behind but debts, an admission that would have resonated deeply with many in the Depression-era audience when the film was originally released. Ziegfeld's faithful valet Sidney reminds him that he leaves behind "memories of the finest things ever done on the stage." His attempt to comfort his dying employer gets to the heart of the paradox of the great showman's influence. Ziegfeld's *Follies* and most of his musical comedies were never intended to last more than a season, to delight in a particular moment in time, or provide a platform for a star's special talents—and yet his disposable, frivolous "follies" live on in the kicklines, clever lyrics, and risqué humor of many later Broadway shows.

SALAD BOWL VERSUS MELTING POT

Ziegfeld lived during the height of American variety entertainment. His life spanned the vaudeville era, and his own *Follies* were the most enduring of the revue format. The aforementioned *Ziegfeld Follies of 1919*, which Ziegfeld and many critics agreed was the best he ever did, opened with a small chorus number, "A Follies Salad" by Ziegfeld's standby songwriting team Gene Buck and Dave Stamper. In an extended metaphor for putting on a show, the chorus girls were dressed up as the ingredients of a salad. Lettuce and Oil formed the musical base; Oil is described as "a melody to soothe," for "everything must run quite smooth" to produce a lavish affair like the *Follies*. The Follies Salad was flavored by Sugar, Spice, Paprika, and of course Salt and Pepper, played by well-known siblings, the Fairbanks twins. The meat of the salad was Chicken, which the 1919 audience would have understood to signify the girls in the *Follies* (chicks, get it?). The Chicken must be not only "young and tender," but alive and, in a double-entendre coup, "kicking."

The genres discussed in this chapter attempted nothing more than to live in the moment, full of topical satire and wit, set to music that was in fashion, unconcerned with posterity. Salad is a perfect metaphor for a variety-based show: light and refreshing, its ingredients mixed together but still separate. To stretch the metaphor even further, there was another group of writers a few blocks away who longed for a more substantial musical theater meal than salad, and were experimenting with fondue, if you will. These writers aspired to solidify a uniquely American sound from diverse influences, and to pair it with the seamless dramatic integration of European opera. It was the beginning of

Broadway shows meant to stick to your ribs—and to endure beyond the era of their creation.

3

THE BEGINNINGS OF INTEGRATION

Very Good Eddie, Shuffle Along, and *Show Boat*

In his autobiography, *Musical Stages*, composer Richard Rodgers writes, "The sound of a Jerome Kern tune was not ragtime, nor did it have any of the Middle European inflections of Victor Herbert. It was all his own—the first truly American theatre music—and it pointed the way I wanted to be led." He was writing of *Very Good Eddie* (1915), which, with a book by Guy Bolton and lyrics by Schuyler Greene, was one of the first Broadway musical comedies to make a concerted attempt at integrating songs, dialogue, and character. Rodgers saw it multiple times as a teenager, absorbing the emerging sound of uniquely American music engendered by the interaction of European American and African American sounds.

Jerome Kern, born in New York City to a middle-class Jewish family in 1885, was intended for a stable, respectable career in business. After a famous mishap in which he ordered two *hundred* pianos instead of just two for the department store where his father had gotten him a job, Kern embarked on a music career, showing much more aptitude for business when it came to becoming a composer. He started out as an administrative assistant at a music publisher, quickly moving up the ranks to be a song plugger, a job unique to the height of the sheet music publishing trade whose epicenter was **Tin Pan Alley**.

TIN PAN ALLEY

Before the advent of recording technology and mass-produced re-corded music, the home entertainment system was a piano. Families with any significant social standing had a piano and at least one member who could play it competently, and the popular song industry was driv-en by sheet music sales. In the nineteenth century, it was the publishers who got rich while songwriters, even those of such renown as Stephen Foster, often died in poverty. In the mid-1880s, a number of songwrit-ers decided to go into the publishing business themselves, and many of the successful ones set up shop on a stretch of Twenty-Eighth Street between Fifth and Sixth Avenues in Manhattan. This block, and eventu-ally the popular song industry, came to be called Tin Pan Alley after the pianistic cacophony of song pluggers demonstrating new songs for po-tential buyers.

A music publisher's office was a busy scene, with lyricists and song-writers running back and forth to arrangers who solidified the piano part. The final product, a new potential hit, was "plugged" to perform-ers and managers coming and going from the office. Publishers would try to convince big stars to perform their songs, giving them the sheet music for free, and sometimes printing the singer's likeness on the cover. Singers who weren't famous had to fight, sometimes literally, for the right to sing a great new song—songwriter Irving Berlin, working as a staff lyricist, fell in love with his first wife, singer Dorothy Goetz, when he saw her win a physical tussle over a song.

One of the first megahits of Tin Pan Alley was "After the Ball" by Charles K. Harris, written in 1891. It is a prime example of one of the dominant genres of Tin Pan Alley, the sentimental ballad. Its slow waltz tempo is typical of the style, as are the lyrics that tell a story that is both nostalgic and tinged with regret. "After the Ball" sold two million copies of sheet music, and was used in several films and Broadway shows over the next few decades, including *The Great Ziegfeld* and *Show Boat*.

The second main Tin Pan Alley genre was initially known as the coon song, which, as can be inferred by the racist epithet in the name of the genre, was a continuation of minstrelsy's parodying of African Americans. Coon songs often portrayed African Americans as lazy, vio-lent, or hypersexualized, furthering the exploitation of them to circum-vent cultural taboos. These stereotypes were usually the creation of white songwriters, though some African Americans also contributed to the lucrative genre.

In fact, most popular songs around this time were associated with a specific ethnic group, the vividness of different cultures in close proximity with each other for the first time painted in stereotypes characterized by certain dialect and musical patterns. The word "ragtime" came into use for coon songs in the 1890s (also a term for solo piano compositions such as Scott Joplin's "The Entertainer," ragtime then more commonly referred to up-tempo vocal songs). After around 1900, ragtime and other ethnic parodies began to lose their racial associations, with lyrics becoming more generalized and musical characteristics assimilated into the general language of pop music. The most fundamental, lasting effect of ragtime on American popular music is syncopated rhythm. In many African musical traditions, several interlocking rhythmic patterns happen at once, resulting in accents repeatedly coming *between* the underlying pulse instead of on it. The popular instrumental genre of the late nineteenth century was the march, descended from British and Central European band music, in which the important notes in the melody and accompaniment land on the beat, resulting in sturdy music for, well, marching. The music that evolved from these two backgrounds is a combination of an oompah march accompaniment pattern outlining the harmony and the beat, and a "ragged" melody that dances on and off the strong beats. The operative word is "dance": ragtime's irresistible rhythm was inextricably linked to titillating dance moves that also came from African American dance. The genre was predictably hailed in the establishment as a harbinger of doom, or otherwise dismissed as a passing fad. Similar undertones of racism, classism, and sexual taboo had accompanied the emergence of the waltz centuries earlier in central Europe, and would later be heard in the emergence of swing and hip-hop. A debate raged between ragtime's detractors and those who thought it should form the basis of a new American school of composition.

THE PRINCESS MUSICALS

Jerome Kern's skill as a song plugger soon led to opportunities as a rehearsal pianist for Broadway shows, where he was not above nonchalantly playing his own tunes during rehearsal breaks. In early 1900s Broadway, it wasn't unusual for shows to contain songs by multiple songwriters, selected by the shows' producers or stars. Kern was a masterful melodist and was steeped in both Tin Pan Alley and classical music, and soon his songs were being interpolated into Broadway shows.

Though Kern did quite well getting songs piecemeal into shows, he aspired to write a full score and have more artistic control over the finished product. He shared this aspiration with architect turned playwright Guy Bolton, whom he'd befriended where many of the best theater friendships are forged: in the trenches of an unsuccessful show. While working on the flop *Ninety in the Shade* in early 1915, they bonded over their mutual ambition to improve musical comedies by making the songs and the comedy flow naturally from the story instead of interrupting it. Not long after, an opportunity presented itself when Kern's agent, Bessie Marbury, approached him about helping write a musical for the tiny, failing Princess Theatre. Kern accepted Marbury's offer, and recommended Bolton as a librettist.

The constraints of the Princess's building and budget conversely freed them from the over-the-top conventions that so bored them. The pit could comfortably accommodate about eleven musicians, far fewer than the typical operetta orchestra, and there was no room onstage for the fifty-member choruses of other musicals and revues. There were still pretty girls in the Princess musicals, but they were few enough that they could be recognized as individuals. More than simply objects of Ziegfeldian glorification, young women in these "small-part roles" had appetites and opinions.

In the late 1910s, Bolton and Kern wrote several more musicals for the Princess, most famously with British expatriate P. G. Wodehouse. The shows had a variety of singing, dancing, and comedy, as in the best of the revues, but they were melded together with a more of a plot than other musicals of the time—a roux rather than the salad described in the *Ziegfeld Follies of 1919* (chapter 2). In Dorothy Parker's oft-quoted review of Princess show *Oh, Lady! Lady!!* (1918), she praises "the way the action slides casually into the songs." The Princess musicals, particularly the collaboration of the witty and formidable triumvirate of Bolton, Wodehouse, and Kern, came to be viewed as landmarks in the evolution of the American musical from variety to dramatic integration.

CAST RECORDING: GOODSPEED OPERA HOUSE *VERY GOOD EDDIE* 1975 REVIVAL

As you unwrap the compact disc of the cast album of the 1975 revival of *Very Good Eddie*, you note that the watercolor caricature on the cover is reminiscent of artwork that appeared on the covers of Tin Pan Alley sheet music. The figure of a fashionable man is superimposed over that of a woman drawn on a much larger scale, a difference in sizes that is at the root of the story of the second Princess Theatre musical, which originally opened in 1915. The title character is short, meek Eddie Kettle (Charles Repole), who is newly wed to domineering Georgina (Spring Fairbank). When embarking on their honeymoon cruise up the Hudson River, they run into another pair of newlyweds, Eddie's tall, masculine classmate Percy Darling (Nicholas Wyman) and his sweet, petite bride Elsie (Virginia Seidel). Through a farcical series of events involving last-minute telegrams and forgotten luggage, Georgina and Percy both miss the boat, leaving their timid spouses up a creek, as it were. The farce intensifies when Eddie and Elsie find themselves stranded at the honeymoon destination with no return boat, no spouses, and everyone assuming that they are married *to each other*. A handful of other characters, including a singer named Madame Matroppo and her small female ensemble of voice students, round out the action.

In the decades that passed between the 1915 Princess production and the 1975 revival, audiences had come to expect seamless storytelling in musicals, even in the lightest comedies. Several songs that fit the story line were interpolated from other Kern shows, such as "Good Night, Boat" with lyrics by Anne Caldwell (other lyricists supplementing the songs with lyrics by Schuyler Greene are Elsie Janis, Harry Graham, Harry B. Smith, Frank Craven, Herbert Reynolds, and, last but not least, P. G. Wodehouse, with two songs from later Princess shows). In this case, the interpolation of songs makes the plot *more* cohesive, while preserving the charm and sophistication of the original production. The well-received revival transferred from Connecticut's Goodspeed Opera House to Broadway's Booth Theatre in December 1975 and ran for 304 performances.

While not as focused on current events as a revue, *Very Good Eddie* contains enough 1915 references to satisfy the fashionable set who attended the Princess musicals. "Some Sort of Somebody," a duet that occurs between secondary characters Dick Rivers and Elsie Lilly (not to be confused with Percy's wife Elsie), makes reference not only to numerous European stereotypes, but also to World War I, which had been raging in Europe for over a year when *Very Good Eddie* opened at the Princess. Rivers mentions Italian and French girls among his conquests; Elsie Lilly retorts that "now we know who started the war." The fight for women's suffrage was also in full swing during *Eddie*'s original run, as we are reminded in "Isn't It Great to Be Married," a quartet between the two primary couples. The exchange about giving the women the vote would have been topical satire of the highest order in 1915, especially given the context of who wore the metaphorical pants in Eddie and Georgina's relationship.

We begin to understand poor, henpecked Eddie through his solo "Thirteen Collar." A size thirteen collar is quite small, and Eddie wistfully sings of a nineteen collar, a size eleven shoe, and the assertiveness that must naturally emanate from a man of that stature. "Thirteen Collar" is a patter song, but one that is rooted in Eddie's character. He is not a razzle-dazzle kind of guy, and rather than the focused, near-monotone delivery found in many such wordy songs, it has a widely meandering melody and a moderate, slightly rubato (elastic) tempo. This is the sort of sad-sack song a star like Eddie Cantor might have performed in the *Ziegfeld Follies*; however, here it is tied to the plot and comedy of the show, rather than standing alone as a specialty number in a series of unrelated acts.

The evolution from variety to integration didn't happen overnight, and much of act 2 is made up of old-fashioned musical comedy business, marking time with song and dance until Percy and Georgina arrive and the simple plot can resolve itself. In the original 1915 production, act 2 began with "On the Shores at Le Lei Wi" with music by Henry Kalimai. The interpolation was irresistible: hula songs were very popular at the time, and thus hula numbers were all the rage in musicals, regardless of how ridiculous they made the plot. Broadway was also still in the habit of giving patrons plenty of time to settle in at the beginning of each act. Nothing important happened right away, in case one was a little late getting back from the bar or the loo. The Goodspeed revival opened act 2 with the more topical "Honeymoon Inn" for its 1970s audience.

Madame Matroppo, who has become enamored of the hotel clerk, has two songs in which to impress him. Her second attempt at seduction, "Katy-Did," begins in the operetta vein and ends as an upbeat rag. Actress Travis Hudson as Matroppo gives a two-minute demonstration of the evolution of popular vocal styles as Harry B. Smith's lyric coyly refuses to reveal exactly what Katy did. As the number progresses, Matroppo's diction becomes less crisp, her vocal placement heavier, and her negotiation of the melody allowing for "blue" notes that fall between the pitches of the scale.

Accusations fly when the newlywed couples eventually find each other. All is resolved when Eddie, having grown stronger through this ordeal, stands up to Georgina at last. The full company launches into the finale, with lyrics that address the audience directly, bidding them good night and hoping they enjoyed the play. In the tiny Princess Theatre, the nearness of the performers created a personal effect that bigger shows could not duplicate. The intimate musical with a charming story presented a novel concept of what a Broadway musical could be.

SHUFFLE ALONG

When *Shuffle Along* strode into the 63rd Street Theatre to open on May 3, 1921, it had been over a decade since a musical written, produced, and performed by African Americans had played Broadway. After World War I, racial tensions and discrimination were high, and the theater Henry Cort managed to lease for *Shuffle Along* was dilapidated and located several blocks north of most Broadway houses. But news of the show's impressive performances and tuneful score spread by word of mouth, and *Shuffle Along* became a sleeper hit with a diverse audience. Black and white audiences were still seated in separate sections, but for the first time, African American patrons could purchase seats in the orchestra section. Curtain-time traffic jams were so intense that Sixty-Third Street was made into a one-way thoroughfare to mitigate them.

Shuffle Along's composer Eubie Blake, lyricist Noble Sissle, and book writers Flournoy Miller and Aubrey Lyles all had backgrounds in vaudeville. Blake, born James Hubert Blake in Baltimore in 1887, studied piano from an early age and began to play professionally at age sixteen. (In later years, Blake always claimed he was born in 1883, though official documents back up the 1887 birth year. His gravestone reflects the year he preferred and grants him a full century of life. Either way, being a ragtime composer was apparently good for his health.) In 1912, Blake played in prominent bandleader James Reese Europe's Society Orchestra, which dancers Vernon and Irene Castle hired to play for their ragtime dance act. The Castles, who were white, were instrumental in introducing ragtime dance to white audiences, sparking a dance craze that further increased the popularity of ragtime music.

Blake and Sissle met in Baltimore in 1915; the two immediately hit it off and began writing songs together. During World War I, Sissle enlisted in the 369th Infantry Regiment, the first African American regiment of the war, where he served as drum major and violinist for the 369th Regimental Band, also under the baton of Europe. Sissle and Blake kept in touch during the war, collaborating by correspondence, and afterward formed a musical vaudeville team called the Dixie Duo. They met Miller and Lyles at an NAACP benefit in Philadelphia in 1920, and found that they shared the aim of bringing African American musical comedy back to Broadway. The two teams agreed to collaborate, expanding one of Miller and Lyles's comedy sketches, "The Mayor of Dixie," into a full-length show with Sissle and Blake's songs. They found a financial backer in Henry Cort, the son of a white theater impresario, who gave them enough funding to develop the show on a shoestring budget. The author-performers (Miller, Lyles, and Sissle acted in the show, and Blake played piano and led the band) finessed *Shuffle Along* as they played a series of short engagements through Pennsylvania and New Jersey. Although the production was eighteen thousand dollars in debt when it opened on Broadway, its triumphant and ultimately profitable 484-performance run launched the careers of numerous performers and spurred the development of African American musical comedies for over a decade.

Among the stars who got their start in *Shuffle Along* were Adelaide Hall, Josephine Baker, and Paul Robeson. Robeson, who also played professional football and earned a law degree from Columbia University, was at the beginning of a meteoric rise in theater and music when he worked in the cast of the long-running show. African American performers also appeared in shows by white authors and producers, such as

Show Boat (where we will see Robeson later in the chapter) and Lew Leslie's revue *Blackbirds of 1928*, which had a score by Jimmy McHugh with lyrics by Dorothy Fields. Leslie produced three further editions of *Blackbirds* in 1930, 1933, and 1939, though the first, which starred tap dance legend Bill "Bojangles" Robinson and *Shuffle Along* alumna Adelaide Hall, was the most successful. The 1930 edition was authored by *Shuffle Along*'s Blake and Miller, with lyrics by Andy Razaf.

The success of *Shuffle Along* was a mixed blessing. While it represented African American writers and performers on Broadway and encouraged the development of other African American Broadway musicals, it also created a sort of formula for them. Shows that attempted to progress beyond those boundaries were typically stymied at the box office. Music historian Eileen Southern explores the paradoxical phenomenon in a section of her book *The Music of Black Americans: A History*: "The box office made the final decision, and Broadway audiences tightly specified the roles that African Americans could play on the stage. But within those constraints, all was possible, so black show people invaded Broadway again and again with revues and musical comedies. Wisely, they drew upon their folk roots for materials and, in the process, put an indelible stamp upon the development of American musical theater."

Shuffle Along was originally called a revue, showing how porous the boundaries between musical comedy, vaudeville, and revue were in the early twentieth century. It had a plot—certainly less than we would expect of a contemporary musical, but more than a *Ziegfeld Follies*—about a mayoral race where two candidates promise each other that the winner will appoint the other as chief of police. It turns out they are each out to swindle the other, and they are ultimately supplanted by a reform candidate, Harry, who also gets the girl, Jessie Williams. Audience expectations changed rapidly over the course of a few decades, and the 1932 and 1952 revivals of *Shuffle Along* with updated libretti ran only a handful of performances each.

As of this writing, a production entitled *Shuffle Along; or, The Making of the Musical Sensation of 1921 and All That Followed* is slated to open on Broadway in the spring of 2016, starring Audra McDonald. As the title indicates, an updated libretto written by the production's director George C. Wolfe will infuse the book with the backstory of the original production. Adding the story of the four showmen who both authored and performed in the 1921 hit adds more scope for the amount of plot expected by twenty-first-century musical audiences. Moreover, it provides an opportunity to celebrate the contribution of African American artists—not just as performers but also as authors—during a formative time in Broadway and popular music.

RECORDING: SONGS FROM *BLACKBIRDS OF 1928* AND *SHUFFLE ALONG*

Like that of the *Very Good Eddie* album, the cover art on the RCA Victor album featuring songs from *Shuffle Along* and *Blackbirds of 1928* is stylized and indicative of the nature of the shows it represents. The caricatures of the two mayoral candidates in motion hint at the energy and minimal plot of *Shuffle Along*, and the woodblock image of three blackbirds on a branch imply the plotless revue nature of *Blackbirds of 1928*. On the back of the booklet is a photograph of Eubie Blake at the piano. Blake was instrumental in putting together the revival of his show, and he conducted the orchestra for the recording of selections from *Shuffle Along*. Four songs from each show were recorded in 1952 for RCA's "Show Time" series, a set of ten-inch LP records that featured songs from Broadway's past. The two albums were combined and rereleased on compact disc and online in 2011. The *Shuffle Along* songs feature the vocals of Thelma Carpenter and Avon Long, who starred in the 1952 revival; Carpenter is paired with the swing-era great Cab Calloway for the *Blackbirds* selections.

Fields and McHugh's "I Can't Give You Anything but Love" became a jazz standard after the success of *Blackbirds*. Calloway, renowned as a scat singer and bandleader, first sings a faithful statement of the chorus melody, then, after a rendition of the rarely heard introductory verse, shows his improvisational skill the second time through the thirty-two-**bar** chorus. He is backed by the hard-swinging band for the *Blackbirds* selections, which features full sections of both strings and winds and is led by prominent Broadway conductor Lehman Engel.

Dorothy Fields's proclivity for using slang and topical references, which Sondheim would imitate in *Follies* (chapter 7), can be heard in the lyrics of "Diga Diga Doo," as she incorporates the title of 1927 hit song, "Fifty Million Frenchmen Can't Be Wrong." Fields, whose father made a career as half of a comedy duo "Dutch act" (an act portraying a German immigrant stereotype), grew up immersed in the colloquial language of show business and the ethnic stereotypes that defined it at the time. Stereotypes common to the era are also prominent in the song in its images of a "Zulu king" and its tale of tropical seduction. Such stereotypes were not exclusive to white songwriters: hints of the idealized antebellum South that were so commercially successful in minstrel songs can be heard in the imagery of "cane and cotton" in the Sissle and Blake song reminiscing about "Bandana Days."

Sissle and Blake were also skilled in the language of operetta, as can be heard in the ballad "Love Will Find a Way," a duet between Jessie and Harry. The love scene embodied in this song was the first between African American characters on Broadway that was not a spoof. Blake gives the couple long, legato (smoothly articulated) phrases and sustained melodies even in the typically conversational introductory section of the song. The tuneful writing sets off Sissle's romantic images of skies and clouds, Cupid and fate, and the two lovers repeat the chorus, weaving in and out of harmony and counterpoint. All these elements, and the vocal interpretation of revival cast members Louise Woods and Lawrence Watson, place the song firmly in the operetta territory where Broadway romance blossoms.

Shuffle Along's other big hit, "I'm Just Wild about Harry," also started out as a waltz in the operetta vein. Blake rewrote it with syncopated rhythms at the request of Lottie Gee, who originated the role of Jessie. The ragtime setting was even better for Sissle's modern colloquial lyric than an old-fashioned waltz would have been. The peppy rhythm also made the song useful to Harry Truman in 1948, when he used it as the theme song for his presidential campaign. Like Kern's writing in *Very Good Eddie*, Blake's songs from *Shuffle Along* show fluency both in long-phrased romantic melodies and rhythmic, ragtime-influenced tunes, melding together into a uniquely American sound.

SHOW BOAT

The emerging style of American music and theater had a major landmark in the 1927 musical *Show Boat*, by Jerome Kern and Oscar Hammerstein II. Hammerstein was a third-generation member of a theatrical dynasty. He was named for his opera-obsessed grandfather, a German immigrant who repeatedly gambled all of his and his family's money on producing grand opera in New York. Having been through the wringer that was his father Oscar I, prominent vaudeville manager Willie Hammerstein's dying wish at age forty was that his teenage son Oscar II stay far away from show business. Luckily for Broadway, Willie didn't get his wish. Young Oscar met Jerome Kern while working on the 1925 musical *Sunny*. The two were of the same artistic mind, wanting to create musicals of more substance than fluffy, variety-based star vehicles would permit. They agreed to be on the lookout for appropriate material to adapt into the kind of show they dreamed of.

They found that material in Edna Ferber's 1926 best-selling novel, *Show Boat*. The Pulitzer Prize–winning novelist (for her 1925 novel *So Big*) initially had qualms about having *Show Boat* made into a musical, as the epic story did not fit anywhere on the existing musical theater spectrum of madcap musical comedies and fanciful operettas. Kern managed to wrangle an introduction to Ferber through a mutual friend, and his in-person enthusiasm worked where letters had not. Though Ferber still had her doubts, she granted Kern and Hammerstein the rights to develop *Show Boat* as a musical.

This was no Princess show, nor was it a run-of-the-mill operetta or musical comedy. It was a show with a cast of over a hundred performers, telling a story that takes place over a period of forty years (condensed by a decade from the novel) in many settings on and around the boat and in Chicago and New York. It was clear that there was but one producer in town with the bold vision and financial daredeviltry required for such a production: Florenz Ziegfeld.

In the 1920s, musicals were still thrown together in a matter of months if not weeks, so the thirteen months that elapsed between Kern and Hammerstein getting the rights to *Show Boat* and its Broadway opening in December 1927 was a relatively long gestation period. Early in 1927, Ziegfeld sent Kern a lengthy telegram complaining that Hammerstein's current libretto was "too serious not enough comedy" and that he was "through producing for critics and empty houses." It was an odd thing to say, since Ziegfeld had never tried to please the critics when he knew audiences craved something else. His pragmatic producer jitters came from the fact that *Show Boat* was unlike anything he had ever produced before. It took dramatic integration a step further than the Princess shows: *Show Boat*'s songs are not only related to the plot, some are indispensable to it. *Show Boat* was the first major show to have black and white choruses share the stage. Furthermore, *Show Boat* deals with themes like racism, desertion, and addiction that had never before been treated seriously in a Broadway musical. When the end of the Broadway opening night of *Show Boat* was met with stunned silence, Ziegfeld was sure he was ruined.

But the next morning, ticket buyers were lined up around the block, and the public kept the show open for 572 performances. *Show Boat* is one of the most revived Broadway musicals, and the only musical from the 1920s that is still constantly in production. Its high-profile professional versions include three films, numerous West End productions and Broadway revivals, tours, concert versions, recordings, radio broadcasts, and, more recently, opera house appearances. It is also one of the most revised musicals, throughout the various incarnations of the show on stage and screen; Hammerstein himself continued to tinker with the script for years. As such, there is no one definitive version of *Show Boat*'s libretto and score.

While there are arguments for examining versions that contain more of Kern's score, here we will choose the 1936 film. That film version stays closer to the musical than either the 1929 silent film, which was based on the novel and incorporated some of the songs into the soundtrack, or the 1951 film starring Ava Gardner, which strays far from both the novel and the musical. The 1936 film also features well-known performers from early incarnations of the show, including the Broadway cast, London cast, and national tour. In just under two hours, it tells the epic story quite concisely, eliminating some magnificent music and storytelling, but affording the modern audience an accessible glimpse into a historic performance of the landmark show.

SHOW BOAT, 1936 FILM

You ordered a copy of Universal's classic 1936 *Show Boat* as soon as you found it had been released on the Warner Archive Collection, and the made-to-order DVD arrived just in time for movie night. The opening credits roll by as a parade of paper cutouts, with the figurines in the parade carrying banners bearing the names of actors and filmmakers.

The sound of the band transports you to 1890, after the Civil War but before railroads and vaudeville had reached this part of the South. Riverboats carrying troupes of actors would still travel up and down the Mississippi River and other major waterways, stopping to give performances by riverside towns. Hammerstein made the river a character in its own right, tying together the themes of Ferber's sprawling epic in a way that made sense of it as a musical.

The first singing heard in the film is that of the African American chorus, which fades in midphrase in the introductory verse of "Ol' Man River," tempering the controversial first lyric of the libretto by making it almost inaudible. In this version, it is "Darkies all work on the Mississippi," a milder version of the racial epithet of the original libretto. The lyric has been changed many times in subsequent productions to "Colored folks work" and "Here we all work." The lyrics, which speak bluntly of working while "de white folks play," are not intended to degrade the characters singing them; rather, they contain a hint of protest that was unprecedented in a mainstream Broadway musical, set as they are to a melody that is reminiscent of so-called work songs from the time of slavery, which were sung in part to set a tempo for the brutal work. The full chorus and impact of the song won't be heard until later; here it serves as part of an overture and to announce the arrival of the *Cotton Blossom*, a Mississippi riverboat belonging to the lighthearted Captain Andy.

The paper cutout parade was evocative of the one that now occurs in live action as Captain Andy (Charles Winninger) and his troupe advertise their show to the eager townsfolk. Song and dance are intertwined with the plot in this sequence, which will introduce all of the show's main characters except for the main couple. Captain Andy's stern battle-axe of a wife is Parthy (Helen Westley), who rules the *Cotton Blossom*'s crew and acting troupe with an iron fist. On the crew are the African American stevedore Joe (Paul Robeson, who turned down the offer to originate the role on Broadway but played it in the London production), and his wife Queenie (Hattie McDaniel), the *Cotton Blossom*'s cook. The acting troupe features romantic leads Julie (Helen Morgan, who originated the role on Broadway) and her husband Steve (Donald Cook), as well as the comedy duo Frank and Ellie (Sammy White and Queenie Smith). Captain Andy's quasi-spoken "Ballyhoo" and sampling of the show are interrupted by a fistfight between Steve and the villainous crewman Pete (Arthur Hohl). Captain Andy passes the fight off as part of the show's advertisement—though the conflict will have consequences later in the story.

We can see musical theater "types" at work in the introduction of each character. Musicals have traditionally used physical type, broad acting choices, and musical symbolism—stereotype, in a word—to imply each character's personality and place in the story from the moment they are introduced. Minstrelsy stereotypes are the underbelly of a centuries-old practice of using archetypes of all kinds as efficient mechanisms to convey complex stories with a large population of characters. The type boundaries are strictly delineated in *Show Boat*'s era: you note Andy's dismissive reaction when Ellie, the comic actress, begs to be considered for the romantic lead if Julie leaves. We will see Hammerstein begin to bend the rules, fleshing out the two-dimensional types in one of the ways that will define his contribution to the Broadway musical.

Show Boat's narrative will follow the life of Captain Andy and Parthy's daughter Magnolia (Irene Dunne, who had played the role on the national tour in 1929), starting with her falling in love with the dashing gambler Gaylord Ravenal (Allan Jones). The music clearly identifies Ravenal as the romantic lead in the story as he makes his entrance. Jones's opera-trained voice is suited to the mellifluous melody of "Where's the Mate for Me," but a closer examination of the song's structure uncovers cracks in Gaylord's character, like the cracks Frank notices in his shoes. Kern provides five phrases of melody for Gaylord's declaration of his fancy-free lifestyle. That is one phrase beyond the usual four, and only the first and third phrases have an identical tune, a deliberate lack of melodic cohesiveness that creates the effect of wandering. Hammerstein writes perfect rhymes only for the final two phrases: "free" and "me." The music and lyrics have given fair warning as to Gaylord's reliability or lack thereof.

We finally meet Magnolia, who is instantly smitten with Gaylord, and she likewise has him at the proverbial "hello." The two maintain a proper distance, but the chemistry between them calls for a duet in true operetta fashion. Having just met, it's too soon for a real love song, so they just "Make Believe" they're in love. This type of delayed-love duet will become something of a specialty for Hammerstein, giving the audience a taste of love in act 1 while leaving the love story room to grow.

The sweeping theme of "Make Believe" covers the fairly wide vocal range of an **octave** and a half. When Gaylord finishes his statement of this melody, Magnolia replies with a coquettish, lilting tune, and they expound on the advantages of living in their imaginations (a denial of reality that will complicate their relationship later on, but let's enjoy it while we can). They repeat the main theme together, their voices blending in octaves as the lyric has described their lips blending. Gaylord takes the last phrase alone, and Jones's usually gentle diction gives special emphasis to the final "I do." As he kisses her hand, the romantic violin melody is overtaken by an ominous brass theme. Those who are familiar with *Show Boat*'s full score will recognize it as the introduction to "Mis'ry's Comin' 'Round," one of several songs cut or abridged for the film that are preserved in instrumental underscore.

Joe doesn't need musical foreshadowing to recognize Gaylord Ravenal's type; he's seen it before, and so has "Ol' Man River." In this song, we sense Joe's relationship with the river: a character he knows intimately that is yet totally impersonal, a symbol of stoic perseverance, and a metaphor for passing into heaven (crossing the River Jordan). The melody of the well-known chorus is based on a pentatonic scale, a five-note scale common in spirituals as well as many styles of folk music around the world, making it seem as timeless as the river itself. Spirituals exhibit aspects of African singing and European hymns, having developed among African American slaves who converted to Christianity. Many in the overwhelmingly white audience would have been familiar with spirituals through concerts by singers such as Robeson, which were wildly popular in New York in the 1920s. Beginning on low F in Robeson's rich bass voice, the chorus rises steadily and reaches its peak nearly two octaves higher on the lyric "He *just keeps* rollin' along." The chorus is AABA form, a construction that had by *Show Boat*'s original 1927 production become a common pop form, with an eight-bar A-section of melody stated twice, punctuated by a contrasting melody (B-section or bridge), and stated again. By combining the ubiquitous AABA form with a slow tempo, a pentatonic melody, and lack of predictable rhymes, Hammerstein and Kern fuse the most definitive aspects of the spiritual and the Tin Pan Alley pop song.

The next scene introduces a song that is not only thematic like "Ol' Man River," but actually intertwined with the action throughout the course of the show. Julie begins "Can't Help Lovin' Dat Man" as a cautionary tale against Magnolia falling in love too easily. In this time when music was starkly segregated, Queenie is surprised at Julie singing a song that is well known only in the African American community. When Julie begins again from the introductory verse, you hear the characteristics—the use of the call to attention "Hey listen, sister!" and the flatted blue notes in the melody—that would have identified the song as black to audiences at the time. The second verse, sung by Queenie and Joe, further describes the stereotypically lazy object of the singer's affection, giving Queenie another chance to henpeck her husband. When the chorus joins on the second refrain, Magnolia begins to dance, with steps that are clearly from African American dance, as evidenced by the similar moves of the African American ensemble.

The next scene explains Julie's surprising knowledge of "Can't Help Lovin' Dat Man": she is in fact mixed race; her mother was black. In the eyes of the law in this time and place, this makes her black and renders her marriage to Steve, who is white, illegal. Pete has outed them to law enforcement to get revenge for the events in the first scene. Steve and Julie had just enough warning to execute their emergency plan: he cuts Julie's hand and drinks a few drops of her blood, so that all present at the rehearsal can truthfully say that Steve "has Negro blood in him," and the cop cannot arrest them for miscegenation. Still, Julie and Steve leave the *Cotton Blossom*, because they will be barred from performing with the rest of the white acting troupe. The haunting underscore of "Mis'ry's Comin' 'Round" began as soon as Ellie entered with the news that the law was on the way, and the brass theme again coincides with the appearance of the deputy we saw at the end of "Make Believe."

The silver lining of Julie and Steve's sad departure is that Magnolia gets her first acting break and romance. Over Parthy's vocal disapproval, Captain Andy gives Magnolia a chance to play Julie's part, and hires Gaylord to replace Steve. The new romantic leads are a big hit all along the river, in large part because neither one of them has to pretend to be in love (luckily so, because Gaylord can't act his way out of a paper bag). A montage of their triumph up and down the river is underscored by an instrumental of another cut song, "Life upon the Wicked Stage."

Their forbidden love grows to the point where casual conversation is awkward, and they share in another delayed-love duet that was written specifically for the film. In "I Have the Room above Her," they each confess their love, knowing the other can overhear. The melody sighs with yearning, punctuated by flirtatious woodwind figures such as the one that accompanies Gaylord's "conversation" with Magnolia's stocking, which is fluttering in the wind to dry after she washes it postperformance. His use of the stocking as a proxy for Magnolia may seem strange to viewers accustomed to overt sexuality, but neither of them seems to mind. In fact, the unrealized romance of it leads them to hum the rest of the refrain, having run out of words, and ultimately to meet secretly on the top deck of the *Cotton Blossom*. Having gotten Magnolia to agree to meet up there every night, Gaylord's final "I go sadly back to mine" is not sad at all, sung with more of a lilt than a sigh.

The comically good bad acting in "The Parson's Bride," a regular part of the *Cotton Blossom*'s repertory, shows the echelon of show business on which the *Cotton Blossom* exists. When the end of the play is disrupted by a hillbilly audience member who is both ignorant and armed, Captain Andy finishes the play as a virtuosic one-man performance, trying to give the audience their money's worth, and buying Magnolia enough time to get into her blackface makeup for the next segment, which he introduces as the olio (chapter 2). During the first part of "Gallivantin' Around," Magnolia accompanies herself on the banjo, an instrument popular in minstrel shows. As Magnolia sings, you note Parthy's positive reaction and how it differs from her expression when she caught Magnolia dancing (not in blackface) at the end of "Can't Help Lovin' Dat Man." Parthy seems comfortable with Magnolia "gallivantin' around," so long as she does it as a minstrel.

It is a night like any other on the *Cotton Blossom*, with a show followed by a clandestine meeting between Magnolia and Gaylord, but we are privy to this particular night because it is the night Gaylord asks Magnolia to marry him. Here Kern and Hammerstein provide their leading couple with a proper love duet. No longer coyly making believe, they explicitly state, "You Are Love," in 3/4 time, of course, that waltzing lover-not-a-fighter of time signatures. In the first of the three sixteen-bar sections that make up the refrain, the phrases tumble out in irregular lengths as the voice sweeps up and down over a range of an octave. The following sections begin the same way, but the phrases are of regular length, as if the lover has begun to get used to the idea of being in love. Magnolia takes the second part of the refrain, and the two finish the song together in the climactic mid-upper register of their voices. However, the music once again conceals a warning: the word "love" is always either set to a slightly dissonant note or a minor chord. The music and the way Hammerstein set the words to it tells us that even in its resolution, this is no easy love affair.

Magnolia and Gaylord's wedding takes place about halfway through the story, marking the end of act 1 in the stage version. The middle of a show is a structurally unusual time for a wedding to take place; tradition calls for the wedding to occur at the very end. However, Gaylord and Magnolia's marriage marks the beginning of a new phase of obstacles, rather than the beginning of happily ever after (which sounds lovely but is boring to watch). Short reprises underscoring the proposal and time lapse after the wedding remind us that "Ol' Man River" just keeps rollin' along through all the ups and downs and milestones of life.

"I Still Suits Me" was written for the 1936 film to expand the roles of Joe and Queenie; it was difficult to get a star of Robeson's stature for what is essentially a one-song role, no matter how good the song. The duet allows a further glimpse into Joe and Queenie's relationship, which for all Queenie's haranguing of her easygoing husband, is constant and true. Their loyal partnership provides a contrasting foil for Magnolia and Gaylord's marriage. When Magnolia goes into labor, it is Queenie, Ellie, and Parthy who help, and Joe who moves with uncharacteristic haste into the storm to fetch a doctor—Gaylord is out gambling.

He uses the winnings from one of his streaks of good luck to leave the *Cotton Blossom* at last, moving to Chicago with Magnolia and their baby daughter Kim. Another montage and a series of scenes show the good times that ultimately cannot last, culminating in Magnolia's lowest point, when she receives a good-bye letter from Gaylord. This part of the film is underscored by a sequence of music bookended by "Why Do I Love You?" Though we never hear the lyrics of that song in this version of *Show Boat*, those in the know will recognize that both the wistful tune and the title are appropriate to the moment: Why *do* these mismatched misfits love each other?

It is Gaylord's desertion of Magnolia, along with a few lucky coincidences, that leads to Magnolia becoming a star of the stage. One of the most common criticisms leveled at *Show Boat* is the number of coincidences that occur in act 2. Fifteen years later, it would be considered cheating to get the protagonist out of a jam with a coincidence. Fifteen years earlier, they still would have been dragging the plot to Hawaii just for a hula number. Baby steps. Coincidence number one: Frank and

Ellie happen upon Magnolia just after Gaylord leaves her, and they invite her to audition at the Trocadero where Frank is now working. Before we get to the audition, we catch a glimpse of Gaylord on his way out of town. He bids good-bye to Kim with a little white lie and a reprise of "Make Believe," with lyrics modified to befit the father-daughter relationship.

Coincidence number two, of which Frank and Ellie somehow seem to be unaware: starring at the Trocadero is none other than Magnolia's long-lost Julie. The years have not treated Julie well; her beloved Steve has deserted her, which has driven her to drink, and she channels her despair into the new song she's rehearsing. "Bill," in which a woman tells of her love for an imperfect man, was originally written for *Oh, Lady! Lady!!* with lyrics by P. G. Wodehouse, but was cut from that show and later from *Sally*. Kern finally found a home for it in *Show Boat*'s score, with some slight modifications—though Hammerstein generously made sure Wodehouse always got exclusive credit for the lyrics.

Morgan was known for moving audiences with her emotional singing perched atop an upright piano (she was also known for flouting Prohibition laws, which got Ziegfeld lots of free publicity during the original run). Though she merely leans on the piano in the film, you can imagine the charm and pathos her persona and small soprano voice created in a live setting. Indeed, the song's sentimentality comes from its performance rather than the song itself. The melody never lingers longer than a couple of beats on one pitch, and the lyrics rest on the melody one syllable per note, which together create a conversational effect. The verse and chorus of "Bill" are of nearly equal importance, both being sixteen bars long and having a similar tempo and feel. This verse-chorus parity was characteristic of popular songs around 1900, making it a likely form for a song Julie would have had in her repertoire in 1904, the year indicated in the stage libretto for this part of the story.

We continue to see the evolution of popular music and dramatic integration in Magnolia's audition scene. Magnolia tells the producer, Mr. Greene, that she sings "Negro songs," causing him to immediately peg her as a "coon shouter" (a term that usually referred to a white female performer who "shouted" coon songs, rather than singing operetta repertoire and style). Greene is then puzzled when Magnolia's performance of "Can't Help Lovin' Dat Man" doesn't fit in with his expectations, and he dismisses her out of hand. Backstage, Julie over-hears the familiar tune and slips away, sacrificing herself to give her beloved Magnolia her second big break of the show. The producer doesn't think "Can't Help Lovin' Dat Man" is up to date enough for his crowd, but he's put in a tight spot when he learns Julie has quit. The pianist suggests "ragging" the song, and though Magnolia at first has trouble keeping up with the fast, syncopated version, she catches on in time to get the gig.

Despite the producer's preference for ragtime at the audition, Mag-nolia for some reason opens her performance with "After the Ball." It was the megahit of the 1890s, but it is slow, sad, and a little passé at this point; an odd choice for New Year's Eve entertainment, so of course Magnolia gets heckled by the inebriated crowd. Fortunately, Captain Andy is *in* the crowd (another coincidence, but at least he was in Chica-go to visit Magnolia). In the novel, much is made of Magnolia's magical smile, which has the power to transform her plain face into a thing of rare beauty. Hammerstein distills this thread into Captain Andy's re-peated entreaty throughout the libretto to Magnolia to smile. With her smile, father and daughter are able to turn the tide of audience disdain into a sing-along of this well-known popular song, and Magnolia's star is born.

The film wraps up quite expediently after that, indicating the pas-sage of time with a montage that shows Magnolia's illustrious career and eventual retirement from the stage. The montage is bridged with Gaylord still wistfully "making believe," maintaining a scrapbook of his abandoned wife's triumphs—and his daughter's, as Kim follows in her mother's footsteps. In her debut as the star performer, Kim is front and center for a dance number you recognize as an orchestral arrangement of "Gallivantin' Around." In a coincidence that modern audiences might find a little disconcerting (to say nothing of the scrapbook!), Gaylord has somehow managed to land a job guarding the stage door at the theater where Kim is working. He watches from the wings, and thus he and Magnolia are reunited at their daughter's performance, reprising "You Are Love" from the box seats for a delighted audience—and a surprised Kim, who hadn't recognized "Pops" at the stage door as her father. In later shows, Hammerstein would stretch the boundaries of the obligatory union of the primary couple, but here he concedes to tradition by reuniting Magnolia and Gaylord, in a departure from the novel. Thus *Show Boat*'s long narrative arc ends with, as Captain Andy would say, "one big, happy family."

SHOW BOAT'S LEGACY

Show Boat, in its many incarnations and revivals, has "rolled on" through economic turmoil, conflicts at home and abroad, and the ever-shifting discourse on race in the United States. As is common with works that deal with race, it has faced its share of controversy through the years. Even at the time of the original production, the African American press expressed the familiar ambivalence felt by many black performers about the tradeoff between being pigeonholed by racial stereotype and the professional opportunity of being in a Ziegfeld show on Broadway. Revivals have struggled with the use and interpretation of ensemble numbers like "In Dahomey," whose satirical edge doesn't make sense to an audience that has at most a passing familiarity with the 1893 Chicago World's Fair. On the 1988 EMI recording, which includes the uncut 1927 score as reconstructed by conductor John McGlinn, the white Ambrosian Chorus that had been hired for the white chorus material is heard on *all* the chorus music, because members of the black chorus quit rather than sing the racial epithet that was the original first lyric.

Show Boat touches not only on race but on the performance of race, onstage and in life, over a period of several formative decades in American history and entertainment. The theme comes straight from the source material: in addition to Julie's mixed-race heritage and the resulting subplot, Ferber describes Magnolia as having a "black voice" that played a part in her professional success. Todd Decker notes in *Show Boat: Performing Race in an American Musical* that despite the novel's description, Magnolia's role in the musical has no Southern dialect, no blue notes, and she even has a little trouble syncopating "Can't Help Lovin' Dat Man" the first time she tries to "rag it" at the Trocadero audition. Decker surmises that perhaps Broadway audiences weren't ready in 1927 for a white ingénue to sound black; the black/white music story line comes through more in the choice of repertoire ("Can't Help Lovin' Dat Man" with its story line of coming from the African American community) than in the performance thereof. The same holds true in the 1936 film, except in Magnolia's performance of "Gallivantin' Around," though as a minstrel number, that song had precedent in white performance.

The performance practice of the role of Julie has evolved over time. Helen Morgan, who was white, was identified with the role of Julie for years, even after her untimely death at age forty-one. Since the civil rights movement of the 1960s, it has been more common to cast an actress who is light-skinned African American or mixed race in the role of Julie; likewise, the interpretation of Julie's relationship to her ethnicity has evolved. Lonette McKee, an actress of Scandinavian and African American heritage, played Julie in the 1983 revival and the Harold Prince revival of the 1990s, and her performance is preserved on the 1993 Toronto revival cast recording. In comparing the vocal interpretations of Morgan and McKee, one notices that Morgan sings rhythmically and melodically as it is written on the page (a characteristic associated with singing "white"). McKee sings Julie's songs in lower keys for a chestier sound, and improvises more with the melody and phrasing (characteristics associated with singing "black"). Julie may be more successful passing as a white woman with Morgan's vocal interpretation, but Julie proudly singing the black part of her heritage, as in McKee's performance, has been the more popular interpretation of the role in the post–civil rights era, according to Decker.

The ongoing debate about the themes and performance of race in *Show Boat* is as important a part of *Show Boat*'s legacy as its place as the cornerstone of integrated (double entendre intended) book musicals on Broadway. It is "Ol' Man River," not "You Are Love," that gets the last word in the 1936 film and most other versions of *Show Boat*— arguably better capturing the point of the story. While Hammerstein, Kern, and Ziegfeld's groundbreaking musical bowed to musical comedy convention in reuniting Gaylord and Magnolia at the end of the show, the story was about something bigger than its central romance: *Show Boat* ultimately has something to say about the resilience of the human spirit, and it says it *through*—not simply interrupted *by*—glorious music and dance.

4

THE GREAT DEPRESSION AND THE GREAT AMERICAN SONGBOOK

Anything Goes and *Porgy and Bess*

The 1927–1928 Broadway season was a bumper crop for theater. Two hundred sixty-four shows opened on Broadway during that time, and many of them, including *Show Boat*, enjoyed good ticket sales. But it was more than the market could bear, and the following season saw a contraction, which was closely followed by the stock market crash of October 1929 and the ensuing economic collapse. During the lean times of the Great Depression, people sought escape in entertainment if they could afford it, but they often got more bang for the buck from movies than from live theater. Songwriters followed the work to Hollywood, and Broadway went into survival mode, cutting losses with fewer productions and shorter runs. Risk-averse commercial producers and theatergoers favored the tried-and-true formulas of musical comedies and revues. Operettas, though comfortingly familiar, were expensive to produce with their large casts and elaborate sets and costumes, and they experienced what author Ethan Mordden describes in his book, *Sing For Your Supper: The Broadway Musical in the 1930s*, as "a slow and painful death" (but never fear—old art forms never die, they just slink backstage and bide their time).

In terms of dramatic integration, the 1930s are sometimes viewed as a period during which Broadway musicals treaded water between *Show Boat* and the next major landmark in 1943, *Oklahoma!* Yet even in these straitened times, when musicals delivered the zany, escapist musical comedy the dwindling audiences craved, subtle changes were afoot. *Show Boat* had proved that a musical could tell a powerful, quintessentially American story with popular music, and within the formulaic crowd pleasers of the 1930s could sometimes be detected a sharper political edge and a thrust toward narrative.

A sign that musicals were being taken more seriously came early in the decade, when the comedy *Of Thee I Sing* (1932) became the first musical to be awarded the Pulitzer Prize. The goofball political satire, about a bachelor presidential candidate trying to find a wife through a reality show–like popularity contest, had a book by George S. Kaufman and Morrie Ryskind, music by George Gershwin, and lyrics by his brother Ira Gershwin (the Pulitzer did not include George, because the award only applied to text, not music—a technicality that upset Ira so much that he hung the award askew in his bathroom). The score doesn't sound like the jazz standards many associate with Gershwin; its intricacy speaks to the influence of classical concert music on Gershwin's writing at the time. The degree to which *Of Thee I Sing*'s music is dependent upon and woven into the libretto of the show prompts Mordden to cite the show as one of several "missing links" between *Show Boat* and *Oklahoma!* Such integration also made it hard to extract any of the songs as popular hits, so its excellent score is undeservedly obscure.

Irving Berlin's revue *As Thousands Cheer* (1933) was inspired by present-day newspaper headlines; librettist Moss Hart's witty sketches had Broadway stars of the day impersonating celebrities and political figures. It was mostly comedic but had a few serious moments of pointing out injustice and suffering, as when Ethel Waters, the first African American woman in an otherwise all-white Broadway show, sang Berlin's "Suppertime," a song written from the point of view of a woman trying to prepare supper for her children after her husband has just been lynched.

A few shows were overtly political. The company of *The Cradle Will Rock* showed up a few nights before opening in 1937 to find their theater padlocked, because the government, which was producing the show through the New Deal's Federal Theatre Project, feared that the serious, operatic, pro-union show would foment labor unrest. But "the show must go on," so the creators rented a piano and another theater nearby. Because of their union restrictions, actors couldn't perform onstage, so they sang their parts from seats in the audience. The show's composer Marc Blitzstein accompanied them on the piano, as the musicians' union wouldn't let the orchestra perform, either. A fictionalized account of the embattled show is told in the 1999 film of the same title.

Those who got the laughs got the audiences: the second-longest-running show of the 1930s was, like *The Cradle Will Rock*, a pro-labor 1937 musical; unlike *Cradle*, it was a comedy revue. With songs by Harold Rome, *Pins and Needles* was produced by the International Ladies' Garment Workers Union, starring its own members. When the show became a hit, the women quit their day jobs and embarked on an eight-show-a-week schedule, making it, as historian John Kenrick writes in *Musical Theatre: A History*, "the only amateur musical production to ever find success on Broadway."

The longest-running show of the 1930s was also a revue, a fast-paced hodgepodge of comedic sketches and songs called *Hellzapoppin'* (1938), written primarily by Sammy Fain and Charles Tobias. It ran for over three years, with constant changes to keep its political and cultural references fresh. Over time, many songwriters including Louis Armstrong and Oscar Hammerstein II contributed material to the show. There was a movie adaptation of the show in 1941, but it didn't preserve much of the cast or achieve the success of the original show.

By the 1930s, a multicomposer, patchwork score like *Hellzapoppin'* was the exception rather than the rule; most musicals were written by one songwriter or songwriting team. Names like George and Ira Gershwin, Cole Porter, and Richard Rodgers and Lorenz Hart attracted audiences in the way big-name stars had done two decades previously. Many of their Depression-era shows are best remembered by their hit songs, which have become the backbone of what is known as the Great American Songbook. Such gems as Porter's "Ev'ry Time We Say Goodbye"(from *Seven Lively Arts*) and Rodgers and Hart's "My Funny Valentine" (from *Babes in Arms*) have transcended their Broadway origins to be performed and recorded by artists in diverse genres, and have become favorites of audiences around the globe. The following sections will examine songs from Porter's *Anything Goes* and the Gershwins' and DuBose Heyward's *Porgy and Bess*, which are among the few Broadway musicals that survived their tumultuous decade and century to remain popular both as shows and as sources of popular song.

COLE PORTER

Composer-lyricist Cole Porter's songs are known for their sophisticated references and cynical humor. Born in 1891 in Peru, Indiana, Porter came from a wealthy Anglo-Saxon Protestant family, unlike many of his songwriting contemporaries. His iron-willed maternal grandfather was a self-made man who disapproved of artistic careers and wanted Porter to study law. Porter's equally strong-willed mother had him studying music from a young age, determined that her son would distinguish himself in the arts.

Porter's wit and musical talent drew people to him, and he learned early on that these talents were his keys to success. He attended prep school in Massachusetts, where he had a piano in his room and spent hours playing and singing to amuse himself and his classmates. At Yale, he wrote over three hundred songs, including school fight songs and musicals for the drama department. His prolific output earned him extra credit and essentially enabled him to eke out a degree despite his otherwise mediocre academic performance. After Yale, he spent a miserable year flunking out of law school at Harvard while still busily writing musicals. He accepted the offered alternative of switching to the music department, and finally abandoned his studies to move to New York, where he had his first show on Broadway in 1916: *See America First*. It was a flop. *Variety*'s critic advised the theatergoing public to "*See America First* last," and the show closed after fifteen performances.

After that disappointment, Porter retreated to high-society life in Europe, writing few songs for public consumption, confining himself instead to songs intended to entertain his circle of friends until his successful return to Broadway in 1928 with *Paris*. His prospects had been helped by his marriage in 1918 to Linda Lee Thomas, a wealthy and well-connected divorcée. It was an advantageous arrangement for both of them. Porter was gay at a time when being out would have destroyed his career, and Linda provided a respectable cover as well as societal connections. Linda's first marriage had been abusive, and she accepted Porter's homosexuality in exchange for his companionship and the social status brought by marriage. Moreover, Linda and Cole truly loved one another; they shared many interests, and underneath the glitz and glamour, he was an Indiana farm boy and she a simple Kentucky girl. Rough patches and separations notwithstanding, they remained married until her death in 1954.

Porter's cosmopolitan sparkle was supported by down-to-earth midwestern roots. His marriage to Linda lasted through many short- and long-term romantic relationships with men, and he put on a brave face over chronic pain after a crippling horseback riding accident. Such layers can be found in Porter's lyrics and music as well. A master of sexual innuendo, some of the double entendre was not obvious to those outside the gay community. As Graham Payne writes in the introduction to his book *My Life with Noel Coward*, "Cole amused himself by pitching words on two levels, so that the 'coach party' audience was content with the obvious, while the 'in' group relished the real meaning." The emotional complexity of Porter's songs is underpinned by his harmonic language: a favorite technique is to switch abruptly between major and minor tonality, as if allowing a momentary glimpse at the layer beneath the surface before the façade falls back into place.

1954 TELEVISION BROADCAST: *THE COLGATE COMEDY HOUR: ANYTHING GOES*

Spring has come, and with it, the excellent local repertory company's big musical. This season's selection is *Anything Goes*, the classic musical comedy about a motley crew of passengers on a cruise liner crossing from New York to London. The director has given the cast a research assignment: watch the video of the 1954 live televised version of the show. Originally broadcast on February 28, 1954, this version was part of a series called *The Colgate Comedy Hour*. The twists and turns of the original *Anything Goes* plot defy brevity, and the director has warned that drastic cuts and changes were made to fit the show into a one-hour slot with commercials. Don't watch it for plot, she has explained, as they will be using the script from the 1987 Broadway revival, which was also used for the 2011 revival. Watch it instead for the Cole Porter songs and the legendary performers: Ethel Merman in the role of Reno Sweeney, which she created in the original 1934 production; pop star Frank Sinatra in the midst of a career comeback, and Bert Lahr, a vaudevillian who is best remembered as the Cowardly Lion from *The Wizard of Oz*. Enjoy the inevitable gaffes of live television in its earliest years, and see how these star performers, who grew up with vaudeville and knew how to handle live performance, react.

The Colgate Comedy Hour of *Anything Goes* begins by showing the manicured hand of an audience member flipping through the program, while an announcer intones the names and titles printed on it. As Merman announces the show from her dressing room, you can hear the orchestra tuning in the background. There's an long, awkward pause after her speech that betrays live television's novelty as a medium, but then the show is off and running with a Charleston-style dance number. The particular rhythms and dance moves of the Charleston evoke the 1920s, not the 1930s when *Anything Goes* and many of Porter's other hits ran on Broadway. In his liner notes to the DVD, musical theater writer Stephen Cole surmises that perhaps the 1930s were not remembered as enough of a happy-go-lucky, "anything goes" setting for the 1954 audience.

As characters are introduced, anyone familiar with the show will notice major deviations from the original plot. Merman, as evangelist-turned-nightclub-singer Reno Sweeney, enters to great fanfare and applause, already engaged to Evelyn Oakleigh, the man Reno winds up with at the *end* of the original. Later, Frank Sinatra will enter as Reno's erstwhile agent Harry, more or less replacing Billy Crocker from the original—except in this version, he is in love with Reno instead of the ingénue, Hope Harcourt, whose role is cut entirely.

This might be inexcusable in another musical, but *Anything Goes* has a history of major revisions from its very start. The original story line, written by Princess Theatre alumni Guy Bolton and P. G. Wodehouse, was overhauled after a deadly real-life shipwreck made the news and rendered a shipwreck in Bolton and Wodehouse's plot unfunny. They were unavailable for rewrites, or maybe the shipwreck provided the producer with an excuse to revise a book he didn't like. In any case, *Anything Goes* launched a fruitful collaboration between Howard Lindsay and Russel Crouse, who were hired to make the revisions. A 1936 movie version starring Bing Crosby alongside Merman preserves most of the plot but hardly any of the music. Drastic revisions to the plot and song list were made for a revival in 1962, and again in 1987 for a Lincoln Center production starring leading lady Patti LuPone. The 2011 Broadway revival starring Sutton Foster used the same song list as 1987. *Anything Goes* is an excellent illustration of how forgiving audiences will be of changes in a musical comedy: in short, anything goes so long as the songs stay.

Merman stands center screen and beams her star power to the folks at home with the title song. The verse of Porter's tune about changing times opens with a four-note melody outlining a minor chord, declaring that "times have cha-anged." The second half of the verse repeats the four-note melody, this time in major, to state what would happen to the Puritans "*if toda-ay* any shock they should [back to minor] try to stem." Cole Porter succinctly expresses his opinion of Puritan morals with the major chord on "if today," and the almost gleeful setting of the line "Plymouth Rock would land on them" leading into the refrain. Merman's brassy belt voice and emphatic diction perfectly project Porter's lyric about the changing mores from Pilgrim times to permissive times. The refrain goes on to describe the details of modern times in modern rhythm; that is to say, syncopation. The rhythm of the melody and even the rhyme scheme push the beat, as the rhyming word "shocking" appears sooner than expected, while the melody also rises to a higher note for emphasis. The last section, which usually begins "Though I'm not a great romancer," instead uses a new melody and alternate lyrics that include the word "Technicolor"—perhaps a bow to the industry that was just taking off. Merman's idiosyncratic vocal accentuation can be heard on the final "goes."

Over the years, songs from other Cole Porter shows have often made their way into *Anything Goes*. Even this one-hour broadcast managed to find time for three interpolations, and the first of these is "You Do Something to Me," originally from *Fifty Million Frenchmen*. A ballad duet between Reno and Harry, one chorus of it bubbles up in the midst of their argument, and subsides as quickly as it appears.

Harry is a stowaway until gangster Moonface (Bert Lahr) offers him the ticket and passport of his no-show cohort. Little does Harry know the no-show he is now impersonating is Snake Eyes Johnson, public enemy number one! Harry explores the ship and pursues Reno, but she cuts him off by reminding him of a long-ago night when he had his chance to commit and refused. Rapid harp glissandos, symbolic of a change in time period, indicate a flashback. This being live television, Merman and Sinatra need time to get to their positions, so the screen comes back into focus on a barroom pianist playing the blues (a keen observer will notice that the pianist accepts a drink with his right hand, but the melody played by the right hand continues!). The blues and the booze, and the woman with money in her garter scratching her foot set the seedy scene while Merman and Sinatra scurry to their marks as flashback Reno and Harry. After Flashback Harry rejects her, Flashback Reno begins to sing "I Get a Kick Out of You," one of the hits from the original 1934 song list. Reno slowly intones a rising scale accompanied only by the piano that has been playing under the barroom scene; strings and woodwinds add more romance to the accompaniment after the first two phrases. When the orchestra kicks in with a beguine dance rhythm on the chorus, the contrast between the slow-moving phrases of the vocal line and the busyness of the accompaniment highlight the angst Reno is feeling. In the second verse, Reno sings, "Some like that perfume from Spain," instead of the more provocative "Some get a kick from cocaine." Along with the double entendre of some of his lyrics, Porter's not-so-subtle lyrical references to sex and drugs often put him at odds with entertainment censors, and he had written the alternate lyric to meet Production Code standards for the 1936 film. After this verse, the orchestration thins out to accentuate the new vocal melody of the bridge. The beguine rhythm resumes for the final section, where Porter has extended the usual ascent of the melody to climb all the way up the scale, corresponding with the high-flying words "guy in the sky." The orchestra pauses before the final phrase to allow Merman to deliver it with all her rafter-reaching power—but she places the last note so that she can soften it to return Reno to the emotional state where she began the song, even while the orchestra finishes cheerfully.

Harp glissandos return us to the ship, where Harry sings a reprise of the final section of the song and an extended ending, his feet providing a literal "kick" to complement the lyric. Sinatra's casual delivery and the swing of the arrangement feel very loose by comparison to Merman's: the music belies Harry's renunciation of the "free and easy" in favor of Reno's love.

The arrangement of "I Get a Kick Out of You" prompts you to take a detour to Sinatra's album *Songs for Young Lovers*. One of two 1954 Sinatra albums on the Capitol Records label, its release dovetailed nicely with the *Anything Goes* broadcast. Nelson Riddle, who conducted the recording sessions for the album, launching a long-term collaboration with Sinatra, was then hired to orchestrate the music for the *Anything Goes* broadcast along with Buddy Bregman. It was likely Bregman who arranged "I Get a Kick Out of You" (Stephen Cole quotes him in the DVD booklet: "If Ethel opened her mouth, I did the arrangement"). Still, given the timing and crossover of personnel, it makes sense both from a marketing and a performing standpoint that some similarities to George Siravo's arrangement from the Capitol album, which Riddle had conducted, would be heard in the television version.

On Sinatra's album, the slow introductory verse leads into the chorus, where the walking bass and ride cymbal set the foundation for an easy swing. The syncopated echoes between Sinatra's phrases, here dominated by the guitar, are very similar to the ones played by muted trumpets in Sinatra's reprise on the television broadcast. Drums punctuate the word "kick," but Sinatra's delivery remains ever nonchalant even when the band drives into the final section. He **backphrases** frequently; for example, "my idea of nothing to do" is sung far behind the beat, giving the effect that he's improvising the series of internal rhymes in that stanza.

Both Sinatra and Merman take liberties with the written rhythms and pitches of the song, as is customary in popular songs performed and recorded by multiple artists. On the page, Porter wrote languorous half-note triplets (three notes stretched across four beats) for champagne, cocaine, and/or perfume from Spain—all the things that do *not* give the singer a kick. The words "I get a kick" land delightfully on the beat, but the accented "kick" surprises the singer on the relatively weak fourth beat, setting up a delightful syncopation in the way only infatuation can do. These rhythms are, as musicologist Geoffrey Block points out in his book *Enchanted Evenings*, more often seen on the sheet music than heard in practice. However, their goal is the contrast between the ennui-inducing luxury items and the sought-after "you," and both Sinatra and Merman accomplish this contrast in their respective styles, with the help of the instrumental arrangements.

The Colgate Comedy Hour finds room for two more interpolations from other Porter shows: "Just One of Those Things" from *Jubilee* (1935), and "Friendship" from *Du Barry Was a Lady* (1939). "Just One of Those Things" is another song that became a standard, appearing on recordings by dozens of artists, including Sinatra's other 1954 Capitol album, *Swing Easy*. As for "Friendship," Merman and Lahr had worked together on *Du Barry*, and they both requested the song be included when they found out they'd be doing the *Anything Goes* broadcast together. A comedic song-and-dance duet that in this context illustrates the quirky rapport between Reno and Moonface, "Friendship" has been included in almost every version of *Anything Goes* since.

In addition to the title number and "I Get a Kick Out of You," other songs used from the original 1934 song list are "You're the Top," "Blow, Gabriel, Blow," and "All through the Night." A duet between Reno and Harry, "You're the Top" is the quintessential Cole Porter **list song**, a song whose lyrics are mostly composed of a list that creates some kind of metaphor or narrative, a genre that was a Porter specialty. Full of urbane references like "the Tower of Pisa" and "the Mona Lisa," "You're the Top" achieved greater popularity than many of Porter's other list songs that had lyrical references too esoteric or period specific to resonate with a wide audience (for example, inside jokes about his high-society friends). Even "You're the Top," with its relatively accessible references, had to undergo some changes by P. G. Wodehouse to be more comprehensible to London audiences attending the 1935 West End production. At the end of the song, Merman and Sinatra acknowledge the applause and repeat the last refrain. Despite the tight time frame of the commercial broadcast, the producers allowed a couple of these carefully planned **encores**, hearkening back to recent days when "showstopper" was a literal term and stars might have taken a half a dozen encores of a big number.

"Blow, Gabriel, Blow" calls the viewer back from a commercial break with a screaming trumpet riff, acted out by a silhouetted trumpeter onstage next to Reno. The tongue-in-cheek revival meeting is an iconic scene in the original show, where the evangelist turned nightclub singer nature of Reno's character is made clearer by the libretto. In this version, the number comes out of nowhere, but one can still appreciate Merman's trumpetlike use of her voice. Porter uses contrasting minor tonality to distinguish between hell and salvation: at the end of the mostly minor section about hell, he solemnly outlines a minor chord with the lyrics "So I said 'Satan, farewell,'" to make the listener "ready to fly" to the end of the tune.

Harry ends up in the brig near the end of the show, as in the stage version but for different reasons. There he sings the sensuous ballad "All through the Night," accompanied by a richly orchestrated arrangement that sets off the melancholy fluidity of his voice. A descending chromatic scale can introduce a circus act, brisk and **marcato** (marchlike) as in "March of the Gladiators." But performed slowly and **legato** (smoothly) as Sinatra sings this melody, descending chromatic tones are the tune of yearning and desire. Such melodic figures, which also allow for surprising twists in the harmony, appear throughout the entire song; Porter wards off boredom by bringing each section to a different ending. The layers of similarity and variety written into the song create a balance that is as perfect as an imagined night with a lover.

The curtain comes down behind Sinatra, Merman, and Lahr after a reprise of "I Get a Kick out of You," and the ensemble dances across the curtain to "Anything Goes." According to Stephen Cole's liner notes, the dress rehearsal had run three minutes over, so, to ensure that the whole show fit with commercial breaks, the creative team had obediently cut three minutes of the show. Live performance adrenaline being what it is, the show ended with three minutes to spare during the broadcast, the stars standing in front of the curtain at the end with nothing left to do. An encore being the obvious solution, Sinatra suggests that Merman sing "Anything Goes" once again, and the conductor and orchestra follow her without missing a beat.

PORGY AND BESS, A FOLK OPERA

George Gershwin aspired to write an opera. Born in 1898 into a middle-class Jewish family in New York City, he began to study music at the relatively late age of twelve, after the family purchased a piano intended for his elder brother Ira. George's love affair with the piano was immediate and lasting. As soon as it was hoisted into the living room through a window, he was at the instrument, picking out a popular tune he'd figured out on a friend's piano, and at age fifteen he quit school to become a song plugger. Gershwin never needed convincing to take over the piano at parties, and it was at such a party that superstar Al Jolson heard him playing "Swanee," to which Irving Caesar had written the lyrics. Jolson's performance of it made it Gershwin's first international hit in 1920.

The year 1924 was a big one for George: bandleader Paul Whiteman commissioned *Rhapsody in Blue* for a pivotal concert entitled *An Experiment in Modern Music*, curated to demonstrate the new and daring concept of jazz-influenced classical music. The piece, if not the concert as a whole, was a popular success, but reviews were mixed, stating that the composer showed talent and originality but lacked the mastery of musical form and development expected of a "serious" composer. In December, the musical comedy *Lady Be Good* opened successfully on Broadway, his first joint effort with Ira as lyricist. The brothers had a string of hit musicals in the late 1920s and early '30s, including the Pulitzer-winning *Of Thee I Sing*. Still, for all his commercial success, George was haunted by the criticisms of his concert compositions and fired by ambition to write an American opera.

He first approached South Carolinian writer DuBose Heyward in 1926 about adapting Heyward's novel *Porgy*. Heyward and his wife Dorothy had already adapted the novel as a play, and George thought the story had potential as an opera. Heyward was an important figure in post–Civil War Southern literature, and he was recognized as one of the first white Southern authors who—from the perspective of his white contemporaries—wrote about Southern blacks without caricature or condescension. His mother was an avid linguist who studied the speech patterns of the Gullah, who were brought as slaves from West Africa to the islands off the coast of the Carolinas and whose language developed in relative isolation from the mainland. *Porgy* is set in Catfish Row, a Gullah tenement of Charleston, South Carolina, in "the recent past" (of 1935). The story centers around Porgy, a crippled beggar, and the love that unexpectedly enters his life in the form of Bess. Plagued by addiction, Bess struggles to be accepted by the community and to escape the throes of Crown, her virile, violent lover, and Sportin' Life, the dapper purveyor of happy dust (cocaine).

After several false starts because of George's demanding schedule, Gershwin and Heyward finally began work on *Porgy* in late 1933 (the "*and Bess*" was added to the title later, lest the public think it was just a revival of the play). After working by correspondence while Gershwin was finishing a whirlwind concert tour, Gershwin visited Heyward on Folly Island and James Island off the coast of South Carolina, immersing himself in the music of the Gullah people while he worked. The collaboration brought about new processes for both Heyward and Gershwin: Heyward had never written lyrics before, and George was accustomed to writing the music first. George set Heyward's poetic words to his most sustained, soaring melodies. Later, Heyward came to New York, where Ira joined the collaboration. The songs for which Ira

provided the lyrics were the Tin Pan Alley–esque tunes, such as Sportin' Life's "It Ain't Necessarily So" and "There's a Boat That's Leavin'
Soon for New York."

Porgy and Bess opened on October 10, 1935, at Broadway's Alvin
Theatre. The first aria the audience heard that night was a tune that
would permeate the world. Gershwin's melody and Heyward's lyrics,
both influenced by an existing African American song used in *Porgy* the
play, have inspired thousands of cover versions across all genres of
music from artists and groups in many nations.

"SUMMERTIME"

The jazz combo meets on Tuesday nights at the university, a group of
six music majors led by a graduate student. Tonight they are rehearsing
an arrangement of "Summertime" based on jazz trumpeter and bandleader Miles Davis's 1959 recording from his *Porgy and Bess* album.
The trumpet player in the combo begins without preamble, muted,
playing the same slight variations on the melody that Davis recorded. As
the song continues, he deviates further from the original melody. The
trumpet student has spent hours listening and copying the exact notes
and inflections that the master jazz trumpeter improvised. The rest of
the ensemble provides the accompaniment for this solo, with the bassist
and drummer laying down a steady, mellow four-beat groove, and the
pianist and two saxophones playing a repeated figure behind the solo.
Miles Davis's ensemble had eleven players (himself included, with
some players doubling on more than one instrument), and Gil Evans
arranged and conducted the piece. Much of this student combo's rehearsal time is spent figuring out how the piano and two saxes can
imitate the subtle changes in the background figure with each verse.
With only three players, their options are limited. The piano is a mixed
blessing, for it can play full harmonies, but its chords must sound gentle, like the wind instruments on the recording. Nothing should be
jarring in this arrangement, and the whole thing should evolve subtly,
inviting the listener to pay attention to the changes, and to the wordless
melody played by the trumpet.

The next day, the pianist from the combo accompanies a voice lesson
for a soprano opera student. Her assignment: the aria "Summertime"

from *Porgy and Bess*. The pianist has never given much thought to the origins of "Summertime" before. Hasn't it always been there? She vaguely recollects hearing it as a lullaby, and clearly remembers blasting Janis Joplin's version of it, *not* as a lullaby. Now encountering it twice in one week, in two equally different guises, she decides to investigate.

The original aria version is in fact a lullaby, sung by the supporting character Clara to her baby at the beginning of *Porgy and Bess*. The germ of "Summertime" came from the play version of *Porgy*, which included a number of preexisting African American choral and folk tunes. In it, Bess sings a lullaby that includes the lines "Hush, little baby, don't you cry / Mudder and Fadder born to die." Such a matter-of-fact attitude toward hardship was common enough in songs from the time of slavery, and Gershwin attempts to capture the essence of the spiritual in this aria. Heyward's lyrics omit the reference to death, instead stating that "Yo' Daddy's rich, an' your Ma is good-lookin'," and assuring the baby of his safety and his ability to rise up and fly. Still, the specter of death remains, as the haunting harmonies beneath the soprano melody are minor. Only the line "Hush, little baby" is supported by reassuring major chords.

A quick search at the music library yields numerous recordings of *Porgy and Bess*, among them a 1942 performance with Anne Brown, the original Clara, released on the Decca label in 1959. Juilliard-trained Brown worked closely with Gershwin, helping him by singing through most of the female roles while he was writing the opera. Her voice seems to float effortlessly above the orchestra even on the last stratospheric wailing note, her formidable technique allowing her to negotiate the challenging **tessitura** with a softness that reminds us this is, in fact, a lullaby.

The first popular music release of "Summertime" was Billie Holiday's 1936 recording. The guitar, bass, and drums lay down every beat to create the swing feel, and trumpeter Bunny Berigan and clarinetist Artie Shaw improvise simultaneously, responding to each other and to Holiday's vocal. The arrangement is in B-flat minor, only a half step lower than the original aria, but Holiday sings the melody the octave down in the speaking part of her voice. She takes liberties with the melody and rhythm, and her manner of singing "blue" notes that are lowered from their usual position in the scale exemplifies the African American style of singing that influenced Gershwin's writing, even as he mixed the melodic language with classical vocal production and inflections. Holiday ends on a hopeful note, literally: she alters the melody at the end of each verse to end on the note that indicates a major key, and the band follows suit with a cadence in major.

Having discovered hundreds of cover versions, the pianist decides to take in just one more recording of the song before calling it a night. In 2004, *American Idol* contestant Fantasia Barrino's performance of "Summertime" won praise from the judges and helped her gain the votes from the public that earned her the title for the third season of the televised singing contest. This "Summertime" is in E minor, about halfway between the operatic key and Billie Holiday's key, which puts the melody in the silvery mix range of Fantasia's voice, heavier than **head voice** but lighter than **chest voice**, perfect for a lullaby in the R&B idiom. She starts simply, singing the melody as written, only subtly reattacking the third syllable of the title lyric: "Summer-*ti-ime.*" As the song continues, Fantasia adds ever more elaborate vocal fireworks to sustained words ("your daddy's *riiiiiiich*"), and alternately incorporates an idiomatic flip into breathiness ("don't *you* cry") and a cry ("one of *these mornings*") into her tone. In a fusion of classical and popular music that would make Gershwin proud, the orchestration that accompanies Fantasia's performance is notable for both its prominent rhythm section, and the string and wind parts that borrow heavily from the opera score.

OPERA OR MUSICAL? (WHO CARES?)

While George Gershwin achieved tremendous success as a performer and composer of popular song during his lifetime, the accolades he so craved for his long-form works eluded him. Composer and critic Virgil Thomson was typical of Gershwin's detractors from the "serious" music world when he reviewed *Porgy and Bess* for the November/December 1935 issue of *Modern Music*: "Gershwin's lack of understanding of all the major problems of form, of continuity, and of straightforward musical expression is not surprising in view of the impurity of his musical sources and his frank acceptance of them . . . at best a piquant but highly unsavory stirring-up-together of Israel, Africa, and the Gaelic Isles." (Note also Thomson's racist snobbery toward Gershwin's multiplicity of musical sources, which have come to be frankly accepted as some of the richest veins in American musical tradition.)

Gershwin went to great lengths to have *Porgy and Bess* accepted as an opera. He studied classical composition for years before starting work on it, and he insisted that the entire libretto be set to music, except the few lines spoken by the two Caucasian characters. Even the conversational parts would be spoken on pitch in an operatic construct known as **recitative**. The themes—the definition of manhood, acceptance into a community, gambling, murder, substance abuse—were certainly operatic, especially compared to other musicals of the time (*Show Boat* was still an anomaly as a Broadway show dealing with heavy themes). Even so, the 1935 Broadway run of *Porgy and Bess* did not elicit the accolades Gershwin had desired from the opera world, receiving mixed reviews and closing at a loss after 124 performances. At a loose end, George and Ira went to Hollywood to score a Fred Astaire and Ginger Rogers film musical. It was there that George began to suffer from terrible headaches and exhibit strange behavior. The cause turned out to be an inoperable brain tumor, and he died a few weeks before his thirty-ninth birthday.

In the years since Gershwin's death, *Porgy and Bess* has been performed in both theaters and opera houses. A 1942 Broadway revival that made huge cuts and changed some recitative to dialogue scenes was commercially successful. In the 1950s, a European tour not only played one of opera's most revered houses, Milan's Teatro La Scala, but went behind the Iron Curtain to Russia and East Germany at the height of the Cold War. Houston Grand Opera (which also revived and recorded the unabridged *Show Boat*) restored all of the cuts for its 1976 production and subsequent tour. The 2011 Broadway revival toured the United States until mid-2014 in a format friendly to twenty-first-century theater audiences, with a two-and-a-half-hour running time, dialogue, and modernized orchestrations. The full four-hour sung-through version remains a frequent fixture in the seasons of opera companies and festivals around the globe.

The designation of what is "opera" is part art, part business, and part politics. Early on, Gershwin and Heyward had an offer from the Metropolitan Opera in New York City. Premiering at the Met would have undoubtedly marked the work as an opera, and the prestige was tempting, but for one problem: the Met wouldn't hire black singers, and

Gershwin insisted that the cast be African American, not Caucasians in blackface. So instead he and Heyward accepted an opportunity from the Theatre Guild, a theatrical society formed in 1918 to promote new, noncommercial American works (they had also produced the play version of *Porgy* in 1926). The leaders of the Theatre Guild worried that their target audience would be put off by the term "opera," so Gershwin compromised and allowed them to bill it as a "folk opera."

Over time, jazz, one of the manifestations of the very melting pot of which Thomson complained, passed the Top 40 torch to other styles of music and has come to be regarded as America's classical music. Gershwin didn't live long enough to experience that shift, but his music lives on, transcending cultural boundaries in the way he himself willfully ignored musical ones. *Porgy and Bess* has become a part of the operatic canon, and several of its arias—"It Ain't Necessarily So," "I Loves You, Porgy," to name two in addition to "Summertime"—have become popular songs in their own right. As to whether a piece is a musical or an opera, composer Stephen Sondheim, whose own works often fall in the gray area between the genres, perhaps comes closest to settling the argument in pinpointing the distinction in the expectations of the audience, responding to the "opera versus musical" query in interviews with words to the effect of "If it's performed in an opera house, it's an opera, and if it's performed in a theater, it's a musical." Such chameleonlike classification is one of the strengths of musical theater: it can meet people where they are used to going, be it the opera house, the theater, or, especially in the era discussed in this chapter, the Great American Songbook.

5

A GOLDEN AGE OF BROADWAY

Rodgers and Hammerstein

When NBC televised *The Sound of Music Live!* in December 2013, the network reached not only those familiar with the Broadway show or classic film, but also viewers who had discovered show tunes through musical-themed shows like *Glee* and *Smash*, and voice competition shows like *American Idol*. Fans of Carrie Underwood could see the *American Idol* season four winner play the lead role of Maria von Trapp alongside stage luminaries such as Audra McDonald and Laura Benanti. Over eighteen million viewers tuned in during the Thursday night broadcast, a number that prompted NBC, despite mixed reviews of the production, to proceed in the following years with live broadcasts of *Peter Pan* and *The Wiz*; the Fox network followed suit with plans for *Grease* in early 2016. These prime-time broadcasts recall the era when musicals were a larger part of mainstream popular culture.

The golden age of Broadway musicals was kicked off by an adaptation of Lynn Riggs's play, *Green Grow the Lilacs*. When producer Theresa Helburn of the Theatre Guild first approached Richard Rodgers with the idea, there were two hurdles: Rodgers's collaborator Lorenz Hart was in a downward spiral of self-destruction and not in a mood to work on anything, least of all a show about cowboys and farmers; and the Theatre Guild, an organization devoted to producing noncommercial works, had suffered a string of flops in recent years and had no money. Hart gave Rodgers his blessing to work with Oscar Hammerstein II, a fellow Broadway veteran and a colleague who could be trusted—but who hadn't had a hit since *Show Boat* in 1927. It's hard to believe in retrospect, but producers were not exactly lining up at the door to fund the first collaboration between Rodgers-without-Hart and Hammerstein-without-a-hit. Rodgers, Hammerstein, and Helburn had to call in old favors and hit the so-called penthouse circuit, auditioning for wealthy investors in order to secure funding for their project (working title: *Away We Go!*). The musical that was to transform Broadway was by no means a surefire hit: the widely quoted quip "No legs, no jokes, no chance," usually attributed to producer Mike Todd, refers to the show's dim prospects owing to the lack of basic musical comedy trappings like a big opening number full of high-kicking, leggy girls.

Instead, they were telling an integrated story, writing numbers that suited the plot (like a charming opening solo with just two people on-stage) and casting performers who were right for the characters, regardless of name recognition. Audiences were supportive as the show underwent several weeks of out-of-town performances and revisions in New Haven and Boston. One of the changes, the addition of a big choral number in act 2, gave the show its title: *Oklahoma!* The reviews were unanimously positive when it opened on Broadway on March 31, 1943, and more important, the ticket-buying public loved the show. *Oklahoma!* ran for over five years—a record-smashing 2,212 performances—making it a boon to the investors who had taken a chance on the show.

Nothing succeeds like success, so of course everyone wanted to make a "situation show," as Irving Berlin called shows like *Oklahoma!* Since *Show Boat* had stunned theatergoers in 1927 with its integration of story and songs, there had been a handful of other dramatically integrated shows, but none had been commercial breakthroughs. Musicals during the lean years of the Depression had tended to play it either very safe or very left field; many songwriters had done well for themselves in Hollywood, where work was plentiful but creative control was next to nil. Now, with the success of *Oklahoma!*, the improving economy, and a corps of talented musical theater writers, conditions were ripe for the era of what historian Gerald Bordman, in *American Musical Theatre: A Chronicle*, terms "the American musical as a conscious art form." Everyone jumped on the integration bandwagon, even masters of the old musical comedy form who felt less at ease with integrated shows: Berlin wrote *Annie Get Your Gun* (1946) with librettists Dorothy and Herbert Fields, and Cole Porter wrote *Kiss Me, Kate* (1948) with Samuel and Bella Spewack. The twenty-odd years after *Oklahoma!* opened on Broadway saw a panoply of memorable characters, songs, and stories from shows like—to name just a few—*My Fair Lady* (1956; Alan Jay Lerner and Frederick Loewe), *Guys and Dolls* (1950; Frank Loesser with librettists Jo Swerling and Abe Burrows), and *Fiddler on the Roof* (1964; Jerry Bock and Sheldon Harnick with librettist Joseph Stein). Composer Leonard Bernstein teamed up with librettists Betty Comden and Adolph Green for *On the Town* (1949), and with librettist Arthur Laurents and a young lyricist named Stephen Sondheim for *West Side Story* (1957).

RODGERS AND HAMMERSTEIN

In an age crowded with great musicals, Rodgers and Hammerstein were the clear titans, as their *Oklahoma!* debut as a writing team was followed by years of fruitful collaboration. *Carousel* (1945) played a respectable 890 performances and has been revived four times on Broadway; *South Pacific* (1949), *The King and I* (1951), and *The Sound of Music* (1959) each played over a thousand performances in their original Broadway runs. All five of their "greatest hits" have had at least one major Broadway revival, and all received film adaptations, the best known being the 1965 film version of *The Sound of Music* starring Julie Andrews. Even their "lesser" Broadway shows (*Allegro*, *Pipe Dream*, *Me and Juliet*, and *Flower Drum Song*) had runs of several hundred performances each. Rodgers and Hammerstein collaborated on *State Fair* for the big screen and *Cinderella* for small screen, both of which have been adapted for stage and produced on Broadway. They became producers in their own right, producing a number of shows including *Annie Get Your Gun* and six of their own musicals starting with *South Pacific*. They were household names, and that fact plus having a business stake in their work gave them a great deal of creative control on their shows.

Their work has earned the title "classic," because it has stood the test of time and become familiar to multiple generations through stage, screen, and any number of recorded versions. It's easy to take these stories for granted because they have been familiar to so many for so long, but a look beneath the brand name reveals how daring they were and, in some ways, still are. Rodgers and Hammerstein expanded the range of what stories could be told in the musical form, doing things that had previously been the milieu of nonmusical plays, books, and dramatic operas. Characters die (so they do in *Porgy and Bess*, but remember Gershwin was trying hard to call it an opera when it first came out), couples don't always live happily ever after, people are conflicted and contradictory, and there is a mix of triumph and loss—just like in real life, but with singing and dancing. Hammerstein didn't break musical conventions to be contrary; he did what was necessary to be true to the story and characters he was adapting for the stage. As in real life, there is much important information that goes unspoken, and Rodgers, musical dramatist that he was, imbued Hammerstein's text with the musical clues that "tell the rest of the story" and give us something that feels very real to connect to. To contemporary ears, attuned to amplified sound and driving rhythms, Rodgers's music may sound sweet, but make no mistake, Rodgers and Hammerstein do not sugarcoat their subject matter. Not one of their "greatest hits" has a simplistic, "happily-ever-after" ending; rather, they find something positive to say within the bittersweet denouements of stories that were more ambitious than other musicals up to that time.

Aside from being the tipping point to a golden age, *Oklahoma!* also has the distinction of being the first Broadway show to receive a comprehensive original cast recording. Music from some British shows had been recorded with their original performers, but that idea had not yet leapt across the pond. The recordings of music from Broadway shows were either incomplete, or featured different singers or musical arrangements from those heard in the theater. The *Oklahoma!* album featured the original cast and orchestra, led by the show's original conductor, Jay Blackton. Released in late 1943, the *Oklahoma!* album became a chart-topping success, selling over a million copies and leading to the production of cast albums of other Broadway shows.

One advantage of integrated shows and thoroughly written characters is that they can outlive their original cast in a way that loosely scripted star vehicles cannot; if there is integrity in the script and score, it can be brought to life by other talented performers. Still, there's something special about the performers who are chosen to originate roles in a new musical. Original Broadway cast albums combined these advantages—the sound of the original casts could be heard in living rooms across the nation, *and* preserved for generations to come.

OKLAHOMA!—1943 ORIGINAL BROADWAY CAST

It's a Sunday afternoon in early spring in 1945; from the news, it seems the tide of the war is turning in the Allies' favor, but it isn't over just yet. Sunday seems a good time to stay away from the radio and opt for the record player instead, so you pull your ten-record set of the original Broadway cast of *Oklahoma!* from its spot on the shelf. You have never seen the show, not having had the opportunity to travel from your small hometown to New York or to one of the stops on the national tour that began last year, but thanks to the cast album you know the music by heart. Some days, you play the records in order; other days, like today, you skip around, focusing on one character at a time, as if spending time with a very musical friend.

Oklahoma! is a simple, approachable story: Laurey must choose between two young men, the charming cowboy Curly and the sinister but compelling farmhand Jud, who both want to take her to the box social (a kind of combination fund-raiser and matchmaking event wherein the community's men bid money on elaborate boxed meals and the privilege of lunching with the girls who prepared them). Hammerstein brought out the layers inherent in the play, and they were given resonance in the added dimension of Rodgers's music: Laurey is on the verge of womanhood, living in a Wild Western territory on the verge of statehood; her friend Ado Annie is courted by men who bring news and products from the outside world, as well as comic relief; times are changing, and there is much to fear, but also much to anticipate.

In a breathtaking change of pace from the hectic chorus numbers that usually opened a musical, Curly (Alfred Drake) begins *Oklahoma!* by praising the serene pastoral morning while Aunt Eller (Laurey's aunt, played by Betty Garde) sits by, churning butter. As Curly describes the picturesque scene, his plain words follow a tune up and down the first five notes of the major scale. His observations grow to joy in the refrain, with his exclamation of "Oh, What a Beautiful Mornin'" built on wider melodic intervals than the scale-based verse. The pitch for "morn-" is taken from outside the key, adding a tonal color that suggests this particular morning's beauty is rare and special (of course it is, it's the morning of the box social!). Drake's voice is round and full, and he sings simply but with expression. As the opening number, his solo sets the tone for the whole show: this will be a story about people who take pleasure in simple things, love the land and what grows upon it, and have an optimistic outlook.

Shortly thereafter, Curly uses the time-honored technique of bragging about his vehicle—"The Surrey with the Fringe on Top"—in an effort to entice Laurey to go with him to the box social. The very first lyric of the song, "when" rather than "if," implies Curly's assumption that Laurey will go with him (which might be why she thinks he's so darn cocky—what makes him think she'll be available, asking on the morning of the dance?). But the lyrics also show Curly's good side, that he cares for Laurey's social status and comfort: only the best for her, a top-notch surrey and horses that'll impress the neighbors and transport her comfortably in all kinds of weather. In Curly's optimistic imagination, Laurey will enjoy his company so much that she'll stay out all night with him, and feel at ease enough to fall asleep on his shoulder as they ride home at dawn. The tempo and **dynamic** level (volume) of the music drop dramatically during this imaginary ride home, and he sings softly, lest a sound or a bumpy ride wake Laurey from "a dream worth a-keepin'." For all his arrogant posturing, Curly really does care about Laurey.

By contrast, Curly's rival for Laurey's affection broods over his plan of action in his "Lonely Room." Jud (Howard Da Silva) observes his surroundings, which include a creaky floor and a rodent infestation, in a stepwise melody accompanied by persistent dissonance. Here Rodgers simultaneously accomplishes tension and stagnation by sitting on a single chord for the first couple of phrases, resisting resolution to a key center that would at least tell the listener where home is. The music does finally land in a minor key as Jud begins to fantasize about a better version of his life, but it is volatile, continually shifting keys, as Jud moves through his dream back to reality. As Jud's voice rings out the last three dissonant notes of the final phrase "git me a woman to *call my own*," you note that Laurey is no longer *the* girl that Jud wants (wants, not loves), but rather *a* bride, *a* woman to fill the void. Nowhere in the lyric is there any hint of love, any concern about Laurey's wishes or comfort. On the other hand, Rodgers and Hammerstein have given us a rare glimpse of universal human experience in a villain in letting us hear Jud's loneliness. Allowing Jud this moment of humanity is a step in the direction of dramatic gold: evoking complex feelings in the audience about the characters in the story.

Curly is no angel, either, as you notice in "Pore Jud Is Daid." Curly pays Jud a visit at home to confront him about Laurey. He points out a rope and a roof beam strong enough that Jud could hang himself on them, and imagines aloud what people would say if Jud killed himself. While the choice of words and the use of dialect set us squarely in the American West, the musical setting of this song is decidedly European. The long-long-short-long rhythm of "Pore Jud Is Daid," which recurs throughout the song in the melody and accompaniment, is taken direct-ly from the language of heroic funeral marches (e.g., Chopin's *Marche Funébre*). Rodgers's use of the solemn classical form for Hammerstein's darkly humorous lyrics hints at the serious intent behind Curly's errand. Jud's response to Curly's veiled insults reveals that he would like to be well regarded; he is not thoroughly evil. The two men sing the two final cadences in thirds, a harmony usually reserved for duetting lovers or siblings. Musically speaking, Curly has gotten Jud around to his way of thinking, at least for a moment.

Laurey (Joan Roberts) declares her independence from men (or at least from any one particular man) in "Many a New Day," which is almost martial in its on-the-beat melody; yet, like many people in real life, Laurey proves to be self-contradictory. At the end of act 1, she puzzles out her feelings toward Curly and Jud in "Out of My Dreams," a dream sequence brought on by a "potion" sold to her by a peddler who told her it would reveal her heart's desire. This narcotic-induced song reveals much about Laurey: the song is in 3/4, or waltz time, a musical signifier of romance, and its melody uses many notes from outside the key of the song to connote danger, sensuality, or a combination of the two, as the lyrics paint images of shadow and light. A decisive cadence accompanies the final lyric as Laurey and the ensemble women sing of going "into a dream with you"—quite the opposite sentiment of "Many a New Day." The song leads directly into a ballet sequence (the music for which is omitted on the cast recording) choreographed by Agnes de Mille and considered to be another of the advances *Oklahoma!* made in integrated storytelling. The ballet continues the narrative rather than suspending it, as Laurey envisions life with Curly as a happy dream that turns to a nightmare when Jud kills him.

Laurey has already all but admitted to being in love with Curly in "People Will Say We're in Love," a duet whose chorus begins with a tune outlining that brightest of chords, the major seventh chord. As he did in *Show Boat* with "Make Believe," Hammerstein prevents the couple from openly confessing their love so early in the show. The playful rising and falling intervals of all the "don't" phrases, and the sensuous closeness of the **chromatic** notes of each "people will say we're in love" give the audience something to hope for, while the sinister turn of the "Out of My Dreams" ballet heightens the sense of threat from Jud. The hope, the threat, and Laurey's own internal conflict, make for an exciting ride.

Another trio of characters provides a comedic foil for the Laurey-Curly-Jud triangle: Laurey's friend Ado Annie, who "cain't say no" to men, is courted both by dim-witted but good-natured Will Parker and by Ali Hakim, the unscrupulous peddler who sells Laurey the potion. Ado Annie appears in *Green Grow the Lilacs*, but Will Parker is only mentioned, and Ali Hakim doesn't exist at all in the source material; these characters are largely Hammerstein's creation. Will returns from "Kansas City" with the latest news about technology and culture, including (in a dance break that is omitted on the album) the ragtime dance that is sweeping the country. Ragtime had lost most of its racial associations by this time, but its syncopation was still associated with youth and sex. It's fitting, then, that Rodgers gives Ado Annie and her outsize libido most of the few prominent ragtime-derived rhythms in the score in her solo, "I Cain't Say No." Celeste Holm's vocal interpretation of Ado Annie, with its strong dialect and comedic inflections, is wildly different from Roberts's melodious Laurey. The music of the Annie-Will-Ali triangle is designed for comedy, the untrained sound and thick accents recalling the broad ethnic stereotypes that played as comedy in the previous generation's music. Holm actually had a highly trained voice, and when she auditioned for *Oklahoma!*, Rodgers asked if she could sing as if she had never had a lesson. She replied that she could call a hog, proceeded with a long, shrill "sooooooo-weeee," and booked the job.

Act 2 opens at the much-anticipated box social with a big ensemble number, "The Farmer and the Cowman," which efficiently provides music for the dance while adding a political layer to Curly and Jud's enmity: cowboys and farmers compete for land and water rights as well as for marriageable girls. Many of the events in act 2 take place in scenes, short reprises, or dance sequences that are not included on the album, which must have made the elusive theater tickets all the more desirable for those who had become attached to the characters through their act 1 music. In summary, Curly outbids Jud for Laurey's lunch basket, and Jud tries to kill Curly but is thwarted by Aunt Eller. Jud then approaches Laurey in a desperate bid to win her love, but ends up frightening her instead. She banishes him and calls out for Curly, finally ready to concede that she loves and needs him. They get engaged, celebrating with a short, satisfying reprise of "People Will Say We're in Love." Jud, drunk and out of his mind (remember the harmonic instability of "Lonely Room"), returns and attacks them at the wedding party. Jud is killed in the struggle, but things look down only for a moment, as Curly is acquitted in an impromptu trial. Curly and Laurey are joined by the full company in reprises of "Oh, What a Beautiful Mornin'" and "People Will Say We're in Love" as they ride off for their honeymoon—in the surrey with the fringe on top, of course.

Marrying Laurey means Curly will have to give up his cowboy lifestyle to settle down on the farm, but he looks on this change with a positive attitude, thereby also resolving the play's conflict between cowboys and farmers. The song "Oklahoma" starts with the full orchestra ramping up a major scale to Curly's first joyful proclamation of the land to which he belongs. Rodgers again gets great mileage out of simple stepwise melodies for Hammerstein's words extolling the beauty of the land. While there are notes taken from outside the key in the melody and accompanying chords, the harmony progresses in such a way that it never strays from the key throughout the form of the song. Curly's future becomes even brighter when he finishes his verse and the entire community takes the whole song up a key, in harmony, ending with tension-building spelling of O-K-L-A-H-O-M-A and a triumphant "Yeow!" There is an introductory verse not included on the album that references Oklahoma's impending statehood explicitly, tying it in positively with Laurey's status as a "brand new wife" and Curly's new career as a farmer. In 1953, the state of Oklahoma adopted "Oklahoma" as their official state song, the only Broadway song to be so honored. *Oklahoma!* begins and ends by looking forward, and the title number brings into focus the story's themes of simple pleasures and optimism in the face of the changes that were in progress in early 1900s Oklahoma. The music and characters who carry that message are tonic to your soul in your own uncertain time.

CAROUSEL—1994 BROADWAY REVIVAL CAST

Fast-forward to the mid-1990s. Other wars have scarred the nation, and times seem to be changing faster than ever, in ways that are both thrilling and terrifying. While popular music and Broadway music parted ways decades ago, you still find that Rodgers and Hammerstein manage to capture the nature of real people, painting them in all their layered contradictions. Certainly the characters of *Carousel* are complex. Rodgers's favorite of the forty musicals he wrote in his lifetime, *Carousel* transplants Ferenc Molnár's play *Liliom* from Budapest to the New England coast in 1873. The title character Liliom (slang for "tough guy" in Hungarian) becomes *Carousel*'s Billy Bigelow, a charismatic carousel barker, who dies by his own hand less than halfway through act 2, and spends the rest of the show trying to earn his way into heaven, having failed to do so in life. One of Billy's main failings in life was hitting his wife, Julie Jordan. *Carousel* is sometimes mistakenly written off as condoning domestic violence, even though the libretto takes a clear stance that Billy is in the wrong. What the libretto *doesn't* do is take a simplistic or moralistic view of Julie's choices, nor for that matter those of her best friend, Carrie Pipperidge, who makes up half of the secondary couple. Carrie and her man, Mr. Snow, seem at first like the usual comedic foil, but their relationship is layered, too, albeit in a more socially acceptable way. We will see how the words and music work together to help us understand Billy, Julie, Carrie, Mr. Snow, and the world they inhabit.

Rodgers and Hammerstein expanded their technique of dramatic integration in their second collaboration, largely leaving behind standard popular song forms in favor of extended musical sequences that develop thematically along with the characters they represent. The original cast album, while wonderful, had to trim some of the music that best captures Billy and Julie's love to fit on the 78 record format that was prevalent in 1945, so today you choose instead the 1994 Broadway revival album. Instead of an overture made of snippets of songs from the show, *Carousel* starts with a richly developed instrumental "Prologue," popularly known as "The Carousel Waltz." The stepwise fall and rise of the main melody suggests the motion of horses on a carousel, while the use of Lydian mode (similar to the major scale, but with the fourth note raised) gives it a slightly detuned quality reminiscent of an actual carousel organ. We see the palpable attraction between the carousel barker Billy Bigelow (Michael Hayden) and the mill worker Julie Jordan (Sally Murphy) before they utter a word, as the music of the carousel swirls around them and the people of the town.

It is such a powerful connection between Billy and Julie that they each allow themselves to be fired from their jobs in order to stay longer in each other's company, and their very first conversation leads to a confession of how each would feel and behave "If I Loved You." This song, another of Hammerstein's delayed-love songs, is part of a longer musicalized scene known as "the bench scene" to Broadway aficionados. Julie is ordinarily taciturn; in "Mister Snow," her best friend Carrie Pipperidge (Audra McDonald) calls her "a queer one" for her secrecy and reserve. But Julie opens up to Billy; *he* calls her a queer one because she doesn't seem to be afraid of him. Likewise, Billy catches himself slipping from his usual tough-guy persona with Julie as their conversation develops.

As they chat and flirt lightly at the beginning of the scene, they are accompanied by gentle **boom-chuck** pattern outlining common chord progressions, but their conversation keeps going unexpected places, and the music follows, winding through multiple keys with cadences and tempo shifts that seem surprising and yet, paradoxically, preordained. Rodgers has taken Hammerstein's words (which, in this section of the show, are very close to the original play) and imbued them with subtext: Billy and Julie's love *is* a paradox, both beautiful and dangerous. This can be heard in the song proper, as the strings and harp lay a delicate foundation, filled with rich chromatic harmony, for the words foreshadow the course their relationship will take. The peak of the song articulates the magnitude of "how I loved you"—but they each backpedal, as the melody drops with the reminder that they are speaking hypothetically, "*if* I loved you." You hear the song twice in the course of the scene, because they sing it separately. In fact, they never sing together; rather, they really listen to each other, and, in another measure of affection, are capable of being silent together while the music says it all.

Carrie and Mr. Snow (Eddie Korbich) could not be more different from Billy and Julie. We first meet Carrie's intended through her description of him in "Mister Snow." It's clear she is excited about marrying this upstanding fisherman, as her voice ascends with each adjective in the final phrase that sums up her "*o*-verbearin', *dar*-lin'" fiancé. The lyrics suggest there may be a hint of pragmatism in hitching her fate to an "almost perfect beau" who smells like fish, but it may be Mr. Snow's own pragmatism that attracts Carrie. He is a man with a plan, which he details in "When the Children Are Asleep." Mr. Snow has a similar ascending figure in the verses of this duet, describing first the fleet of boats and then the fleet of children he plans to build. Carrie is not quite on board with having so many children, but she comes around to Mr. Snow's way of thinking by the end of the song (one of Carrie's verses, "When children are awake," is cut on this recording as it is in many productions, an unfortunate cut because it makes clearer Carrie's own viewpoint *and* her choice to settle for Mr. Snow's plan). These ascending melodies imply intention and success, represented by marriage, and for Mr. Snow, building a big business and family. Rodgers and Hammerstein show that these two are the type who plan, who say "when" rather than "if" (except when they teasingly sing "if I still love you" in the chorus of "When the Children Are Asleep"). Their charming dreams of a stable, conventional life together are underpinned by stable, conventional harmony to match; the accompaniment is generally absent of the harmonic non sequiturs that unfold in Billy and Julie's logic-defying relationship—less exciting, certainly, but perhaps a better foundation for a long marriage.

Billy and Julie never plan, and before long, the unemployed couple is expecting a child. Rodgers and Hammerstein saw in this moment of the story an opportunity for Billy to be relatable to the audience. In a seven-and-a-half-minute "Soliloquy" about his impending parenthood, we hear excitement and fear and narcissism all rolled into one, as Billy's lyrics focus on himself as much as on his son ("my boy Bill," of course). Music for a new section often begins as Billy sustains the last note of the previous phrase, as if his thoughts are tumbling over each other faster than he can finish them. Then, while fantasizing about giving his teenage son "pointers" on how "to get 'round any girl," he has a thought so startling that it interrupts the music: his unborn son could turn out to *be* a girl. With the word "girl" returns the anxious minor music from the beginning of the song. As it did the first time, this section soon cadences in major as his anxiety melts into a vision of a "neat and petite little tintype of her mother." "Soliloquy" *has* to be a soliloquy—tough guy Billy would never be able to show such a tender side in a conversation with someone. But alone, he can dream about his little girl, who comes home to him when she "gets hungry ev'ry night."

Hungry! Home! Me! Billy is jolted by the reality of having a child as the low instruments of the orchestra play a portentous figure, a chromatic descent that in this case spells doom. Rodgers has Billy's voice move the other direction, fighting the orchestral tide of destruction that would drag him down on the heartbreaking line "I never knew how to get money." The fanfare-like phrases that accompany "she's got to be sheltered" and "I'll go out" allow for the possibility that Billy and his good intentions may triumph. But Billy's melody holds a clue about his fate: the orchestra's descending figure is the inverse of the ascending figure that permeates the score, including Carrie and Mr. Snow's melodies. Suddenly having to plan for a child, Billy has a similar ascent on the final phrase "I'll go out and make it . . ."—but Rodgers doesn't let him complete it. Practically speaking, there are few voices that could both sustain the high B-flat and carry the requisite heft in the lower range of the rest of the song. That aside, Billy's newfound willingness to change his behavior for someone else's benefit is too little too late, and the aborted ascending figure predicts that Billy will fail, at least in his earthly life.

Billy agrees to participate in an armed robbery as a way of supporting Julie and their unborn child. The plan goes awry, and Billy kills himself rather than go to prison, fulfilling the sad foreshadowing of "If I Loved You." It's not even halfway through act 2, and the protagonist is dead—now what? The action briefly transfers to just outside the back gate of heaven, where Billy is given the opportunity to earn his way in by returning to earth for one day to do something good for his daughter Louise, now fifteen. Back on earth, he tries to give Louise a star he stole from heaven, but when she refuses it, he slaps her.

Herein lies the difficulty of *Carousel*. Louise runs off to get her mother, and on Julie's entrance, she catches a fleeting glimpse of Billy as the orchestra begins playing a reprise of "If I Loved You"—the sound of all the feelings for each other flooding back to them. As the orchestra approaches the climax of the song, Louise, telling her mother about the encounter with the mysterious stranger, asks if it's possible for someone to hit you and it not to hurt at all, and Julie replies in the affirmative. This exchange occurs during a pause at the final cadence, giving it the weight of dogma. Did Rodgers make a mistake setting these lines at such an important musical moment? The dialogue is omitted on the recording, but having used all the powers of **rubato** in a vain effort to avoid that cadence, this feminist conductor assures you that the music is structured to land with the line. Rodgers, expert dramatist that he was, knew exactly what he was doing. Earlier, when the ensemble women try to get Julie to corroborate their claim that men are inherently bad for the women who love them (an adage they find to be so true that "Stone-cutters Cut It on Stone" and Julie of all people should know), she not only refuses to go along with what they're saying, she actually contradicts them with the fatalistic, stand-by-your-man anthem, "What's the Use of Wond'rin'?" Julie has a stubborn streak, which we first heard when she deflects Carrie's questioning in "You're a Queer One, Julie Jordan." While she may not make the decisions a friend would want her to make, Rodgers and Hammerstein allow Julie to make them without judging her or robbing her of her agency. For Julie, the answer she gives her daughter *is* dogmatic; it is her truth from experience, disquieting though it may be to watch.

Carrie's more subtle relationship concessions, too, were freely chosen. In act 2 we see the tradeoffs Carrie has made for her prosperous life with Mr. Snow, in tolerating Mr. Snow's controlling, hypocritical behavior, and acquiescing to his master plan, which included raising more children than she might have chosen to have. The clues were all there in act 1, had we known to look for them. Carrie copes with the outcome of her decisions with humor, Julie with stoicism. Do we avoid stories of such complexity, whose thorniness the addition of music increases exponentially? Are storytellers limited to telling the tales of those who make what society deems the "right" choice? *Good Life Decisions! The Musical* would be a short show indeed (and boring, plus you'd never understand the words to the "Brushin' My Teeth" production number). Theater is a forum for empathy, catharsis, and community; do we quash the stories of the people who may need those things the most?

The real moral of the story lies in the theme of community. The ensemble numbers show the townsfolk coming together to celebrate changing seasons and life milestones in songs like "June Is Bustin' Out All Over," "This Was a Real Nice Clambake," and the reprise of "Mister Snow." Billy, in his stubborn pride, isolates himself from the community; this point is underscored in the fact that he sings very little and is always alone. Rodgers and Hammerstein, as they often do, have a matriarchal mezzo provide the moral authority in the story: at the emotional nadir of the story, when Billy has just died in Julie's arms, it is Julie's older cousin Nettie (Shirley Verrett) who gives her strength to carry on, telling her "You'll Never Walk Alone." The song acknowledges life's challenges; it begins "when you walk through a storm," not "if you ever happen to walk through a storm." But Hammerstein paints images of the beauty beyond the storm, and Rodgers sets the concluding phrase to two different melodies, the better to draw attention to the text, first with determined repeated notes and again with resounding emphasis on "you'll *nev*-er walk alone." The point is reiterated at the end of the show. The ending of the original play was considered too gloomy for a musical, so, in a change approved by Molnár himself, Billy finally earns his passage into heaven with a few words of encouragement to his daughter at her high school graduation. Whether she hears him or merely senses his presence, the previously lonely, outcast teen appears to change direction, ending the show on a hopeful note by joining her community in the harmonized choral finale of "You'll Never Walk Alone."

SOUTH PACIFIC—1949 ORIGINAL BROADWAY CAST

Based on several short stories from *Tales of the South Pacific*, James Michener's Pulitzer-winning collection of anecdotes from his experiences during World War II, *South Pacific* was the first of Rodgers and Hammerstein's collaborations to be set outside the United States (or soon-to-be United States). Writing about the military was also foreign to Hammerstein, and director Joshua Logan, who had served in the military, helped write the libretto and eventually received coauthorship credit. Rodgers was initially hesitant to write the score, thinking he'd have to employ ukulele and slide guitar, two instruments he disliked, but Michener assured him that he'd never heard those instruments during all his time in the South Pacific. Rodgers instead applied techniques similar to those used by classical composers to evoke the setting: for example, **whole-tone** scales (with tones evenly spaced at the interval of a whole step), which had been used to conjure sonic images of Asia by composers such as Claude Debussy, appear frequently in the score of *South Pacific* amid Rodgers's usual character-specific songwriting. When Bloody Mary sings of "a lonely island," her voice and words evoke a place shrouded in mist, helped by the whole-tone progression of chords in the orchestra.

On this unspecified island in the midst of a world war, characters' identities are suspended against a backdrop where ideologies and cultures collide. The central story concerns Emile De Becque, a forty-something French expatriate with a mysterious past, and Nellie Forbush, the young "cockeyed optimist" army nurse from Arkansas with whom he has fallen in love. Much of the comedy in *South Pacific* comes from Seabee Luther Billis, who is an amalgamation of several Michener characters, and Bloody Mary, an enterprising Tonkinese woman from Bali H'ai. Neither character is merely a comedic stooge; Bloody Mary may engage in banter with the soldiers who buy her wares, but when she uses all her tactics to induce handsome young lieutenant Joe Cable to come to "Bali H'ai," she is motivated by her determination that her daughter Liat will marry a rich foreigner and escape to a better life. The comic relief in musicals traditionally came from the secondary couple, but in this case both couples have a serious plot. The romance of Joe and Liat is based on Michener's "Fo' Dolla," which Hammerstein felt was too similar to the Puccini opera *Madame Butterfly* to be used as the primary plot of *South Pacific*; Michener's "Our Heroine" was the basis for the story of Emile and Nellie.

Ezio Pinza, a bass from the Metropolitan Opera, was cast as Emile, opposite established Broadway star Mary Martin as Nellie. Martin, writing in her memoir, *My Heart Belongs*, that her voice had dropped "about twelve octaves" as a result of belting out eleven songs per show on the tour of *Annie Get Your Gun*, quipped, "What do you want, two basses?" She was concerned about duetting with an operatic bass, and Rodgers mostly avoided having them sing at the same time, expertly weaving their thoughts around each other's in "Twin Soliloquies." Pinza, whose contract stipulated that he sing no more than fifteen minutes per show, nevertheless ascended to middle-aged matinee idol status with the vocal gems written with his voice in mind, "Some Enchanted Evening" and "This Nearly Was Mine."

Rodgers and Hammerstein decided against having an official chorus or ballet; such stylized elements didn't fit the realism of the setting. Instead, they relied on superb, character-driven songs that called for the occasional participation of the enlisted men (male ensemble) and nurses (female ensemble). The few moments of group singing are very satisfying: the unison male singing of "Bloody Mary" and "There Is Nothin' Like a Dame" is charged with the masculinity of a group of men stuck on an island with no prospects for female companionship (the nurses, as commissioned officers, were off limits to them). The nurses live vicariously through Nellie in her indecision about Emile, joining in "I'm Gonna Wash That Man Right out-a My Hair" when Nellie decides against committing to a man about whom she knows so little. A little reassurance and a marriage proposal from Emile persuades Nellie to change her mind, and Nellie backpedals from her shampooing spree in "A Wonderful Guy." The beginning of the song shows her sheepishness about the sudden change of heart with a minor key and rhythmic orchestral figures between the vocal phrases, but as Nellie gives in to her feelings, the stubborn resistance of minor gives way to the infectious joy of major, and the rest of the nurses join in the last chorus.

But racial prejudice gets in the way of love: Nellie changes her mind again after meeting Emile's two children, whose mother, now deceased, was Polynesian. Lieutenant Cable, too, may have felt "Younger Than Springtime" the first time he made love to Liat, but he balks at taking her back to his family on the East Coast. Despite her best efforts (shown in an above-average number of melodic themes for a pop song), Bloody Mary's "Happy Talk" does not convince Cable to marry her daughter. Emile, brokenhearted, questions Cable about these strange American prejudices, and Cable bitterly replies that "You've Got to Be Carefully Taught." Though the song is a waltz, the alternating bass notes and tense **offbeats** in the accompaniment convey more self-loathing than romance. This antiracist song resulted in *South Pacific* being banned in a number of Southern locales, but Rodgers and Hammerstein refused to cut it, stating that that song encapsulated the show's meaning. Shortly after Cable rejects Liat, he and Emile leave for a dangerous mission and he is killed. The primary couple's story ends on a more conventional hopeful note: Nellie overcomes the bigotry she was carefully taught, and Emile returns home from the mission to find his white Arkansan love learning "Dites-Moi," Rodgers and Hammerstein's take on a French nursery rhyme, from his Eurasian children.

THE KING AND I—1951 ORIGINAL BROADWAY CAST

South Pacific and *The King and I* share several common threads. *The King and I* was intended as a star vehicle for veteran leading lady Gertrude Lawrence from its inception; Rodgers could once again tailor his writing for a specific voice. Inspired by accounts of real-life Anna Leonowens's time as governess to the children of King Mongkut of Siam (modern-day Thailand) in the 1860s, all but the opening of the show is set in the King's palace in Bangkok, and Rodgers, as he writes in his autobiography *Musical Stages*, employed his "usual custom of writing the best music I could for the characters and situations without slavishly trying to imitate the music of the locale in which the story was set. . . . It would look like Siam, but like Siam as seen through the eyes of an American artist." This approach can be heard in all of Rodgers's work, but is clearest in these two shows whose settings are most foreign to Rodgers's European American background.

And, once again, Hammerstein breaks with convention in the central relationship, this time completely eschewing the musical-results-in-marriage equation. The adversarial professional relationship of Anna and the King grows into one of respect and affection, and indeed a love that is no less compelling for all its cultural impossibility. Hammerstein, as always, is an expert at keeping romantic resolution out of reach: they never kiss, and the one thrilling moment when they touch is near the end of the show in the duet "Shall We Dance." Rodgers helps to keep the romance at bay by making this song not a waltz but a polka. There is a delightful moment in the score when Anna begins to teach the King to dance, and he counts in three, against the music that the audience hears. As Anna and the King are only hearing the music in their heads, his hearing a waltz hints at his romantic feelings for her. Anna, whatever her feelings may be in this moment, counts "one-two-three-*and*," keeping it strictly business in a 4/4 time signature. This moment is cut from the cast album but can be seen in the film.

Gertrude Lawrence, for whom the show was written, was a star of rare skill and charisma, but limited vocal range. Rodgers wrote melodies with little vocal sustain and relatively small range, giving Lawrence a comfortable musical platform for expressive dramatic moments. Impetuous Anna shows her young son how to face an intimidating situation ("I Whistle a Happy Tune"), finds a way to connect with her new employer's wives ("Hello, Young Lovers"), and bonds with her pupils ("Getting to Know You"). You can hear Lawrence's expressiveness come through in the largely spoken "Shall I Tell You What I Think of You," in which she rails at the King's condescending treatment of her.

Hammerstein reserves the conventional romance, and Rodgers his most soaring melodies, for the star-crossed secondary couple, Tuptim (Doretta Morrow) and Lun Tha (Larry Douglas). Near the beginning of the show, Tuptim, a well-educated young Burmese woman who is fluent in English, has been escorted to the palace by scholar Lun Tha to be presented to the King as a gift. The melody of Tuptim's solo, "My Lord and Master," is almost entirely based on the **pentatonic scale**, a five-note scale associated with folk music from many places around the world, and another of Western music's ways to imply, in this case, an Asian setting. This pentatonic scale contains no half steps, the smallest interval in most Western music, which give major and minor scales their sense of tension and resolution. Thus it has a serene quality to it; Tuptim is perhaps trying to appear calm as she contemplates her future in the King's court. The climax of the song is the A-sharp of "I love an-*oth*-er man"—it is both the highest note and a note that doesn't belong to the scale on which the rest of the melody is based (the A-sharps in the bridge—"Something young"—don't have the same effect because of the way they are used and harmonized). The music and lyrics work together to make the audience feel her desperation and let them in on the dangerous secret of her forbidden love.

Passion is not calm, as shown by Rodgers's use of tension and release in the major-scale melodies of the lovers' duets "We Kiss in a Shadow" and "I Have Dreamed." The title line "I have dreamed" is based on a half-step interval, and the pitches to which it is set ascend twice in each of their solo verses: it is a melody filled with yearning that is *this close* to being realized. Tuptim, who had earlier borrowed Harriet Beecher

Stowe's *Uncle Tom's Cabin* from Anna, adapts the novel as a narrated dance sequence, "The Small House of Uncle Thomas" (not included on the original Broadway cast album). You note the many twists a work of art can take: an American novel whose stage adaptations have often been decried for minstrel-like stereotypes is used in *The King and I* by a well-educated Burmese concubine to not-so-subtly protest slavery in general, and specifically her captivity, in the form of stylized dance performance.

Tuptim's narrative brings together the abolitionist and feminist themes that are among the "new" ideas that the King finds a "Puzzlement." He hired Anna for precisely the purpose of instructing his children and wives in Western thought and customs, as a way to protect his kingdom against encroaching colonialism. The imperfect English of the King's lyrics place him as a member of the generation that came of age during isolationist times, but they also reveal his alacrity of mind and ability to pick up new phrases, ideas—"et cetera, et cetera, et cetera" (a phrase he picks up from Anna early in the show that becomes one of his favorites). It is ultimately his internal conflict between old and new ideas that causes a rift between him and Anna and speeds his death. In the end, the young new King Chulalongkorn decrees that there will be no more kowtowing in front of the King, which could be seen as a victory for both Western cultural imperialism and equality—a typically complex Hammerstein ending.

Needing an actor whose stage presence could match that of Lawrence, *The King and I* creative team cast Russian-born actor Yul Brynner. He defined the role, playing over four thousand stage performances of the show including the original Broadway run, and starred opposite Deborah Kerr in the 1956 film adaptation (Lawrence had died of undiagnosed cancer in 1952). The creative team of *The King and I* had originally hoped to cast British actor Rex Harrison (best remembered for his portrayal of Henry Higgins in *My Fair Lady*), who had played the King in the 1946 film *Anna and the King*. Notable as the first serious Broadway musical to have mostly Asian characters, few of the performers in the original Broadway cast were of Asian parentage. Over the years, through the activism of the Asian American performing arts community, the practice of yellowface (a Caucasian actor cast as an Asian character) has decreased; the 2015 revival at Lincoln Center is cast with actors of Asian descent in the roles of the King and his court.

Rodgers and Hammerstein's shows, progressive in their day, are still provocative, because the issues they encompass—bigotry, imperialism, fetishization of Asian women, to name a few that appear in *South Pacific* and *The King and I*—remain relevant and sensitive issues. It was 1910 when Bert Williams broke the Broadway color barrier in the *Ziegfeld Follies*. While challenges to diversity persist in the development and casting of Broadway shows, Hammerstein was part of the slow slog of progress (slogress?) from the days of the segregated stage and audience.

THE SOUND OF MUSIC—1959 ORIGINAL BROADWAY CAST

With music by Rodgers, lyrics by Hammerstein, and book by Howard Lindsay and Russel Crouse, *The Sound of Music* is the fictionalized account of the real-life von Trapp family's escape from Nazi-occupied Austria in 1938. Maria (Mary Martin), a postulant nun who loves to sing and is always late to mass, is sent to tutor the seven children of retired, widowed naval captain Georg von Trapp (Theodore Bikel). She brings music back into their lives, and she and the Captain fall in love and marry, but they decide they must flee when the German authorities demand that the Captain come out of retirement to join their regime. *The Sound of Music* opened on Broadway in 1959 to mixed reviews. Still, audiences granted it a healthy run, and its 1965 film adaptation, starring Julie Andrews and Christopher Plummer, won five Academy Awards and boasts a soundtrack that has never been out of print. The film (screenplay by Ernest Lehman, who also adapted *The King and I*) omits three songs from the stage version, and adds two: Maria's solo, "I Have Confidence," and the Captain and Maria's duet, "Something Good." Rodgers (with help from the film's music department) wrote the lyrics for those songs; Hammerstein had died in 1960.

You listen to the original Broadway cast, starting with the songs that were omitted in the film: "How Can Love Survive," "No Way to Stop It," and "An Ordinary Couple." The latter, an act 2 duet between Maria and the Captain, draws the contrast between wholesome Maria and Baroness Elsa Schräder, the Captain's erstwhile fiancée. But you can see why the song was replaced with "Something Good" in the film; a couple that will "Climb Ev'ry Mountain" with seven children is an *ex-*

traordinary couple (as in *Carousel*, the moral of the story is sung by a matriarchal mezzo, in this case the Mother Abbess, played by Patricia Neway). The other two songs absent from the film involve Elsa and the other secondary character, Max Detweiler, and develop the stage version's more obvious political message. Act 1's duet, "How Can Love Survive," establishes Max and Elsa as fun-loving sophisticates, and the act 2 trio, "No Way to Stop It," reveals them as people who look out for number one in the midst of political turmoil. The music of the latter song is staccato and unresolved as they urge the Captain to compromise with the Nazi regime. For Elsa, the song is a dramatic "can this relationship be saved" moment; in the stage version, it is a difference in politics, not Maria, that causes Elsa to break off her relationship with the Captain.

Now back to the beginning, a very good place to start: Maria's devotion to nature and music is evident in her first solo, "The Sound of Music," which parallels the worshipful, eternal imagery in the nuns' Latin liturgical music that precedes it. Such parallels mark "The Sound of Music" as Maria's own personal liturgy, telling the audience two things about her: nature and music are where she finds God, and her free spirit chafes under the cloistered practice of the abbey. The huskiness of Mary Martin's voice and the way she often scoops from one note to another (as in the first "the hi-ills are alive . . .") are a contrast to Julie Andrews's interpretation in a higher key: more refined, less earthy, each good in its own way.

Maria, aghast that the von Trapp children have been deprived of musical education, begins their instruction with solfège, a pedagogical system of associating syllables with each note of the scale, the first three notes of which are "Do-Re-Mi." Maria teaches the children a mnemonic device for remembering the syllables by linking them to images: doe, ray, and so forth, corresponding to the syllables of the major scale "do-re-mi-fa-sol-la-ti-do." The song shows the children's musical progress, as they join with more confidence in each chorus. The significance of "Do-Re-Mi" develops throughout the show: "far, a long, long way to run" takes on a deeper meaning when the Captain sings it in an act 2 reprise, as he prepares to escape rather than accept a commission with the Nazis. At the end of the show, when the family performs an elaborate concert arrangement of "Do-Re-Mi," the children's singing skill, which the Captain resisted so strongly in the beginning, becomes his family's chance to flee.

The children's first public performance is "So Long, Farewell." At the beginning, the orchestra evokes the "sad sort of clanging" from the clock and the nearby steeple bells, with slightly dissonant chords that move parallel to the mostly stepwise vocal melody. A masterpiece of writing for young performers, almost the entirety of the singing in the chorus is composed of the same short "so long, farewell" melody (Maria probably taught them "mi sol, mi sol, mi do re mi fa sol-la" and took the rest of the day off). The sprightly orchestral phrases between each verse, and the delightfully character-specific solo each child takes before his or her exit, balance the repetition. Furthermore, when the children exit in a different order during the reprise in act 2 (which is not included on the original cast album), the younger children's solos change the least. Such elegant simplicity saves rehearsal time, which can then be used for refining the performance instead of drilling an overcomplicated arrangement.

Rodgers and Hammerstein evoke Austria as vividly as they did the American West in *Oklahoma!* and the Far East in *South Pacific* and *The King and I.* The Alpine signifiers of goatherding and yodeling (a type of singing, used in goatherding, whose distinctive sound comes from quickly alternating between head and chest voice) are used in "The Lonely Goatherd," which Maria uses to comfort the children during a thunderstorm. While not an official music lesson, the song shows evidence of ongoing music tutelage: Maria and the children sing in call-and-response style at the end of the song, with wider, more challenging melodic intervals that show the solfège study is working. Whatever Mary "twelve-octave drop" Martin may have said about her voice, she dexterously reaches a high B-flat at the end of the song.

Austria is closely associated with the waltz, and *The Sound of Music* has many songs and dances in three: the fast three of "Maria" (which transitions into a march based on a triplet rhythm); "My Favorite Things"; the instrumental "Laendler" where the Captain and Maria first dance together; and, perhaps most famously, "Edelweiss," an ode to the tiny flower that is a national symbol of Austria. The simple melody, which uses only notes from the major scale and stays under an octave in range, is a skillful concoction wherein Austria meets Tin Pan Alley in **AABA form**; it has sometimes been mistaken for an Austrian folk song and functions as such in the show. When the Captain sings it at the act 2 concert in front of an audience of his countrymen, "Edelweiss" is a covert protest song against the Nazis who have invaded his country. It is also a good-bye; a final "may you bloom and grow forever" as he prepares to flee with his family, not knowing if he will ever see his beloved homeland again.

On the other end of the rhythmic spectrum, there is very little ragtime-style syncopation in this score. Of the five Rodgers and Hammerstein shows discussed here, the score with the most musical comedy and popular music moments is *South Pacific*, where it suits the time period and characters of the piece. While *The Sound of Music* is set only a few years earlier than *South Pacific*, it makes sense that syncopated rhythms from American popular music wouldn't yet have permeated the cultural psyche of these Austrian characters, except perhaps those young enough (Rolf and Liesl in "Sixteen Going on Seventeen") or sophisticated enough (Max and Elsa in "How Can Love Survive") to have soaked up popular music coming from the United States. "How Can Love Survive" is the lone fox-trot among the waltzes in the music for the party scene; the song survives in this form in the film. As for Maria, she sticks to Central European on-the-beat rhythms, except in "Sixteen Going on Seventeen (Reprise)," when she is relating to her new stepdaughter Liesl.

But "wait a year or two," and syncopation, amplification, and all manner of cultural change will be ubiquitous. If some consider Rodgers and Hammerstein dated, it is not their complex, daring, unconventional characters (how many widows do *you* know who tutor a prince in a foreign country?), or the societal issues their shows tackle that have become passé. It was music—the actual *sound of music*—that changed so dramatically, right around the time *The Sound of Music* had its first Broadway run. It is the dawning of the Age of Aquarius. . . .

6

ROCK ON BROADWAY

Hair

When *Hair* opened in 1968, it was the first musical to put rock music on the Broadway stage—and mean it. As critic Clive Barnes writes in reviewing the show for the *New York Times*, *Hair* was "the first Broadway musical in some time to have the authentic voice of today rather than the day before yesterday." Until the mid-1950s, pop songs on the radio sounded much the same as show tunes: closer to romantic classical music, with orchestral instrumentation and rubato (ebb and flow in the beat), or a slicker version of the big band swing whose popularity had peaked around 1940. Songwriters often wrote for multiple markets, including Broadway, Hollywood, and pop music. It was commonplace to hear show tunes on the radio and see them on popular music charts, either from cast albums or as cover versions by artists like Rosemary Clooney and Perry Como.

By the 1940s, African American artists like Big Joe Turner and Roy Brown were developing rhythmic styles that grew out of blues and swing; these stylistic precursors to rock became popular on African American radio. White DJs like Alan Freed, who played music by African American artists on the segregated airwaves, helped to popularize the exciting new sound among the Caucasian audience in the early 1950s. As had happened with ragtime and jazz, once it was seen that there was demand in the populous white markets for the styles coming from the African American music scene, white-owned music businesses started marketing white artists playing these sounds. In 1954, Big Joe Turner's recording of "Shake, Rattle, and Roll" hit number one on the Billboard Rhythm and Blues (R&B) chart (music popularity charts were, and to some extent continue to be, segregated; Rhythm and Blues was the name of the chart that tracked music marketed to African American audiences at that time). Later the same year, Caucasian group Bill Haley and His Comets recorded a version of the song that sold over a million copies. Haley had an even bigger hit in 1955 with "Rock Around the Clock," which many historians mark as the beginning of the rock-and-roll era. Haley's sound, and that of Elvis who hit the scene hot on his heels, showed the cross-pollination of the blues and country music. Over the next decade, the air became filled with the sounds of Little Richard, Chuck Berry, Johnny Cash, the Four Seasons, the Beatles . . . just listing the artists and their various styles could fill this whole chapter. What ties them together is the steady, driving pulse of the music, and an increasing reliance on amplification. Amplified sound would especially influence styles of singing; we will hear over the next couple of chapters how vocal writing and interpretation changed after rock and roll, especially for women on Broadway.

As rock's sound evolved and its popularity grew, Broadway seemed more and more out of touch with mainstream popular culture. There was the occasional one-off rock song in a revue, as in the final 1957 edition of the *Ziegfeld Follies*. In 1960, the musical *Bye Bye Birdie* poked fun at the kerfuffle Elvis and his publicity machine created when he was drafted into the army in 1957. The Elvis character, Conrad Birdie (a play on the name of Conway Twitty, a singer as popular as Elvis at the time), sings rock-and-roll songs, but he is not the hero of the show. The rest of the score is typical Broadway music of that time, including "Kids," in which the parents complain about "kids today." *Bye Bye Birdie* is therefore not a rock musical; it is a musicalized generation gap.

And what a generation gap there was to sing about. The seismic changes in the music were reflections of upheaval in the world at large, a world that was trying to return to "normal" after World War II, amid fear of the spread of communism and the very present threat of nuclear war. Meanwhile, the children of the post–World War II baby boom were growing up, forming the largest, best-educated, most affluent group of American youngsters ever. Though there was plenty of money in the economy, schools and the job market were not equipped to absorb the sheer number of baby boomers. Conditions were perfect, in other words, for a small percentage of the young population to step off the overcrowded cultural conveyor belt in the 1960s and become, as they came to be called, hippies, or flower children. Building on the values of the antiauthoritarian Beat generation of the 1950s, the hippie movement centered around valuing human life and love (including the sexual expression thereof), nature, and spirituality (often aided by hallucinogenic drugs). Hippies rejected the mainstream "establishment" values of materialism, organized religion, and authority they saw as corrupt and destructive. They were particularly vocal in protesting the Vietnam War, which took the lives of many of their contemporaries.

The movement originated in the Haight-Ashbury neighborhood of San Francisco, epitomized by a "Human Be-In" in January 1967, which took its name from the antisegregation sit-ins that had begun in South Carolina in the early sixties. Not far from San Francisco that summer, tens of thousands of people heard Jimi Hendrix, Janis Joplin, and other artists perform at the three-day Monterey Pop Festival, which kicked off the retroactively named Summer of Love. There was a strong identification between the hippie movement and certain styles of music. The otherworldly sounds Hendrix drew from his guitar and amplifiers, and the extended jams of bands like the Grateful Dead mimicked the effects of meditation or psychedelic drugs. There was a sense of optimism that their voices, lifted as a group (chanting "Om" around the Pentagon, for instance), could really change the world for the better. While the hippies' lax attitudes toward recreational drugs and sex had some negative repercussions, movements such as the continuing struggle for civil rights were also born of or supported by the ideals of the counterculture.

THE NEW YORK SHAKESPEARE FESTIVAL AND PUBLIC THEATER

It is a truth universally acknowledged that there will be long lines for anything in New York City that is both free and good. This is why you get up before dawn on a beautiful Saturday morning in summer 2008, arming yourself with breakfast from the twenty-four-hour deli to fortify yourself while you wait in line for free tickets to the New York Shakespeare Festival's production of *Hair* in Central Park. The mood in the park this morning is festive despite the early hour, as theater fanatics and savvy tourists mix with people who remember the first production of *Hair*.

The outdoor summer revival represents a kind of coming full circle for the New York Shakespeare Festival and for *Hair*. Impresario Joseph Papp's populist vision of making Shakespeare's plays available for free began with acting troupes touring the city on a flatbed truck. The truck broke down in Central Park in 1957, and the Delacorte Theater was built on that site, opening in 1962. In 1967, Papp opened the Public Theater, an indoor, multistage performance complex in the East Village, several miles south of Central Park and Broadway theaters. The Public expanded Papp's mission to include producing original American works. That fall, Papp inaugurated his new Off-Broadway theater with James Rado, Gerome Ragni, and Galt MacDermot's groundbreaking musical about a group of young, iconoclastic hippies.

James Rado and Gerome Ragni had met in 1964 when they played opposite each other in *Hang Down Your Head and Die*, an ill-fated Off-Broadway show about capital punishment. Rado was a classically trained actor, having studied with Lee Strasberg; Ragni was active in the experimental theater scene that thrived downtown in Manhattan, where venues like La MaMa were stretching the boundaries of how stories could be communicated in live performance. Rado and Ragni were both fascinated by the hippie culture that centered in Greenwich Village, and they set out to learn more about these young people. Around late 1964, they started writing the words that would eventually comprise *Hair*, and in 1966 were introduced to Galt MacDermot as a potential collaborator. The Canadian composer didn't look like the most likely candidate to provide music for a hippie musical, but beneath MacDermot's short haircut lurked a musical mind with a great breadth of style. He had earned a bachelor of music at Cape Town University in South Africa, and had won a Grammy in 1960 for jazz saxophonist Cannonball Adderley's recording of his composition "African Waltz." MacDermot's understanding of classical composition, knowledge of African tribal rhythms, and abiding love of what he calls rhythm music gave him the diverse palette he needed to paint Rado and Ragni's lyrics, which contained everything from acid trips to Shakespeare references.

In 1967, Illinois politician Michael Butler had been planning to run for the Senate on an anti–Vietnam War platform when he saw *Hair* at the Public during a trip to New York. Suddenly he had a new mission: to get this show in front of many people as possible. He obtained the rights to the show, and after a short stint at a discotheque called the Cheetah, *Hair* was Broadway bound. *Hair*'s subject matter was controversial, there had never been a rock musical on Broadway, and, to top it off, it was simply unheard of for an experimental downtown show to transfer to Broadway. Butler left behind his Senate ambitions, borrowed money, and, when most Broadway theaters refused to rent their spaces to him, used family connections to secure the Biltmore Theater, where *Hair* opened in April 1968 and ran until July 1972, a total of 1,750 performances. *Hair*'s 1968 cast album sold millions of copies and topped Billboard 200's Top 20 list for thirteen weeks in 1969; several of its singles also had chart success.

Most shows will only have one, maybe two other companies touring the United States while still running on Broadway, but Butler worked like a zealot, starting no fewer than eleven companies of *Hair* to tour or play in other U.S. cities by 1970. Numerous international productions were next, taking the show's message around the world. A number of the companies faced censorship or even violence, but *Hair* was seen and heard by many millions of people all over the world, and probably had more influence than Butler's one U.S. Senate vote would have had.

The Nixon years came and went, and American combat troops were pulled out of Vietnam in 1975. By the late 1970s, the optimistic era of the Summer of Love was long gone. A 1977 Broadway revival of *Hair* fared poorly, too old to be topical but too recent to be a period piece among audiences that had grown disgusted with the unproductive aspects of hippie culture. A *Hair* movie was released in 1979, featuring many wonderful musical arrangements but completely missing the point of the story, changing characters, gutting any spiritual meaning, and adding a nonsensical plot. These changes prompted Rado and Ragni to state their view that the movie version of *Hair* has yet to be made.

Hair has, throughout its existence, been deeply influenced by the directors who worked on it. Director Gerald Freedman, who came from a traditional theater background, shaped the show's material at the Public in 1967. For the original 1968 Broadway run, Tom O'Horgan, Rado and Ragni's original first choice, brought exercises from his experimental theater background to build a close-knit ensemble. Diane Paulus directed the 2009 revival as well as the outdoor production that led to it, bringing her historical lens to the work to create a coherent period piece. She placed the action very specifically in 1967, the year *Hair* played at the Public, before a series of horrifying events in 1968 (the My Lai Massacre in Vietnam, the assassination of Dr. Martin Luther King Jr., the riots at the Democratic National Convention, to name just a few that involved Americans) laid waste to some of the optimism of the early years of the counterculture.

HAIR 2009 BROADWAY REVIVAL CAST ALBUM

There are few experiences on par with sitting outside on a summer evening with thousands of people watching a show that celebrates life and love. The New York Shakespeare Festival production moved indoors to Broadway's Al Hirschfeld Theatre in spring 2009, along with most of its cast and **creative team**. The cast album released later that year is an excellent vehicle to take you back to that lovely evening, which in turn transported you to 1967. Often described as plotless, *Hair* contains many songs that are more "be-ing" than "do-ing." Unlike the plotless musical comedies described in chapters 2 and 3, however, *Hair* uses its short songs to develop its characters, known collectively as the Tribe, and the world they live in, sometimes suspending space, time, and other conventional theatrical boundaries to do so. The structure of *Hair* may elude the casual listener, but a closer examination reveals how the sequence of apparently abstract songs draws the audience progressively deeper into the world of the Tribe. This chance to experience what the score describes as "the fluid-abstract world of the 1960's as seen by, for, and about the 'Flower Children' of the period" was an important foothold for a 1960s audience, most of whom weren't hippies and may have had mixed or negative feelings about the counterculture.

The show opens with the band onstage and members of the Tribe mingling with the audience. The interactive group dynamic in *Hair* is thematic, speaking to the communal values of the hippies. Though some characters are more prominent, *Hair* is really an ensemble show, with the Tribe joining in as a group on almost every song. The group dynamic is also crucial in the band: unlike most Broadway shows in which each instrumental part is fully written and played note for note, the band parts for *Hair* leave much more room for improvisation, and details are determined between the music director and band for each production. Galt MacDermot himself led the band for the original production. The 2009 revival, music directed by Nadia DiGiallonardo, features big-time session musicians Wilbur Bascomb and Bernard Purdie on bass and drums, respectively, as well as *Hair* composer's son Vincent MacDermot on trombone. Rounded out by guitarists Steve Bargonetti and Andrew Schwartz, percussionists Joe Cardello and Erik Charlston, trumpeters Elaine Burt, Ronald Buttacavoli, and Christian Jaudes, and Allen Won on reeds, each player in the band is at the top of his or her game, both technically and within the musical styles of the show.

The deep, funky groove of "Aquarius" solidifies out of the ambient electric guitar and percussion sounds that start off the album. In the early 1960s, celestial bodies aligned in a way that astrologers believe heralded a new age, the Age of Aquarius, ruled by peace and love. "Aquarius" acts as a call to the Tribe to gather onstage, and they sing together about "harmony and understanding." With its positive lyrics, "Aquarius" invites an audience that may or may not share its worldview to relax and stay awhile, enjoying the riffs lead vocalist Dionne (Sasha Allen) adds to the melody. The women in this *Hair* revival live up to a precedent set by Melba Moore, the original Dionne, with her high belt voice.

The next few songs introduce members of the Tribe, as well as some of their edgier viewpoints on religion, drugs, and sex. Rado and Ragni have earned some edge by starting with the warm embrace of "Aquarius"; still, a sense of fun prevails early in the show, communicated through the tongue-in-cheek lyrics and popular styles of music. In "Donna," Berger (Will Swenson), the extroverted ringleader of the Tribe, makes pointed references to Catholicism in frenetic verses about looking for "my Donna" (always pronounced "Madonna"), but refers to Eastern religion and drugs in the relatively sustained notes of the bridge. The lyrics of "Hashish" are nothing more than a list of mood-altering substances, with a few nondrug references thrown in for good measure (such as IRT, the former acronym for part the New York City subway), set to an appropriately hypnotic slow groove and three-note melody. The unison singing expresses a rock ethos in which authenticity and shared experience take precedence over beauty and precision.

Next, we meet Woof (Bryce Ryness) and Hud (Darius Nichols), two characters who each bring something new to the Broadway stage: Woof is the first character to be (sort of) openly gay. He lists sexual taboos in "Sodomy," a "prayer" that mocks religion with its gospel-style accompaniment and background vocals. Hud is the first African American character in a mainstream musical to be portrayed as the equal of his peers onstage. In "Colored Spade," he subverts a list of minstrelsy stereotypes and pejorative names for African Americans, proclaiming himself the "president of the United States of Love."

Claude Hooper Bukowski (Gavin Creel) is the one character in *Hair* with something of a traditional story arc. Over the course of the show, he's compared to Hamlet, Jesus Christ, and the embodiment of Aquarius—a bright hope for the future. Here at the beginning of his story, though, he's just a confused, film-obsessed kid from Queens, offering a way in to the story for audience members who could recognize their own interests and ambivalence in him. Claude likes to imagine he's from "Manchester, England," complete with an accent and the chipper British Invasion beat of his song. In the second chorus, Claude refers to prominent counterculture figure and LSD advocate Timothy Leary and Leary's catchphrase "Turn on, tune in, drop out." Leary explains in his autobiography that his exhortation to live with awareness was often misinterpreted to mean "get stoned and abandon all constructive activity." Whether or not this is Claude's interpretation, he has apparently tried Leary's way and is still searching for answers, through a thicket of internal rhymes: dreary, weary, query, Leary, dearie. Claude, who lives in his imagination and hides in the movies, is the introspective counterpart to flamboyant, extroverted Berger. Claude and Berger's relationship is a semiautobiographical reflection of the creative and romantic partnership between Rado and Ragni, who also played those parts in the original Broadway production.

There's no explicit conflict or dramatic action yet, but now that we've met a few of members of the Tribe, the music will continue to take us deeper into their identity and values and the themes of the show. In "I'm Black," Claude follows Hud's, Woof's, and Berger's declarations of identity by singing, "I'm invisible," foreshadowing his path in act 2. "Ain't Got No" is a rejection of materialism, a laundry list of all the things that the members of the Tribe don't have. Noticing how many of the songs consist of lists, free of rhyme, and often seemingly created by free association, you wonder how hard it is for performers to memorize these "fluid-abstract" lyrics.

Sheila (Caissie Levy), an idealistic student at "NYU, second semester," arrives with a trumpet fanfare. Woof calls her Joan of Arc, a fitting sobriquet, for she is the social crusader behind the Tribe's activism. The lyrics, bouncy pop beat, and female trio background vocals of "I Believe in Love" add up to the perky sound of someone whose belief system includes faith in her own power to effect political change. Sheila manages to reference both a typing exercise ("Now is the time for all good men . . .") and a patriotic song ("My Country 'Tis of Thee") in urging her cohorts to join in a protest chant. This juxtaposition of the familiar and the confrontational is another technique used frequently in *Hair* to draw the audience in. The lyrics of the protest march "Ain't Got No Grass" evolve into a stream of uninterrupted nouns that by the end of the song are abstract sounds rather than intelligible thoughts, in an echo of visual art from the era. The aural bombardment eases in the final seconds of the song, as the Tribe gasps for "air—air—air!"

This stream of consciousness segues to "Air," in which Jeanie (Kacie Sheik), pregnant and wearing a gas mask, sings a satirical paean to the polluted environment. While on the surface "Air" seems to be a musical comedy non sequitur, it is actually a perfectly integrated character sketch. The duality of the song, with its sardonic lyrics and cheerful doo-wop background vocals, reflect the layers of Jeanie's personality: though seemingly ditzy, she is perceptive, acting as a sort of Greek chorus with her asides to the audience later in the show. Additionally, according to *Hair: The Story of the Show That Defined a Generation*, the character Jeanie is pregnant because Sally Eaton, the actress who created the role, was pregnant at the beginning of the original production. Jeanie's pregnant state adds a layer of resonance to "Air" for anyone who feels concern about bringing a child into a violent, polluted world.

Even though we have yet to meet an **antagonist** in human form, a picture is emerging of the conflict between the members of the Tribe and the establishment as represented by their parents' generation. The abstract foe finally takes shape in a scene with Claude's parents, who urge him to get his life together—cut his hair, join the army, be a man. Their arrival catalyzes a section of the show focused on the generation gap, where anthems of hippie identity alternate with old-fashioned songs commenting on the establishment. When Claude's parents ask what 1967 has got that makes it superior to 1947, Claude responds with "I Got Life," another list song, this one an anthem to the Tribe's values, tallying what they *do* have. The spiritual aspect of the song is clear from the beginning, when Claude imitates an African American spiritual, to the full Tribe "amen" at the end. Musicians Bascomb and Purdie add gospel energy to the up-tempo rock feel indicated in the score with a walking bass line and hi-hat playing every offbeat like a gospel tambourine. The Tribe joins Claude with full, syncopated choral backgrounds to show their solidarity with his joy of life and the body with which he experiences it. Material goods are notably absent from the list, in another rejection of keeping-up-with-the-Joneses consumerism. The Tribe brings the song to a close with a resounding "amen, amen" to Claude's intention to "spread it around the world," sincerely proclaiming their own beliefs while spurning a moral code based on materialism, sexual repression, and conformity.

The word "amen" is almost always sung to the same distinctive chord progression, called a **plagal cadence**: a chord built on the fourth note of the scale ("Ahh . . .") resolves to a chord built on the first note of the scale (". . . men!"). While that chord movement is also a common progression in rock and other blues-based music, when it forms a **cadence** at the end of a phrase of music, it can add a dogmatic undertone to text. This is obvious when the last word is "amen," but plagal cadences also appear in a number of other prominent "beliefs/values" moments throughout *Hair*, befitting the spiritual dimension of the show. In "Going Down," Berger describes his expulsion from high school with his characteristic combination of sarcasm and glee: Rado fits in references to oral sex, Milton's *Paradise Lost*, and Yale's perennial a cappella group the Whiffenpoofs ("baa, baa, baa"). But his deeper point is made when the Tribe sings the final "going down," as the plagal cadence lends a sense of prideful "amen" to the Tribe's distancing itself from mainstream values even if it means going "down, down, down" in the eyes of society. Whether this is an intentional or subconscious "amen" on Mac-Dermot's part, its effect is that of incontrovertible conviction.

The last of the identity anthems is prompted by a pair of tourists, apparently a respectable middle-aged man and woman. The woman questions Claude about his hair, and Claude responds with an ode to that most visible indicator of belonging to the Tribe. Always thoughtful, he starts slowly (notice Creel's suggestive riff on the word "low"), soon joined by Berger and the rest of the Tribe for a euphoric up-tempo celebration. Free association is a driver in the rest of the lyrics, as when a list of hairstyle adjectives ending in "spangled and spaghettied!" gives way to the first phrase of "The Star-Spangled Banner." By quoting the first line of the national anthem and turning it into a statement about hair, the Tribe expresses their belief that they could bring about change in their country—a return to freedom, symbolized by their natural hair, "long as God can grow it."

In contrast to the identity songs, Berger's vocal mockery of his parents' pop music is accompanied by the passé style of light swing in "The Stone Age," which is called "1930s" in the score. Similarly, the lyrics of "Initials" are set to a rigid minuet, turning what could be a nonsense song into a send-up of the acronym-intensive military-industrial complex. "My Conviction" reveals a more porous age-values boundary than the show might otherwise imply. Following a short monologue in a broad upper Midwest dialect, the female tourist analyzes the male hippies' "gaudy plumage" as "the birthright of their sex." There are hints of musical comedy in the exaggerated sustain of the word "aaaaaaaactually," and of baroque opera in the song's accompaniment and vocal ornaments. The accompaniment pauses for the vocal trill on the song's penultimate word "most" before playing one more phrase to finish the song, a musical convention baroque composer Handel would have recognized if he were to travel 225 years after his *Messiah* was first performed. As the tourist couple leaves, she is revealed to be a man in drag, and the Tribe nicknames her Margaret Mead, an anthropologist born in 1901 whose work influenced the 1960s sexual revolution.

Hair gives the audience a good long time to get to know the Tribe before introducing conflict between its members. The Tribe has been portrayed as such a united front that it's jarring when Berger and Sheila have a falling-out after he rejects a shirt she tries to give him. Sheila, who is in love with him, wonders how he can show such compassion for strangers yet treat her with such insensitivity, concluding that it must be "Easy to Be Hard." The song's gentle groove belies Sheila's feelings, but the harmonic and melodic setting of her questions, and the fact that the melody of her answers is higher than that of her questions, show that the answers she finds are not the ones she wants. A comparison of the revival recording with the original cast album (with Annabel Leventon as Sheila) illustrates how deeply embedded the metallic sound of a belted vocal in listeners' consciousness became between 1968 and the turn of the twenty-first century. The 1968 album has a much folkier interpretation, with acoustic guitar accompaniment and Leventon singing most of the song with the lighter sound of the head voice. By 2009, Broadway had become accustomed to rock, and listeners expected the impressive, athletic sound of belting. Levy's flawless belt, accompanied by electric guitar, conveys Sheila's passion in a way suited to a twenty-first-century audience.

At the Public in 1967, the opening number was the next track on the revival recording, "Don't Put It Down" ("Aquarius" then appeared in act 2), a much more confrontational choice that would have set a very different tone for the show and probably curtailed its reach. The later placement of the song gives the audience a chance to understand the Tribe's worldview and the space-time-bending theatrical language of the show before hitting them with the provocative symbolism of the American flag. Even so, and despite the fact that O'Horgan made sure the flag was folded to military specifications, the satirical song was one of the biggest sources of controversy during the 1968 Broadway run. A Buddhist mantra underscores the reverent folding of the flag; then, courtesy of experimental theater, Woof, Hud, and Steve (Tommar Wilson) fall through space-time "through a hole in the flag" and into a metaphor in Selma, Alabama, a site of civil rights protests and violence in the mid-sixties. The song uses country music and a caricature of Southern dialect (a sort of regional and political stereotype not unlike the ethnic stereotypes of the early 1900s) to censure those who would revere the symbolism of the American flag more than the actual lives and liberty of their fellow Americans.

Meanwhile, back in New York, the Tribe is passing out flyers to invite the audience to a Be-In, and innocent Crissy (Allison Case) sings earnestly about trying to find "Frank Mills," a motorcycle aficionado who "resembles George Harrison of the Beatles." The lyrics are entirely prose, based on a letter to the *Village Voice*, which in turn was written by an anonymous person who combined lines from various personal ads in a 1966 issue of the British rock magazine *Rave*. MacDermot sets the words to a wandering melody, using the repetitive AABA form to lend some organization to Crissy's thoughts as she comes somewhat circuitously to her point: she and her friend don't want their money back, just

Frank. Twenty-first-century fans of the song have used the Internet as a forum to wonder if Frank Mills was sent to Vietnam. Though the authors have said nothing to this point, it's an interesting and poignant interpretation of an otherwise transitory song.

At the Be-In, the Tribe chants "Hare Krishna," only slightly modified from the genuine Hare Krishna chant (MacDermot added two notes to the end of the melody and reharmonized it to be in a minor key). Improvisation, be it on "drums or an old tin pot," is valued at this Be-In, and you hear flute, trumpet, and marimba solos among the chanting and drumming. Not included on the cast album is the dialogue performed by the actors who play Claude's parents. Though their words are far less graphic than those on the original 1968 cast album, they still represent the counterprotesters' view of the hippies as naïve at best and a menace to society at worst, what with their drugs and their "sex mess." Undaunted by the counterprotesters, the Tribe continues making music and getting high, conflating the use of marijuana with spiritual enlightenment by substituting the word for "Hare Krishna" in the chant. Part of the purpose of this gathering was for the young men to burn their draft cards, an action that had been made a federal offense in 1965. The sudden silence that accompanies Claude's last-second decision *not* to burn his card sets his fateful decision in sharp relief.

Torn between the expectations of his parents and those of his peers, Claude asks "Where Do I Go?," searching for answers in images from both nature and industry. When the Tribe joins, they add a vocal accent to the first "I," making it a universal question: "Where do *I* go?" The staging of the last part of this number is worth mentioning because it so concisely served both artistic and commercial purposes: the Tribe members emerged nude, symbolizing their union with nature and peace. Though dimly lit and behind a scrim for under a minute, the nude scene garnered attention from both proponents and detractors in 1968. As there's no such thing as bad publicity, this was good for the life span of the show. Act 1 ends on Claude's question mark, still searching, backed by the Tribe reprising their chant of "Beads, Flowers, Freedom, Happiness," ending, significantly, with a full-voiced "Freedom" on a D minor chord. Another important audience foothold, Claude's struggle resonated with those who may have felt ambivalence about the war, even if they disagreed with the drug use, sexual and religious practices, or other facets of the counterculture movement.

The beginning of act 2 functions as a palate cleanser, something light after the climax of act 1, and a breather before the intensity yet to come. "Electric Blues" is sung by a quartet (Steel Burkhardt, Nicole Lewis, Andrew Kober, and Megan Lawrence) that warns of the consequences of an electrified world, its declamatory tune interrupted by a sweeping "old-fashioned melody" that mimics Kern and Rodgers. The cautionary tale comes true when a blackout occurs at the height of an amplification-fueled jam. "O Great God of Power" is a hymn to Con Ed, New York City's utility company. (You note the irony of the electric accompaniment in this moment; then again, everything in the show is coming through a sound system, so why not suspend your disbelief just a bit more for the orchestration. Such is the magic of theater.) In this ritual to call back the light, the Tribe anthropomorphizes Con Ed and equates "him" with Aquarius. When the lights come back on, they reveal Claude, drawing him once again as a symbol of bright hope.

The next two songs express ideas that were quite radical when *Hair* first came out: interracial relationships and female sexual agency. "Black Boys" is marked "Tequilla [*sic*] Tempo," and you can hear the similarity in the groove to the 1958 Champs hit, "Tequila." A trio of black boys (Nichols, Wilson, and Brandon Pearson) introduce the background vocal pattern "I've got" on the accented beats, connecting act 1's corporeal celebration "I've Got Life" to the lead vocals of three white girls (Megan Reinking, Jackie Burns, Kaitlin Kiyan) who sing about their craving for "choc'late flavored treats." The Motown-driven ode to "White Boys" is performed by a "Supremes trio" (Allen, Lewis, and Saycon Sengbloh). Allen's text-driven vocal shows the inspiration of Diana Ross, and she adds some of her own style in the high belted notes and riffs of the last verse. Lewis and Sengbloh support her with precise backup vocals, most in the lighter head or **mix** voice, imitating the Supremes, whose femininity was treated as a strength rather than a liability. The lyrics contain vestiges of the contrasting portrayal of Caucasian and African American female sexuality in American culture, wherein black women are often shown as hypersexual and exploited thus, while their white counterparts' sexual desire is concealed, their chastity carefully guarded or enforced. The white women use food as a metaphor in describing their hunger for "Black Boys," whereas the black women sing about bodies and sensations in "White Boys." However, in treating femininity as strength and sex as life affirming, and in showing women who choose their words and their partners, the songs are ultimately a celebration of human wholeness—including desire, male and female, across color lines.

Hair now begins an extended trip sequence that will take us into Claude's subconscious mind. As the Tribe gathers to smoke, Berger hands Claude a "special" hallucinogen-laced joint, possibly to help him with his indecision about the draft. A slow, syncopated bass line sets the tone for "Walking in Space," which is a window into the hippies' rose-tinted attitude toward psychedelic drugs. The intentions of self-aware-ness and coming face-to-face with God are supported musically by the use of a gong, like those of Eastern meditation practices. As they begin to experience heightened sensation, the Tribe members sing "my body" in a tone like that of a boy soprano in sacred music—pure, free of **vibrato**. The evolution of the collective trip is represented by changes in the tempo and feel of the music, as the Tribe members experience waves of visions of the cosmos and the beauty of life. The Tribe chal-lenges the military-industrial complex that would bury them in soot and ship them off to war: "How dare they try to end this beauty?"

Claude's internal conflict now manifests as a bad trip, and as the sound of helicopters fades in at the end of "Walking in Space," we enter his hallucination of parachuting into the jungles of Vietnam. What comes next is a swirl of images, the boundaries of space, time, fact, fiction, gender, and ethnicity distorted by the trip. It is peppered with well-known characters from literature and history: familiarity with a twist, for twisted times. While it conveys nonlinear, nonrepresentational moments through techniques from experimental theater, the trip se-quence itself has a precedent in a classic Broadway musical in which another protagonist takes a "potion" to clear her mind: Laurey's dream ballet in *Oklahoma!* Claude's "dream ballet," if you will, consists largely of cycles of killing, fueled by his conflicting values and fear of going to war. The cycles include characters from all over Claude's subconscious, including Abraham Lincoln played by an African American woman (Sengbloh).

In the Abraham Lincoln sequence that follows the first cycle of death, three African witch doctors become a trio for "Yes, I's Finished on Y'all's Farmlands." The word "y'all's" is emphasized, indignantly pointing out the injustice of slavery. This point of view renders satirical the echoes of minstrelsy in the on-the-beat banjo figure and dialect of the lyrics; these free men upend stereotypes by praising "Massa Lincoln" for being the "Emancipator of the Slave" (augmenting the lyric with a colorful repetition). The anachronistic device of doo-wop background vocals lends a civil rights–era bent to the Gettysburg Address. "Four Score" fills Lincoln's 1863 speech with rhythm-and-blues riffs, and a couple of additions to the text that, especially when performed by a black woman, cast the words "all men are created equal" in a new light.

The next, extended circuit of carnage begins with four Buddhist monks, led by a thousand-year-old monk who recites a monotone chant before setting herself on fire. This event was a topical reference in the original production, when the 1963 self-immolation of the Vietnamese monk Thich Quang Duc in protest of South Vietnam's treatment of Buddhists was fresh in people's minds. The remaining monks are then strangled by three rosary-wielding Catholic nuns, who are followed by groups of astronauts, Chinese, Native Americans, and finally Green Berets, each group killing the one that preceded it, with the Green Berets offing each other with their machine guns. As a trumpet plays a funereal reprise of "My Country 'Tis of Thee," Claude's parents talk to their son. Even amid all the images of death, earning the approval of his parents is still foremost in Claude's mind.

The dead bodies littering the stage rise twice more, first to play children's games that devolve into war games until all are dead again; then, zombie-like, for "Three-Five-Zero-Zero." Inspired in large part by Allen Ginsberg's antiwar poem, "Wichita Vortex Sutra," the title refers to a passage in which U.S. general Maxwell Taylor reports the number of Viet Cong losses in a month, then repeats the number digit by digit for emphasis. The song begins with an explosion, its decay accompanied by Hendrix-like electric guitar riffs and distortion. The bass's emphatic downbeats are answered by the snare drum's insistent backbeat, laying the bellicose foundation for the vocal. The vocals here are the opposite of the enlightenment-seeking tones of "Walking in Space." The tone is harsh, the diction is aggressive, and the on-the-beat setting of the text is martial—Mars, the god of war, being the root of the words "march" and "martial." The band further supports the text, building the groove throughout the first section of the song, climaxing with wailing guitar behind the head count of "two hundred and fifty-six Viet Cong captured."

A livelier beat brings with it a major key as it builds from a whisper to a full Dixieland jam. This New Orleans style is rooted in that city's tradition of musical funeral processions, which typically play a mournful hymn on the way to the cemetery and a rousing march on the way back. Multiple soloists improvise simultaneously, weaving around one another a tapestry of sound to celebrate the life of the deceased. But the lyrics in this song, developed from the last lines of Ginsberg's poem, decry both the senseless loss of life in Vietnam and racial inequality at home. Placed amid the explicit images of war, "prisoners in Niggertown" refers to the inhabitants of an African American ghetto in Wichita, for whom the struggle is far from over. Significantly, the long, long armies don't *march* home, but drift, as if combat has knocked out their sense of direction. The bitter lyrics and bright accompaniment combine to form a caustic parody of the desensitization to and rationalization of violence: there is nothing to celebrate on the way home from the burials of the young and innocent.

Two Tribe members sing over the bodies an adaptation of a soliloquy from Shakespeare's *Hamlet*. MacDermot's setting of "What a Piece of Work Is Man" places many unaccented syllables on accented beats. Such setting is idiomatic in highly syncopated styles of music, but in this, one of *Hair*'s "old-fashioned" songs, it has the effect of distorting the words: "no-BLE," "MA-jes-TI-cal." This distortion is true to Hamlet's inability, echoed here by Claude as he comes down from his trip, to find mirth in what he recognizes as the perfect form of man and nature. It also paints the more recent, sarcastic connotation of the phrase "piece of work": humanity is a real piece of work, bent on ending its own beauty. The Tribe, waking from their collective trip, repeats lines from "Walking in Space," bookending Claude's trip with a message of peace. But Claude has found no peace or answers in the hippie lifestyle. He just wants to be invisible, so he can go everywhere and perform miracles, a clear Christ parallel just as Claude is about to submit himself as a lamb to the slaughter. How better to be invisible than by getting in uniform?

Before the action proceeds, Sheila gives our psyches a break with "Good Morning, Starshine," its twinkling lyrics and nonsense syllables set to a peppy beat. The song has been used everywhere from *Sesame Street* to *The Simpsons*; it is so easily extractable because it functions as a respite between the intensely visceral sequences in the show. The

Tribe members bid Claude good night with repetitions of "Aquarius," an insistent, martial pulse from the rhythm section replacing the funky, danceable groove of the act 1 opening. Left alone onstage, Claude recites his draft number and begins to sing "Ain't Got No," this time leaving each statement incomplete. Gunshots ring out of the snare drum between the phrases as the song progresses, starting after the fourth phrase. The fifth and sixth phrases of "Ain't Got No" use the same melodic intervals as the beginning of "I Got Life," pairing with the more obvious gunshots to imply "ain't got no . . . [life]." The boundaries of space and time once more dissolve as Claude disappears into the crowd of the Tribe entering for a dawn protest. The members of a generation that believed in the transformative power of their collective voice gather once more to "Yip Up the Sun," and they search for Claude but cannot find him. He is, at last, invisible.

"The Flesh Failures" depicts the chasm between human potential and human reality, the inability to realize our inner greatness because of the weakness of the flesh. After two verses of mourning this disparity, Claude slowly reiterates his own words of youthful promise in a reprise of "Manchester, England." The Tribe joins (in a parallel dimension— they still can't see him) with a solemn recital of Hamlet's and Romeo's last words. "The rest is silence," they repeat as they surround their missing friend.

The revelatory silence that tells Claude "everything, everything" about why he lives and dies comes only with his death and the moments that foreshadow it: when he pulls his draft card out of the fire, when he first appears in uniform, and when the band falls silent near the end of "Let the Sun Shine In," leaving the Tribe to wail, **a cappella**, as they part to reveal Claude's body lying on the American flag. Often misinterpreted as a cheerful button to the show, "Let the Sun Shine In" is not a shallow ditty about opening the blinds but a desperate plea to remove the *blinders*. It asks the listener to be mindful of the life "around you and in you," instead of involuntarily vacillating between the fear and cravings of the flesh. The first two phrases of the refrain, in B minor, speak to the overwhelming need for sunshine. Having started the show with an optimistic view of a new age dominated by peace and love, the third and final phrase resolves G major "shine" to D major "in." As with many other moments in which *Hair*'s writers are making a point, Mac-

Dermot sets this final text to a plagal cadence, and the members of the Tribe sing their hearts out in harmony. Let the sun shine in. Amen.

HAIR'S LEGACY

But it's not quite over! One of the highlights of seeing *Hair* at the Delacorte in 2008 was joining the cast and other audience members onstage after the curtain call for a "Be-In" as the band continued to jam. After such a wild ride, especially the life-and-death journey of act 2, it was cathartic to let loose to exuberant music. The short repeated phrase "Let the sun shine in" gave everyone the opportunity to join in or simply bask in the vibrations of the communal experience.

By the time *Hair* opened in 1968, rock was long since a cultural force to be reckoned with. Change comes slowly to musical theater; it takes visionary artists and producers who are willing to risk trying a new style of music or storytelling in such an expensive and multidisciplinary form. A runaway commercial success on the scale of *Oklahoma!* or *Hair* breaks ground for other shows in a similar vein. *Hair*'s success encouraged the production of musicals that featured up-to-date popular music, a racially diverse cast, and nonlinear storytelling techniques. While there were plenty of flops among the shows that *Hair* inspired, a number of them went on to become part of the musical theater canon. *Jesus Christ Superstar*, *Grease*, and *The Wiz* are just a few of the shows that owe their existence at least in part to *Hair*.

Groundbreaking or old-fashioned, and regardless of the depth of a show's message, a musical must first and foremost entertain. The word "entertain" comes from the Latin root "to hold," and a show must give the audience something worthy of holding their attention, captivating enough to let go of their own troubles for a while and leave the theater with a fresh perspective. Rado, Ragni, MacDermot, and the people who supported the creative development of *Hair*, helped propel Broadway into the latter half of the twentieth century by expanding the notion of who could be a hero and how they could sound.

7

CONCEPT MUSICALS

Sondheim! The Birthday Concert and *A Chorus Line*

The nonlinear type of storytelling that *Hair* pioneered made it ground-breaking not only as a rock musical, but also as a **concept musical**. The standard line about concept musicals is that they have a unifying concept instead of a plot, hence the term. But concept musicals are not simply a return to the revue (chapter 2); the concept musical retains the character development from plot-driven book musicals, and in fact takes it further, deep into a character's mind and environment, like *Hair* did with Claude and the world of the Tribe. Instead of relying primarily on external, interpersonal events ("plot"), drama in a concept musical is largely internal. The self-examination and commentary—and the arc of discovery and growth that happens along the way—is the story.

The score of *Cabaret* (1966), John Kander and Fred Ebb's musical set in Berlin during the Nazis' rise to power in the 1930s, is a kind of hybrid book-concept musical, with songs in the book musical tradition of expressing action through song (like "So What"), as well as social commentary from the cabaret numbers that occur in the Kit Kat Club (like "Maybe This Time"). The 1972 film adaptation eliminated the book songs and kept the cabaret numbers, making it an early concept movie musical. Kander and Ebb's *Chicago*, which covers a sensational-ized murder trial, uses the framework of vaudeville numbers to comment on the interplay between entertainment and justice. Its 2002 revival has been much more successful than its original 1975 run, when it was overshadowed by the megahit concept musical, *A Chorus Line*. More on the latter show later in the chapter; first, an overview of a composer-lyricist whose work both defined and extends beyond the concept musical.

STEPHEN SONDHEIM

It is impossible to overstate the importance of Stephen Sondheim to Broadway, in his decades of work in musical theater and his influence on other lyricists and composers. The characters that inhabit his shows are complex and contemporary, and in terms of character development, musical form, and subject matter, he continued Oscar Hammerstein's expansion of what stories could be told and how. Hammerstein was, in fact, an important mentor to Sondheim, critiquing his early work and giving him writing exercises to develop his skills. This fortunate relationship came about because Sondheim's mother, divorced, preoccupied with her work, and something of a social opportunist, moved them near Doylestown, Pennsylvania, a conveniently short distance away from the Hammersteins, and Sondheim became like a member of the family. It was on Hammerstein's advice that Sondheim took two important lyricist jobs early in his career, despite his ambition to write both music and lyrics. The first was *West Side Story* (1957), where he gained valuable experience working with composer Leonard Bernstein, librettist Arthur Laurents, and director-choreographer Jerome Robbins. After Hammerstein told him he would learn a great deal from writing for a star, Sondheim agreed to write lyrics for the Ethel Merman vehicle *Gypsy* (1959), with music by Jule Styne. Sondheim finally made his composer-lyricist debut on Broadway in 1962 with the farcical *A Funny Thing Happened on the Way to the Forum* (book by Burt Shevelove).

Sondheim became known for sophisticated and intellectual writing that speaks to the modern human condition. The quintessential concept musical *Company* (1970, book by George Furth) takes on the minefield of modern marriage. It began as a handful of one-act plays by Furth, and it was director Harold Prince who suggested that they could be developed into a musical. *Company* became a series of musicalized vignettes with no particular chronological order, centered around the thirty-fifth birthday party of stubbornly single Bobby, his pairs of married friends, and his three girlfriends. The show marked the beginning of a long and fruitful collaboration between Sondheim and Prince, who also directed *Follies*. *Company* and *Follies* also benefited from the talent of director-choreographer Michael Bennett, who would go on to be the driving force behind *A Chorus Line*. It was the era of the director-driven show, a manifestation of musicals' ever more elaborate development from page to stage.

Follies (1971, book by James Goldman) ventures even further than *Company* from linear storytelling. Set at a reunion of showgirls from the *Weismann's Follies*, a fictionalized Ziegfeld-like revue, on the eve of the Weismann Theatre's demolition, former chorines and their companions assemble to reminisce, joined by ghostlike figures of their former selves played by younger actors. At the climax of the second act, the two main couples enter "Loveland," a surreal musical extravaganza, as they reach their emotional breaking points. In this thorough examination of choices and regrets, Sondheim had the opportunity to create two types of songs: dramatic songs in the tradition of the integrated book musical, and **pastiche** songs. Pastiche is an evocation of a musical style or composer from the past, in this case artists who wrote for the grandiose revues that inspired the fictional *Weismann's Follies*. Sondheim added his own spin to the musical characteristics of composers and lyricists from the golden age of the revue, such as Victor Herbert, Cole Porter, and Irving Berlin.

Though Sondheim is associated with the concept musical, he is not limited by it. One of his well-known mottos is "Content dictates form," and each of his shows is shaped by the needs of the story and characters at hand. For instance, *A Little Night Music*, adapted from Ingmar Bergman's film *Smiles of a Summer Night*, is a book musical dealing with the romances and liaisons of several couples. Sondheim set himself the challenge of writing the romantic score all in time signatures of three or multiples of three, resulting in a bounty of varied waltzes and triplet figures. His biggest hit, in the Tin Pan Alley sense of a song transcending its show of origin, comes from this score: "Send In the Clowns" has been recorded by many popular artists, including Barbra Streisand and Frank Sinatra.

Sondheim's rules for writing lyrics are printed in a repeated pattern on the inside covers of both volumes of his collected lyrics, *Finishing the Hat* and *Look, I Made a Hat*. These dictums are so crucial that he also states them, typeset as if they were lyrics, in the preface of each volume. Forming the foundation of all his work, they are: "Less Is More / Content Dictates Form / God Is in the Details / all in the service of / Clarity / without which nothing matters." We will also see how he serves clarity by creating a distinct musical language for each score, borne of the themes of that story.

SONDHEIM! THE BIRTHDAY CONCERT

It is New Year's, 2015. You recently saw the film version of *Into the Woods*, and its twisted take on fairy tales and witty but heartfelt songs sparked your interest in Sondheim. On this lazy holiday afternoon, you decide to continue your exploration with something that will show the wide range of Sondheim's work, as well as the tight-knit Broadway community's fanatical devotion to it. You rent *Sondheim! The Birthday Concert*, filmed in 2010 for his eightieth birthday, from the online streaming service to which you have a subscription, realizing later that it is also available at your local library.

A caption sets the scene at Lincoln Center's Avery Fisher Hall, home of the New York Philharmonic. The venerated classical music institution will tonight play host to a bevy of Broadway royalty, first among them conductor Paul Gemignani, who has music directed and conducted Sondheim's shows since 1971. He raises his baton and draws from the orchestra the first dark, dramatic chords of *Sweeney Todd*—a strange start to a birthday party! Seconds later, host David Hyde Pierce enters in a mock panic, telegraphing the first of many inside jokes of the evening. After some repartee between host and conductor, Gemignani launches a much more upbeat overture as the opening credits flash by with the names of stars from both Broadway and opera, and some who inhabit both spheres.

David Hyde Pierce, whose song-and-dance skills were often evident in his portrayal of Dr. Niles Crane on television's Emmy-winning *Frasier*, has a lengthy Broadway resume. He is the perfect host to the evening, embodying the wit that is a hallmark of Sondheim's work. While announcing the first number, Pierce also introduces a leitmotif of the concert's script: veneration of language. The running joke about wanting the concert to be performed in other languages acknowledges both Sondheim's Broadway beginnings as a lyricist and the international reach of his music.

Sondheim has often expounded upon the difference between poetry and lyrics, and, by extension, what makes a good lyric. In his view, poetry allows the reader to digest words at the reader's own pace, whereas the pace of a lyric is, by definition, set by the music. The best lyrics are simple and direct, clear to the listener upon one hearing, with room for the music to deepen their meaning. Lyric writing is, as he writes in the introduction to *Finishing the Hat*, "the art of finding the right balance between saying too much and not enough."

The concert selections will be structured like a show unto itself, obeying the most old-fashioned rules of musicals. The opening segment, which features songs for which Sondheim wrote only the lyrics, will start with a girls' ensemble number and an up-tempo protagonist introduction, both from *West Side Story* (but not in the order they appear in the show). Karen Olivo as Anita and the women from the cast of the 2009 revival of *West Side Story* perform "America," verbally sparring over whether life is better in Puerto Rico or Manhattan. Alexander Gemignani (the conductor's son) follows with Tony's solo, "Something's Coming." In the HBO special *Six by Sondheim*, Sondheim explains the importance of this introductory number making the audience interested in Tony. He draws parallels between Tony's need to break away from gang life, the baseball imagery in the lyrics, and the forward momentum of the music. Bernstein and Sondheim often wrote together during *West Side Story*, streamlining the process of collaboration necessary to achieve verbal clarity with Bernstein's rhythmically busy music.

The concert setting presents an opportunity to suspend musical theater's regimented casting pigeonholes. Gemignani is the first of several performers on the program who are a different type or age than the roles for which their songs were written. Their performances, taking the character-specific songs away from their usual context, highlight the universality of human experience that Sondheim captures.

Sondheim's Great American Songbook heritage is apparent in "We're Gonna Be All Right," a duet with music by Richard Rodgers from *Do I Hear a Waltz* (1965, book by Arthur Laurents). The lyrics that ended up in the show were toned down considerably; tonight, real-life couple Marin Mazzie and Jason Danieley perform the risqué original version. To write words for a couple whose relationship is marked by clever banter, Sondheim took the opportunity to borrow from the playbook of Rodgers's first lyricist, Lorenz Hart. While he roundly criticizes Hart's many tortured rhymes and mis-stressed syllables in *Finishing the Hat*, Sondheim blames laziness and not lack of talent for those lyrical sins. Showing that he could learn from both the strengths and shortcomings of his forebears, Sondheim wrote a lyric that was, as in his summary of Hart's style, "lighthearted but acerbic, bristling with unexpected non-sequiturs." Sondheim takes it a step further, incorporating character development by using Hart's stylistic trademark to imply a relationship based on subtle innuendo.

This segment of the concert is rounded out by Victoria Clark's performance of "Don't Laugh," from *Hot Spot* (1963), a musical with music by Mary Rodgers and lyrics by Martin Charnin, to which Sondheim contributed some of each. This song shows the young woman Sally gaining confidence in herself as the self-deprecation of the first "show me" verse gives way to the can-do attitude of the second, though she never quite loses her youthful way of interrupting herself.

As these four selections demonstrate, Sondheim's songs are miniature plays, musicalized moments that concern plot and character development. In this basic concept, he shows the influence of his mentor Hammerstein, who was instrumental in the development of song as a dramatic device within a musical. But like any excellent mentor, Hammerstein encouraged Sondheim to be more than a pale imitation of himself. On the solid foundation laid by Hammerstein and his generation, Sondheim writes for specifically drawn characters and situations using his own sophisticated vernacular.

The rest of the concert will feature Sondheim's music as well as his lyrics, beginning with a segment introduced by one of the people closest to the music: Jonathan Tunick, orchestrator of most of Sondheim's shows since 1970. In young, romantic Anthony's solo "Johanna" from *Sweeney Todd*, Nathan Gunn's operatic baritone soars over the orchestration that paints Anthony's romantic feelings with lush strings and his determination with brass and percussion.

Sondheim's breadth of style is an orchestrator's dream. Within *Follies* alone, Tunick mentions three distinctly different levels on which the score is built: in addition to the book songs and pastiche numbers mentioned above, Tunick recognizes the surrealistic "Loveland" sequence as a third level of the score, possibly because much of the heightened sensation would come from the orchestration. Jenn Colella, Matt Cavanaugh, Bobby Steggert, and Laura Osnes follow Gunn's performance with the pair of complementary duets from *Follies* that belong to the younger versions of *Follies'* main couples. The melodies in "You're Gonna Love Tomorrow / Love Will See Us Through" are conversational, the better to evoke the clever colloquialism of Yip Harburg and Ira Gershwin, the lyricists who inspired this pastiche. Sondheim, always in a search for new rhymes, adds his own wink to the style by rhyming "warn you" and "*corn-u*-copia." Notwithstanding the full orchestral complement of the Philharmonic, the *Follies* duets recall the chamber ensemble accompaniments of Jerome Kern's Princess musicals (chapter 3) on the verses, and the light drums and acoustic bass underlying the sound of 1920s dance bands in the choruses. Nathan Gunn is joined by Audra McDonald for Ben and Sally's duet "Too Many Mornings," one of the book songs (i.e., nonpastiche) from *Follies*. Every collaborative musical element works toward what dramatist Sondheim has intended: McDonald and Gunn interpret the lyrics with operatic skill but natural expression, and the warm strings and woodwinds deepen their lament of the romance that could have been.

The next segment is a special treat for longtime Broadway devotees, as original cast members reprise songs from roles they originated. John McMartin enters as Ben, the apparently successful middle-aged man he played in *Follies* nearly forty years before. The lyrics of "The Road You Didn't Take," considered by themselves, depict someone at peace with his life. The music tells a different story with its restless accompaniment figures and a melody and harmony that struggle to settle into a key. Sondheim's characteristic use of music to provide subtext to the lyrics is especially effective in this song, where even without the context of the show, it is clear that this character is lying to himself. *Follies'* remembrances are tinged with regret and resignation, but it is Sondheim's large body of work delving into the complexities of human emotion that merits tonight's celebration. Given the retrospective nature of the evening, it's unsurprising that material from *Follies* forms the backbone of the concert's program.

One of the most familiar shows of his oeuvre is *Into the Woods*, whose book by James Lapine draws from several Brothers Grimm fairy tales, making it an attractive choice for school drama departments (there is even a licensed "Junior" version of the show that excises the more sinister parts—like the entire second act). The disparate plots of *Into the Woods* are held together by an original story about a baker and his wife, first played by Chip Zien and Joanna Gleason. The opening lyric—"you've changed"—gets a big laugh, as Gleason plays up the double meaning, unique to tonight, in addressing her stage husband from a quarter century before. In its usual context, that opening line merely lays the groundwork for the character arc of the song. The baker and his wife are in the midst of a quest for certain objects to bring to a witch who promises to cure their childlessness. The lyrics, whose short phrases and monosyllables peppered with numbers are reminiscent of a nursery rhyme, fit the characters' actions and emotional state at this point in the story.

Merrily We Roll Along (1981, book by George Furth) is not well known outside Sondheim fan circles. Despite its excellent score and many moving moments, the plot moves backward through time, so that at the start of the show we meet the protagonist, Frank, when he has already become a jaded and generally detestable songwriter who sold out his best friends and collaborators. The song "Growing Up," performed by Jim Walton, was written in 1985 for a revised production that attempted to make Frank more likable. Sondheim's fundamental principle of "Content dictates form" is evident as this songwriter accompanies himself on the piano while working out a personal problem through song. Steady piano chords place the song firmly in pop ballad territory, while subtly dissonant harmonies and moving lines keep it from being purely commercial—details that paint a clear portrait of a successful man rationalizing the price he's paid in compromised ideals.

Georges Seurat is an uncompromising artist as he is portrayed in the 1984 Sondheim-Lapine work *Sunday in the Park with George.* Inspired by Seurat's painting *A Sunday Afternoon on the Island of La Grande Jatte*, the show is a meditation on art, connection, and art's effect on an artist's human relationships. Seurat was first played by Mandy Patinkin, perhaps best known outside theater circles as Inigo Montoya from the 1987 film *The Princess Bride.* Patinkin mimes his staging from the show, in which George examines his sketches as he justifies his priorities: in his choosing between creative and romantic fulfillment, "Finishing the Hat" takes precedence over nurturing the romance. Although

George mourns the loss of a lover at the beginning of the song, his joy in creating soon overtakes his sense of separation from the rest of the world. At the end of the song, the lyrics and music are both triumphant, indicating that unlike *Follies'* Ben with his untaken roads, George is being honest with himself.

Indeed, finishing the hats and other objects in this painting must have required relationship-compromising levels of dedication. Using a technique called pointillism, Seurat composed the entire work with tiny dots of the twelve colors from his palette without mixing them, leaving it to the eye of the viewer to render the full spectrum of color. In working out his musical language for *Sunday in the Park with George*, Sondheim aimed to do aurally what Seurat did visually, resulting in music whose movement is based not on the idea of melody-plus-chords, but rather of placing certain pitches near each other so the ear of the listener could mix them. Sondheim uses the notes of the scale to create recognizable melodies and harmonies in the way Seurat used paint and canvas to create recognizable shapes. Though their raw material was the same as their fellow artists', the subtly different language of the finished piece comes from a different conception of putting it together.

George's love (named Dot, of course!) was played by Bernadette Peters, who now joins Patinkin onstage for their climactic duet from the second act. Act 2 is set in 1984, when Seurat's great-grandson, also an artist named George (played by the same actor), struggles to find the inspiration for something new. Near the end of the show, Dot appears to him in a vision, bringing the story full circle with "Move On." It is a culmination of the dramatic and musical themes of the show, and Sondheim wrote to the strengths of Patinkin's and Peters's vocal ranges, having them sing in harmony on repetitions of the title lyric. *Sunday in the Park with George*, while not autobiographical, is one of Sondheim's most personal statements (it was his first show after *Merrily* flopped; without the inspiration of James Lapine and Georges Seurat, Sondheim might have made good on his threat to give up theater and write mystery novels instead).

The only way to "move on" from Patinkin and Peters's showstopping performance is to let Gemignani have his *Sweeney Todd* moment at last. It's a tale of two Sweeneys with both Michael Cerveris (from the 2005 revival) and George Hearn (from the original 1979 production). The audience gets a chuckle when they realize Hearn will play the role of the judge tonight: Cerveris, as Sweeney Todd, will spend their duet preparing to slit his predecessor's throat. The judge is Todd's mortal enemy, unjustly sending him to prison and, during his imprisonment, taking Todd's daughter Johanna as ward with the intention of marrying her. Todd is motivated by the urge to avenge his daughter and his wife (who went mad when he was sent to prison), which lends a chilling subtext to Todd's calculated musing about "Pretty Women." For all scholars' attempts to give *Sweeney Todd* a specific classification along the opera-musical spectrum, Sondheim himself considers it "a movie for the stage," inspired by music from the horror films he loved growing up. Horror music needn't be all *Psycho* tone clusters; sometimes the most thrilling choice is the reverse psychology of a tender ballad.

"Pretty Women" gets a decisive ending at the concert; in the show, Todd's decision to savor his revenge backfires when he and his intended victim are interrupted mid-shave. This frustrated attempt is the event that turns Todd from a man with a single homicidal mission into a mass murderer. The resulting bodies provide a solution to his landlady Mrs. Lovett's difficulty finding an affordable source of meat for her savory pie shop, and she first proposes her macabre idea in "A Little Priest." Patti LuPone, who played Mrs. Lovett in the revival, joins Cerveris and Hearn for a one-time-only trio version of the song. LuPone makes her entrance with her usual flair, then signals the instantaneous transition from her own larger-than-life persona to that of Mrs. Lovett with a switch to Cockney dialect. As soon as Todd (both of them) understands what Mrs. Lovett is implying, the song becomes a little game. This song is the end of the first act of *Sweeney Todd*, and in the original Christopher Bond play it is summed up in one line and a stage direction indicating that Todd and Mrs. Lovett laugh helplessly. Sondheim spun this witty act 1 finale from imagining they must be thinking of all the possible human ingredients for their pies.

Sondheim will be remembered for his Broadway musicals, but his prolific career has also included forays into other genres. The second act of the concert opens with an instrumental arrangement from the 1981 Warren Beatty film *Reds*, "Goodbye for Now," interpreted by American Ballet Theater dancers Blaine Hoven and Maria Riccetto. The static bass line and accompaniment **ostinato** (an "obstinate" musical figure, continually repeated) are typical of Sondheim's instrumental writing, providing a spare foundation for the romantic melody interpreted by the dancers.

Next, a star near the beginning of her career and a show from the beginning of Sondheim's career are featured as Laura Benanti sings "So Many People" from *Saturday Night*. On its way to Broadway in 1955, the production fell apart after the lead producer died, and the show went unproduced until 1997. The song shows a command of Great American Songbook writing, with a conversational verse leading to a thirty-two-bar refrain. Like the best of thirty-two-bar standards, the lyrics have a decided point of view—an unabashedly romantic one, a rarity for Sondheim. Also rare for Sondheim, the musical phrases only occasionally break the strictures of the regular four-bar musical setting. This was a few years before *West Side Story*; Sondheim credits Bernstein for inspiring him to consider other phrasing options.

This sort of concert is expected to have myriad **eleven o'clock numbers**, showstoppers of the sort that used to occur around eleven o'clock when shows began a little later in the evening. Six of Broadway's femmes *most* fatales—LuPone, Mazzie, McDonald, Peters, Donna Murphy, and Elaine Stritch—will perform soul-baring solos that reliably bring the house down in their shows of origin. *Follies* continues to be the retrospective-within-a-retrospective, comprising three of the six songs in this set. David Hyde Pierce also uses *Follies* to herald the entrance of the prima donnas, with "Beautiful Girls," a pastiche of the genre epitomized by Irving Berlin's "A Pretty Girl Is Like a Melody." These stars will not be singing the songs they're most closely associated with, which is immediately clear when LuPone rises to perform the evening's sole selection from *Company*, Joanne's scathing indictment of "The Ladies Who Lunch." The iconic interpreter of that song is Stritch, the original Joanne. Stritch warmly congratulates LuPone, who is possibly the only woman who would dare "propose a toast" in her presence.

The accompaniment of "Ladies Who Lunch" is an ironic bossa nova, the kind of music one might expect to hear during lunch at an expensive restaurant. Sondheim uses a similar device in Phyllis's rant "Leave You" from *Follies*, with a waltz underscoring the sarcastic terms of endearment Murphy spits in a tour de force of almost-suppressed rage. Sondheim also often puts a new spin on idioms in his lyrics, as in the expansion of the phrase "another day, another dollar" in "Ladies Who Lunch." *Follies*' "Losing My Mind" is a pastiche, with a rising harmonic line reminiscent of the Gershwins' "The Man I Love" and lyrics for which Sondheim credits Dorothy Fields as the inspiration. The Fieldsian twists on everyday phrases usher Sally through the stages of grief, as performed by Mazzie.

These star performances are marked by a compelling mix of vulnerability and confidence—the willingness to travel the heights and depths of human experience, and the courage to fully inhabit those moments in front of an audience. McDonald's unparalleled ability to transform herself can be seen in her rendering of "The Glamorous Life" from *A Little Night Music*, as Fredrika's ambivalent feelings about her mother's lifestyle flow unselfconsciously from a performer three times the age of the role. In "Not a Day Goes By" from *Merrily We Roll Along*, Peters backphrases fearlessly, stretching the written rhythm to accommodate the enormity of the character Beth's grief.

It takes a certain kind of guts to stand still and be honest, and to take your time in front of an audience as if you presume everyone will be paying attention until you're good and finished. That quality is the closest to a *sais quoi* of the je ne sais quoi that is star power, and nobody embodies it more than Elaine Stritch (1925–2014), who, aged eighty-five at the time of the concert, was the perfect choice to perform the showbiz survivor's anthem from *Follies*, "I'm Still Here." The cymbal texture, acoustic bass, and Harmon-muted trumpet introduction captures a mid-twentieth-century jazz combo sound that enables the imagination to stretch a couple of decades in either direction for the years covered by the lyrics. A sophisticated list song, the lyrics tally the ups and downs of those decades, through the eyes of a performer who made it through the "good times and bum times."

Sondheim's finely wrought musical characters are challenging and satisfying for an actor to inhabit. The finales to both acts of *Sunday in the Park with George* are tableaux of Seurat's painting, poignant statements of how an artist can conjure things—hats, ideas, lives—out of waves of light or sound. The concert ends (not counting the obligatory encore of "Happy Birthday") with "Sunday," sung by hundreds of Broadway performers who fill the stage and aisles of Avery Fisher Hall to show their appreciation to tonight's honoree for all—hats, ideas, lives—he's given them. The widespread choral sound is impossible to capture well on video, but this author can assure you it was thrilling live. Sondheim rarely writes choral singing, finding it difficult to justify many characters expressing the same thought. He made an exception for "Sunday," since the characters in this moment were all manifestations of George's imagination. In this case, the subtext to Sondheim's music and lyrics, added by the organizers of the concert and executed by Broadway's rank and file, is "Thank you."

Sondheim is not escapist entertainment for when one craves mindless sensation. His lyrics and music, developed to detail each character and story, reward the active listener and provide new discoveries on repeated hearings. The initial Broadway runs of his shows have generally met with more critical than commercial success, but the recent big-budget film adaptations (*Sweeney Todd*, 2007; *Into the Woods*, 2014) and steady stream of major revivals point to the likelihood that his work will stand the test of time.

"ONE" SINGULAR SENSATION

Notwithstanding *Hair* and a handful of other commercial successes, Times Square in the 1970s was a depressed and depressing place. Broadway was shrinking, both in the number of shows and the cast sizes thereof, and many Broadway gypsies who had once found steady employment were out of work. The term "gypsy" is a badge of honor, applied to hardworking chorus members who go from show to show, with none of the respect or glory accorded the stars they back up. In early 1974, Tony Stevens and Michon Peacock, dancers who were fresh off a Broadway flop, invited a group of their colleagues to an all-night gathering. Their intention was to talk about forming some kind of collaborative of Broadway chorus dancers, an avenue for creating work when work was scarce, and where they would be respected in a profession that didn't think much of them. They also invited director-choreographer Michael Bennett, who, with *Company*, *Follies*, and several other credits under his belt, was a name that could attract talent and money. He, too, had a nebulous idea of wanting to do a dancer-related project. Bennett almost immediately took charge of the session, which began around midnight, after those who had shows got out of their evening performance. They danced for a while, many wondering if this was an audition, then talked through the night, sharing intensely personal stories with friends, colleagues (some of whom were not so fond of each other), and strangers. They came from diverse backgrounds but bonded over the common experience of being dancers. The company Stevens and Peacock imagined never formed, but that first cathartic session was the germ of *A Chorus Line*.

Once the vague notion of a dancer project began to take shape as a musical, Edward Kleban came on board as lyricist and Oscar- and Grammy-winning composer Marvin Hamlisch (whom Bennett had known since Hamlisch was an ambitious rehearsal pianist) agreed to write the store. Between Kleban's experience at the famed BMI Musical Theatre Workshop and Hamlisch's film and pop background, they were a perfect team to distill dozens of hours of talk therapy–style interviews into an exciting score. One of the dancers, Nicholas Dante, on whose life story the character Paul was based, cowrote the book with playwright James Kirkwood Jr. The Public Theater, which had developed *Hair*, proved once again to be at the forefront of the sea change in how musicals are made, providing space and a shoestring budget to workshop the piece. It was a long road from vague notion to passion project to Broadway musical, and this unprecedented process for creating a show required a lot of trial and error. There was heartbreak along the way, as when most of the dancers unwittingly signed their life stories away for pennies, and when some of them later auditioned unsuccessfully for roles that were based on their own lives.

But all their efforts wrought a commercial and artistic triumph that would provide Broadway with much-needed economic resuscitation, opening at the Shubert Theatre on July 25, 1975, annihilating box office records with a 6,137-performance run that lasted nearly fifteen years. It would change the way dancers were viewed; audience members from all walks of life could recognize themselves in the formerly anonymous faces whose hard work was often underappreciated. The spirit of the show is that each dancer is "one singular sensation," and on opening night those sensational dancers were, in alphabetical order: Scott Allen, Renee Baughman, Kelly Bishop, Pamela Blair, Wayne Cilento, Chuck Cissel, Clive Clerk, Kay Cole, Ronald Dennis, Donna Drake, Brandt Edwards, Patricia Garland, Carolyn Kirsch, Ron Kuhlman, Nancy Lane, Baayork Lee, Priscilla Lopez, Robert LuPone, Cameron Mason, Donna McKechnie, John Mineo, Don Percassi, Carole Schweid, Michael Serrecchia, Michel Stuart, Thomas J. Walsh, Sammy Williams, and Crissy Wilzak. Most (though not all) of them were present for at least some of the taping sessions.

Unlike *Hair*, in which Galt MacDermot uses rock and older styles of music separately to comment on the generation gap, Hamlisch fuses contemporary pop styles with tried-and-true Broadway sounds. Because of the specificity of the lyrics, only one song, "What I Did for Love," had a significant life outside the show. However, the music was memorably fitting for characters who were both Broadway babies and members of the first rock-and-roll generation.

There are ample opportunities to hear the score of *A Chorus Line*; both the original and 2006 revival cast albums have their merits. The revival album includes a little more context for the story, and voices that are a testament to the multitasking ensembles and extremely fierce competition of recent decades (both of which mean that Broadway hopefuls are well advised to train to be **triple threats**, who dance, sing, and act very well). The 1975 cast album has among its ranks several triple threats, plus the raw authenticity of the original cast and orchestrations. Since the show was developed on a small budget, the creative team called in favors from a number of their orchestrator friends. Officially credited are Sondheim's orchestrator Jonathan Tunick, along with Bill Byers and Hershey Kay. Live productions are frequent, as *A Chorus Line* remains a favorite of regional houses, community theaters, and schools.

REGIONAL PRODUCTION: *A CHORUS LINE*

The hum of the crowd is the only noise as you take your seat to see *A Chorus Line* at a prominent regional theater near your home. No sound of musicians tuning comes from the covered orchestra pit, and you fear that the apocalypse has come, that this performance will be accompanied by prerecorded music, until you read in your program that it is *A Chorus Line*'s tradition to cover the pit and ask the musicians to refrain from warming up once the audience has begun to take their seats. In 1975, many theatergoers could still remember the huge dance ensembles of Ziegfeld shows, dozens of anonymous cogs in a machine that also featured lavish sets, costumes, orchestras—and stars. Bennett's intention was to draw as much focus to dancers as possible as the show revealed their individuality and humanity, and that included a bare stage, simple costumes, and a covered pit.

The music begins with a solitary piano, creating the atmosphere of an audition for an unnamed Broadway show. The lights come up on a group of dancers trying to keep up with the barked instructions of star director-choreographer Zach. The piano keeps time, not always a steady four-beat, but following the meter of Zach's instructions. The silence in the covered pit has saved the surprise that comes when the dancers turn downstage to repeat the dance combination facing the audience, and the explosion of sound from the full orchestra takes us from realism to the heightened reality of the concept musical, a dimension where we can hear the dancers' internal thoughts. Edward Kleban's lyrics bring the romanticized life of a dancer down to earth with a universal "I really need this job." As the dancers talk, pray, and berate themselves through the audition, the music matches the choreography and the dancers' collective inner mood. Hamlisch's setting of the text emphasizes the word "need," whether this job would be a dream come true, a stepping-stone, or a step backward for them. Their determination is emphasized by repeating the percussive hit at the end of the last chorus, a "repeated button" device that will recur near the end of the show.

The seventeen dancers who survive the cut that follows the opening number will compete for the eight jobs Zach has to offer. They will have to speak in the show in addition to dancing, and rather than give them lines to read, Zach makes these dancers who may never have opened their mouths onstage before continue the audition by talking about themselves. This construct creates tension, and invites the audience to look beyond the perfect pirouettes to the wheels turning inside dancers' heads. The libretto, which was awarded the 1976 Pulitzer Prize for Drama, arranges the series of songs and monologues in roughly chronological order, creating a mosaic of a dancer's life. The text will float between the internal thoughts of the dancers, as in the opening, and the external words spoken at the audition, as in Mike's solo, "I Can Do That," the first of the vignettes that deal with childhood. As the interviews continue, the text flows between the internal and external, and some of the dancers' stories overlap, creating the opportunity for group numbers like the trio where Sheila, Bebe, and Maggie reveal why they find solace "At the Ballet."

The "Montage," as the word implies, is composed largely of fragments, which overlap and dovetail with one another as the characters bond over stories of sexual awakening, family dynamics, and career beginnings. Hamlisch's diverse musical vocabulary, tailored to each character and situation, paints the tumult of adolescence, capturing its awkwardness in jerky rhythms and its wistfulness—as in Maggie's message to her absent mother—in a gently rocking chantey. Each time the "Montage" chorus returns to bid age twelve and thirteen hello or good-bye, more musical fragments are layered into the texture. The penultimate chorus explodes into thickly orchestrated Motown sound for "Gimme the Ball," fitting Richie's soulful vocals that brim with the brilliance that won him "a scholarship to college." The rest of the cast backs him up like a gospel choir, and, though realizing there is no "scholarship to life," they bid good-bye to their teen years in a buoyant final chorus. The music and lyrics of this section together capture the paradoxical excitement and trepidation of young adults preparing to "go to it." "It," in this case, refers to pursuing a career in the professional dance world. Val's "Dance: Ten; Looks: Three" capitalizes on tropes of old-fashioned Broadway music while she details her successful career strategy of surgical enhancement.

Zach asks Cassie to stay behind while the others leave for a break. The character of Cassie was developed during later workshops, partially based on originator Donna McKechnie's adult life, in which Bennett himself played a role not unlike that of Zach. The high-stakes conflict between Cassie and Zach is one of the hints of "book" that gives shape to the story. Nothing has happened in the show so far in a plot sense, except that several dancers were rejected after the opening. In fact, that is about all that will happen in *A Chorus Line*: there's an audition, eight people will get a job, and the rest will not. Everything else is character exploration, but Zach and Cassie's past may have a bearing on whether she books the job. There is a gentle repeated pattern underscoring dialogue that reveals Zach and Cassie's past as a couple and hints at the source of the conflict between them. Zach's career skyrocketed while hers plateaued and then tanked; she detests his workaholism, and he resents her both for leaving and for selling herself short by showing up to his audition for a lowly spot in the chorus.

"The Music and the Mirror" is a virtuosic piece of acting, singing, and dancing for the performer in the role of Cassie, and a masterpiece of integrating classic and popular styles to fit a story. A proverb of musicals holds that a character bursts into song when moved beyond what can be expressed by speaking, and dance when singing is no longer sufficient. That adage holds true here: though Cassie repeatedly identifies herself as a dancer, she states her case to Zach first through dialogue, gradually bursting into song, then intermittently adding movement. The low-register vocal writing allows for smooth transitions from speaking to singing, and leaves room to build to the catchy "all I ever needed" hook. After the climax of the vocal section, the music drops to almost nothing as Cassie begins a mirror dance that is part seduction and part sheer joy of expression. Here it becomes an internal-reality number, as a "chorus line" of Cassies are reflected in the angled mirrors. The orchestral colors and dynamic build in this section show the symbiotic relationship between music and dance, as Cassie's body articulates and stretches in precise accord with the various colors in the orchestration. As she gathers momentum, so does the music, building into a groove marked by thick brass writing, driving drums, and wah-wah guitar. The brass-dominated orchestration brings to mind another mid-1970s song. Bill Conti's "Gonna Fly Now," the theme from the film *Rocky*, is often used or imitated to accompany images of a protagonist training to triumph against all odds. It was released in early 1977, when *A Chorus Line* had been running for almost two years. Cassie's plea to Zach is successful: against all odds, he sends her down to learn the lyric with the other dancers, so she can continue the audition.

The irony is that for all Zach's wanting to see and hear each dancer's individuality, those he hires will have to subsume that very quality to match each movement, each body angle of group choreography to avoid drawing attention away from the star of the show. With that pressure in mind, the dancers return to the line to the sound of the piano pattern that will turn into the ensemble number "One." It is the only song we will hear from the unnamed musical for which the characters are auditioning, a showy strut reminiscent of Tin Pan Alley with its thirty-two-bar form and modular "repeat until vocal" introduction music. The lyrics, which glorify a female star in best Ziegfeldian fashion, are secondary here to Zach's rapid-fire instructions and the dancers' thoughts as they do their best to execute the steps and win one of the coveted eight jobs. The anxiety and disorientation of the high-pressure situation can be heard in the layered fragments of lyrics and inner monologues accompanied by orchestral chords from outside the key. In dialogue that's cut on both the original Broadway and revival recording, Zach's criticism of Cassie turns personal. The rest of the cast whispers and dances upstage of them like a ghostly Greek chorus as the former lovers level accusations at each other. He gestures to the dancers upstage, moving like clockwork, and asks Cassie if blending in with the group is what she really wants. Cassie declares she'd be proud to dance alongside any of these dancers, for they're all special. The cast's voices rise in the climactic final chorus, repeating the button several times with single-minded focus. Text, music, and movement unite around the theme of the show: each one of these supposedly dime-a-dozen chorus kids *is* "One."

The noblesse of the rank and file is an idea worth applauding, but there's no release yet, as the song fades seamlessly into the next part of the audition. A solemn air falls over the room when Paul injures himself and is taken to the doctor. A dancer's career is fleeting at best, and an injury can end it in an instant. The event prompts Zach's final question: What would they do if this were the day they had to stop? The discussion finds its emotional core when Diana speaks for all of them in "What I Did for Love." Hamlisch uses contrast to paint "the sweetness and the sorrow" of the moment, from the syncopated levity of Diana's first words to the lingering notes at the ends of each short phrase as she contends with the thought of good-bye. The bridge begins in a minor key but returns to major with the realization that love (a metaphor for dancing) is never gone, because—note the bittersweet lowered tones— "love's what *we'll* re-*mem*-ber." At the crest of the melody, Diana declares she'll neither forget nor regret following her passion, and the rest of the dancers show their heartfelt agreement with a harmonized chorus and a key change.

As the tremendous applause begins to fade, the now-familiar piano phrase looms, as the time has come to find out which eight dancers get the job. When the show was in previews at the Public, Zach changed which dancers were eliminated each night, leaving the cast in suspense. However, audience members often complained when Cassie didn't get the job at the end of the show. Cassie's personal story has many universal aspects—the dream, the rejection, the perseverance—and to kill her dream would kill the hope inherent in the idea of doing something for love without a guarantee or even much of a chance for glory. So the script was set with Cassie and the seven other dancers who get the job—although the actor playing Zach may change the order of dancers eliminated each night.

The curtain call (which many think of as the finale, after the subdued ending) is a reprise of "One," as if we have been transported to a fantasy version of the unnamed show-within-a-show where all of the dancers make the cut. Each member of the cast takes an individual bow, instead of the usual chorus group bow, and then they dance together as if they are a single organism, the accents in the music matching the kicks, hat movements, and other showy steps. In the end, the music diminishes to almost nothing before an inconsequential button (on the albums, it simply fades). Such an ending salutes the Broadway gypsies who work so hard for so little glory, and then just fade away.

EXPANDING THE PALETTE

How far the Broadway musical has come since Kern and friends' humble goal of making songs and stories fit together! While musicals still could be and often were about romance and rags to riches, shows like *Follies*, *Company*, and *A Chorus Line* proved that they could also deal with an array of contemporary subjects. The next decade would bring, to borrow a phrase from the obligatory musical comedy wedding, something old and something new: a return to operetta conventions and Ziegfeldian spectacle, and a continued expansion of the subjects and sounds musicals could encompass.

8

MEGAMUSICALS

Andrew Lloyd Webber: Gold Album and *Les Misérables*

It's no secret that big musicals exist near the intersection of art and commerce, and musicals in the era of the pro-corporate leaders Ronald Reagan and Margaret Thatcher took commercialism to new heights. The hit musicals of the 1980s were grandiose productions buoyed by huge marketing machines. The mask of *The Phantom of the Opera* (1988), the waifish image of Cosette of *Les Misérables* (1987), and the amber eyes of *Cats* (1982) are branding symbols recognized by musical theater fans around the world. Musical fashions resurface like a theatrical pair of bell-bottoms, and the scale of these shows recalls the enormous spectacle of the *Ziegfeld Follies*, earning them the term "megamusical." They are also sometimes categorized as poperettas, a twist on another dominant form from the same era. Their fanciful settings are reminiscent of operetta, and incorporate singing styles and technology that has emerged in the decades since operetta's heyday in the early 1900s.

The decade also brought a return to European dominance in musical theater. The number of Broadway shows declined, and though New York produced several excellent long-running shows like *42nd Street* (1980) and *Dreamgirls* (1981), they were somewhat eclipsed by megahits like the ones mentioned above, which originated on the United Kingdom's premier theater district, London's West End. For that reason, this chapter, unique in a book that otherwise confines itself to

American musical theater (so many musicals, so little space), will hop across the Atlantic, considering first a British composer who has continuously had at least one musical running on Broadway since 1979.

ANDREW LLOYD WEBBER

Andrew Lloyd Webber was born in 1948 into a musical family. His father was a professional organist, his mother a piano teacher, and his younger brother Julian is a world-renowned cellist. Lloyd Webber is known equally for his catchy songs and his flair for business—a dual knack that has earned him both praise and censure, and ensured his tunes would be heard around the world. His first three shows, with lyricist Tim Rice, were all concept albums before they were staged musicals. A concept album is a studio recording in which the songs are related by a theme or story: for example, Pink Floyd's 1973 album *The Dark Side of the Moon*—or the Who's *Tommy* (1969), which was staged as a Broadway musical in 1993. The terminology can be confusing; though both genres revolve around "concept," a concept *album* may have more of a plot than a typical concept *musical*, and so may seem more like a book musical when staged (potato, potahto; linear book and nonlinear concept storytelling techniques were mixed and matched in musicals by this point; let's get back to Lloyd Webber's first three shows). *Joseph and the Amazing Technicolor Dreamcoat* was Lloyd Webber's first commission, an oratorio written in 1968 for Colet Court preparatory school. After its positive reception, it was expanded as an album, playing the West End in 1973 and eventually Broadway in 1982. *Jesus Christ Superstar* (1971) ran on Broadway before London, after its concept album became a hit in the United States. Lloyd Webber and Rice also released *Evita* (1979) as a concept album ahead of the stage production, having had two successes with that marketing strategy.

As musicologist John Snelson writes in his book *Andrew Lloyd Webber*, these audio-only beginnings "resulted in a musical language that drew upon bold aural gestures as a form of visual substitute." Lloyd Webber uses obvious, easily recognizable musical symbolism, as if painting with primary colors to aid listeners in following a story they cannot see, using simple forms and harmony and mixing well-known genres of music in an attribute that Snelson labels "musical collage."

The juxtaposition of styles in Lloyd Webber's music is somewhat like pastiche (pastiche and collage are both descended from words that mean "glue"), but absent much of the personal compositional twist such as Sondheim added to his pastiches in *Follies* (chapter 7). The derivative nature of Lloyd Webber's music has been a double-edged sword, as he has fielded criticism and the occasional lawsuit (winning one case against a little-known composer, and settling out of court with the estate of operatic composer Giacomo Puccini). But with only twelve tones in the Western octave, and with popular styles that use idiomatic scales and melodic figures, melodic resemblance is inevitable—and it is that very familiarity and accessibility that has made Lloyd Webber's music so popular.

Musical theater fans who sit firmly in either the Sondheim or the Lloyd Webber camp overlook the fact that there are commonalities between them as well. They both speak of their job as that of a dramatist, and, like Sondheim, Lloyd Webber has expanded the scope of stories told in the musical form. His first three shows dealt with an Old Testament sibling rivalry, an Argentine political icon, and perhaps *the* biblical figure and political icon, Jesus Christ. From there Lloyd Webber went in the fanciful direction of dancing cats (*Cats*, 1982) and roller-skating locomotives (*Starlight Express*, 1987). It was after *Evita* that Lloyd Webber parted ways with Rice as his lyricist; he has since worked with numerous different lyricists. Music is created first in Lloyd Webber's partnerships, meaning that lyrics are molded to fit his melodies. Sondheim provides his own lyrics; the next best thing is to exert a degree of control by choosing the lyricist on a per-project basis. Lloyd Webber liked calling the shots, and post-*Evita* was already in a position to do so, having formed his own production company, the Really Useful Group, which gave him greater control over his creative work. He could choose which projects to pursue and which lyricists he wanted for them.

He chose a very amiable collaborator for *Cats*, his first West End/Broadway project after Rice: poet T. S. Eliot, who had died in 1965. Eliot's *Old Possum's Book of Practical Cats* was a childhood favorite of Lloyd Webber, who had first set some of it to music as a teenager. *Cats* began as a concert in 1980, and came to the West End in 1981 and Broadway in 1982. *Cats'* record-breaking West End and Broadway runs (twenty-one and eighteen years, respectively) were eventually surpassed by other long-running megamusicals; meanwhile, they were kept company by other Lloyd Webber shows. Both *Song and Dance* (1985; lyrics by Don Black and Richard Maltby Jr.) and *Starlight Express* (1987; lyrics for original production by Richard Stilgoe) were relative flops—meaning they "only" ran a year or two on Broadway (for perspective on how much things had changed on Broadway, recall that Ziegfeld's lavish 1927 production of *Show Boat* was considered a great popular success with its run of just under eighteen months).

Lloyd Webber's next projects took a more heartfelt turn. He wrote *Requiem*, a Mass in memory of his father's passing in 1982, featuring the soprano Sarah Brightman, who subsequently became his wife for several years, as well as the inspiration for and originator of the role of Christine in Lloyd Webber's most romantic and long-lived opus, *The Phantom of the Opera* (1988). Lloyd Webber and Cameron Mackintosh (*Phantom*'s producer; more on him later) discovered lyricist Charles Hart at a musical theater writing competition; Richard Stilgoe also contributed to the lyrics and book of *Phantom*. Gaston Leroux's 1910 novel *Le Fantôme de l'Opéra* also inspired a film and two other musical adaptations, but it is Lloyd Webber's version that is most well known. As of this writing, the show is still running in both London and New York, and has myriad professional and amateur productions around the globe. Though none of Lloyd Webber's shows of the 1990s or 2000s has come close to matching the dominance of his earlier blockbusters, his decades-long incumbency on Broadway holds, with *School of Rock* (lyrics by Glenn Slater), an adaptation of the film starring Jack Black, slated to open in late 2015 five blocks north of where *Phantom* has been playing since 1988.

ANDREW LLOYD WEBBER: GOLD—THE DEFINITIVE HITS ALBUM

Familiar names appear on the playlist as you load Lloyd Webber's *Gold—The Definitive Hits* album on your computer's music player. Patti LuPone and Mandy Patinkin, familiar from chapter 7's *Sondheim! The Birthday Concert*, appeared opposite each other in the original Broadway production of *Evita*, and each has a track from that show on this album. Their characters' antagonistic relationship in *Evita* is not apparent here, as their tracks are separated by selections from other shows; the story of the *Gold* album is that of Andrew Lloyd Webber's great commercial success. Released in Britain in 2001, the 2002 American version features all but one of the same songs, with several changes in the performer lineup to feature names more familiar to an American audience. In addition to several selections from original cast albums, the collection contains tracks from artist compilations and singles from concept albums or one-time commissions.

Lloyd Webber's collage technique is evident in the first three tracks of the album. "Superstar," the first single release from the *Jesus Christ Superstar* concept album, begins with a bombastic orchestral introduction complete with timpani, pivoting on a drum fill to the rock beat that underlies the rest of the song. Classical characteristics in rock music are a hallmark of progressive rock, or prog rock. Bands that fit into that pigeonhole, like Jethro Tull and Pink Floyd, reached their peak in the 1970s. Given Lloyd Webber's generation and parentage, it is not surprising that he too was inspired to combine the sounds of rock and classical music. However, where prog rock typically shows signs of "progress" from rock's simple chords and forms to more of the complex ones typical of classical music, almost the entire four minutes, seventeen seconds of "Superstar" is built upon two four-bar phrases, both of which incorporate chords containing flatted "blue" notes. The simple, repetitive structure both invites and demands the improvisation of Murray Head's ad-lib lead vocals.

A power ballad groove begins in the third verse of Barbra Streisand's recording of "As If We Never Said Goodbye" from *Sunset Boulevard*, mandating a steady tempo for that section of the otherwise fluid, romantic ballad. "As If We Never Said Goodbye" bears some resemblance to a typical Sondheim ballad with its use of conversational rhythm and wide melodic intervals. However, the treatment of the melody is different: where Sondheim might prod a melodic figure to evolve and build over the course of an entire song or even the whole show, Lloyd Webber favors direct repetition, building to a climax in each verse of "As If We Never Said Goodbye." The melody of each verse is exactly the same, so that by the time the first lyric of the song recurs after the bridge, the audience could sing along if they wished (to use a metaphor, Sondheim has stamina and is inventive; Lloyd Webber is predictable but multiorgasmic). The overall build in this song comes instead from the development in the orchestration and in Streisand's dynamic voice, ranging from a near whisper to a metallic belt.

The next song, "The Phantom of the Opera," likewise uses key changes to build excitement in the repetitive melodies sung by original cast members Michael Crawford as the Phantom and Sarah Brightman as his beautiful protégée, Christine Daaé. Christine is both a devoted voice student and an object of desire to the reclusive, musically gifted Phantom. Her vocal line in this song expresses the fraught nature of such a relationship, extending nearly three octaves, from a sultry low G all the way up to a glass-shattering high E. There are notable parallels between the relationship of the Phantom and Christine, and the composer's own feelings for his then wife Brightman, and her vocal virtuosity gave him the opportunity to articulate those emotions through her voice. A few tracks later, Crawford navigates the two octaves of "The Music of the Night" with great expression. Crawford, a popular British stage and television figure, was hired to originate the role of the Phantom on the West End shortly before rehearsals began when Lloyd Webber realized that rock singer Steve Harley, who had recorded the promotional single, was not right for the role in the more operatic direction *Phantom* was taking. The Phantom himself is portrayed as a genius of high art; however, the supernatural world he inhabits is scored with drumbeat and heavy synthesizers—the remaining strains of rock in a mostly romantic, orchestral score.

Megamusicals can attract megastars. When the film version of *Evita* was made in 1996, Lloyd Webber and Rice collaborated for the first time since they had split after the stage version of *Evita*. They wrote a new song for the pop star Madonna in the title role; "You Must Love Me" won the 1997 Academy Award for Best Song. The relatively small range of the song—its pitch range is a little less than half as expansive as that of "The Phantom of the Opera"—suits the moment of the story, as Evita struggles to accept that she is dying. It's also skillful writing for a pop icon whose stardom is built on elements other than brassy, powerhouse vocals (recall Ziegfeld's similar stars in chapter 2). Rice's lyrics touchingly emphasize the last word of "you must love *me*," as Evita realizes her husband's choice of her was not purely political.

Lloyd Webber was not the first to cast celebrities in starring roles in his shows, but he was a trendsetter in doing it in an era in which those stars came from outside the musical theater world (since musical theater had long ceased to be the main source of popular music, pop stars by definition would come from a more mainstream sector of entertainment). A 1991 West End revival of *Joseph and the Amazing Technicolor Dreamcoat* featured Australian pop star Jason Donovan. That revival led to a 1992 Toronto production and subsequent North American tour starring Donny Osmond of television's *Donny and Marie* fame. This sort of casting is still often used in long-running productions to boost stagnant ticket sales: a lead role functions as a sort of celebrity turnstile, with a string of famous performers playing the role for a limited time period to attract their fan base to the box office.

The turnstile effect can apply to music as well. The simple structures of "Any Dream Will Do" from *Joseph* have allowed it to be rearranged believably in a variety of styles as years passed—meaning the music could always be up to date in its anachronistic telling of a biblical story. The original 1968 concept album accompanied David Daltrey's vocal with a thick gumbo of late 1960s folk rock, complete with flute solos and backup vocals from the Colet Court school choir for whom *Joseph* was originally commissioned. The 1982 Broadway arrangement, with Bill Hutton as Joseph, begins as a piano ballad, retaining the choral background but building it to the feverish level typical of early 1980s rock ballads. The 1990s revival orchestration used for Donovan and Osmond is based on a quasi-calypso rhythm, and favors the slick sound of 1990s pop, with smooth choral and string countermelodies.

"Any Dream Will Do" was also the name of a 2007 reality television show, in which unknown performers competed to win the title role in a West End revival of *Joseph*. Lloyd Webber first hit upon this concept the previous year with "How Do You Solve a Problem Like Maria," the reality television search for the star of the Really Useful Group's revival of Rodgers and Hammerstein's *The Sound of Music*. Always wearing the bifurcated hat of composer and impresario, Lloyd Webber chooses to see other media as an opportunity rather than a threat. In the absence of an obvious celebrity choice for the starring role, why not create a project that is could be profitable in and of itself, *and* which advertises the upcoming production while simultaneously casting it?

The *Gold* album continues with the most famous song from *Cats* and arguably from Lloyd Webber's whole output, with cover versions by artists around the world. The lyrics for "Memory," unlike the T. S. Eliot poems that form the text for most of the rest of the show, were written by *Cats* director Trevor Nunn from some of Eliot's ideas. Betty Buckley won a Tony for her portrayal of Grizabella, the faded glamour cat chosen to proceed to the Heaviside Layer (metaphorical heaven) in *Cats'* minimal plot; this track features her vocals from the original 1982 Broadway cast album. The main melody fixates plaintively on the first note, a melodic contour befitting Grizabella's existential contemplation. The mix of operatic and rock influence can be heard in the orchestration and in the rubato at the end of the song: the tempo slows dramatically into the final verse, and a key change creates maximum impact in the ending. The higher key sets the melody in the most powerful part of Buckley's belt voice, and the use of grand opera's tradition of lingering on the highest notes is an effective mixture of classical timing with contemporary vocal placement.

The selection of "Pie Jesu" from Lloyd Webber's *Requiem* was first released in 1998 on Charlotte Church's *Voice of an Angel* album when she was twelve years old. The "Pie Jesu" is the most popular part of Lloyd Webber's *Requiem*; not coincidentally, it is the most melodic movement of the piece. The *Requiem*, considered by some critics a surprising foray into "serious" music, contains some of Lloyd Webber's most dissonant writing. It was a commercial success, winning the 1986 Grammy for Best Contemporary Composition. However, it is not programmed frequently, owing to the large and somewhat unusual combination of personnel required to perform it: the soprano, tenor, and treble soloists are backed by a chorus and large orchestra, complete with organ, synthesizer, and drum set in addition to the typical symphonic instrumentation—but *minus* one orchestral standby, the violin section. The predominance of the organ in the "Pie Jesu" is appropriate for liturgical music; the requiems of French composers Faure and Duruflé also rely heavily on organ accompaniment. In contrast to the high drama of most of Lloyd Webber's theatrical vocal writing (and even some of the more turbulent movements of the *Requiem*), the pure vocal straight tone suits the Latin text of this moment of resolution in the Mass: "Pious Jesus, who takes away the sins of the world, give them everlasting rest." Lloyd Webber collages text from two typically separate sections of the requiem liturgy, the "Pie Jesu" and the "Agnus Dei," or Lamb of God.

Yvonne Elliman, who played the role of Mary Magdalene for the *Jesus Christ Superstar* concept album, the original 1971 Broadway production, and the 1973 film, brings belt power and subtle riffs against the background of gentle folk-rock accompaniment of "I Don't Know How to Love Him." Even without the visual input of staging, or the knowledge that Mary Magdalene is a prostitute and a disciple of Christ, the listener can discern both the sexual undercurrent and the internal conflict in the song. In the same way, the vocal writing and performance of *Evita*'s "Don't Cry for Me, Argentina" imparts the flavor of an impassioned political speech. The declamatory, recitative-like verses (speechlike—notice the quick, repeated pitches in the melody), the triplet rhythm of the chorus's *"don't cry for* me," and the short phrases throughout the song all declare that this song is a "stump speech." Patti LuPone, the original Broadway Evita, traverses a great dynamic range in the last vocal phrase of the song, perfectly portraying the ambition and political savvy of her character.

There are advantages and disadvantages to musical repetition. In the pros column, repetition means less new musical information for the audience to digest while taking in a story. On the other hand, wholesale melodic repetition can lead to difficulties in setting the text. "Oh, What a Circus," with Mandy Patinkin as political dissident Che Guevara, demonstrates these pros and cons in action. Though it occurs first in the show, this song is essentially a sped-up version of "Don't Cry for Me, Argentina," with an almost identical melody and form. The use of the exact same tune and timing leads to the ungraceful setting of "we made the front page of all . . ."—wait for the rhythm of the melody—"the world's papers today" (this sort of copy-paste-then-add-different-lyrics is also noticeable in *Phantom*'s ubiquitous "Angel of Music" melody). The advantage of introducing this melody early in the show for Che Guevara's rant is that it's already familiar when it reappears as Evita's big number in act 2. Familiarity breeds sales as well as contempt, and nowhere is that so evident as with Lloyd Webber.

Another example in the category of the mixed blessings of repetition instead of development: when *Aspects of Love*'s "Love Changes Everything" needed a big finish, the obvious choice was to go up the octave in the vocal line. The orchestration had already been building and a key change added after a brief instrumental interlude preceding the last verse. A subtle Sondheim-like melodic development would seem jarring in this song, where all the verses of text are set to the same music, without a bridge or other form of melodic variety. Michael Ball, the phenomenal tenor who originated the role of Alex, tells in the British documentary *The Story of Musicals* how he simply sang the last three notes of the song an octave higher, ending on a high B-flat, much to the chagrin of everyone who has played the role since. That may not seem like much in contemporary musical theater's tenor-centric world, but it is quite a big moment at the top of the show (if your voice cracks on the high note, you have to face the audience for another two hours).

In addition to collage and repetition, Lloyd Webber employs the quintessential symbolism of the theatrical writing trade. Brightman and pop star Cliff Richard's "All I Ask of You," which was one of *Phantom*'s promotional singles, is replete with the sweeping melodic leaps and vocal harmony that signify romance. "The Perfect Year" finds *Sunset Boulevard*'s aging movie star Norma Desmond (Glenn Close) and handsome, conniving, young screenwriter Joe (Alan Campbell) wishing one another a happy new year. Their respective time signatures let the audience know the score of the relationship: Norma, crazy for Joe and also just plain crazy, sings of her vision of happiness in romantic 3/4 time. Joe, sensing an opportunity to build his career, responds in kind, but in the more calculated 4/4 time.

It might seem odd that three of eighteen tracks on this greatest hits album are from a show that never played Broadway; in fact, it is evidence of Lloyd Webber's penchant for cross promotion. *Whistle Down the Wind*, with lyrics by rock writer and producer Jim Steinman, premiered in Washington, D.C., in 1996. It received critical reviews that prompted producers to cancel the planned Broadway run. The UK release of the *Gold* album came on the heels of a more successful revamped West End run and subsequent tour in 1998. The inclusion of the tracks on the American album points to continuing machinations around that time for another crack at Broadway; a U.S. tour did in fact come to fruition for six months in 2007–2008.

Whistle Down the Wind takes place in poor, small-town Louisiana in 1959, and is a coming-of-age tale of a fifteen-year-old girl named Swallow, who encounters a mysterious stranger sheltering in a barn. When she asks who he is, he mutters, "Jesus Christ" before passing out, leaving open the question as to whether he was cursing or claiming a messianic identity. Swallow and the other youths promise to protect the stranger; meanwhile, news has gotten around of an escaped killer hiding nearby. The show contrasts the children's hope and innocence with the adults' fear, and ends with an ambiguity that is new to Lloyd Webber's usual broad-brushstrokes style.

Two of the three selections come from the 1998 *Whistle Down the Wind* concept album; despite exploring new artistic territory, Lloyd Webber stuck to his habitual promotional strategy ahead of the revised West End production. The gospel arrangement of "The Vaults of Heaven," recorded for the concept album by Welsh singer Tom Jones and gospel ensemble Sounds of Blackness, sets up the show's themes of struggle, redemption, and the innocence of children. The end of act 1 finds the children promising the stranger that they'll love him "No Matter What," while the adults, accompanied by dissonant, percussive music, prepare to hunt down the escaped murderer. The concept album version eliminated the dissonant manhunt music and used different Steinman lyrics that are not specific to the show. Recorded by the Irish band Boyzone, the single became a runaway international hit, reaching number one on the charts in nine European and Asian countries; it peaked at thirty-five on the U.S. Billboard Top 40 chart. The **diatonic** melody (staying within the notes of the key the song is in) and common chord progression are predictable, with most of the variety coming from arrangers Angela Lupino and Simon Franglen's subtle variations in the instrumental accompaniment and smooth male harmonies typical of 1990s boy bands. The third selection from *Whistle Down the Wind* is the title track, recorded by Sarah Brightman during the 1995 sessions for her *Surrender* album, but not released at that time. "Whistle Down the Wind" is a key phrase for the main characters in the show to persevere in the face of difficulty. The melody is built almost entirely on the pentatonic scale that is the basis of much folk music from around the world, giving it a timelessness that is well suited to Brightman's pure tone and impeccable diction.

Brightman is also featured on the final track of the *Gold* album, in a duet with Spanish opera star José Carreras. Lloyd Webber's international star status was cemented, if it hadn't been already, when he was asked to write a theme song for the 1992 Barcelona Summer Olympics. "Amigos Para Siempre," which translates as "Friends for Life," has lyrics by Don Black, with the title phrase appearing in English, Spanish, and Catalan. The usual collage element is present in the blend of classical and pop sounds, with castanet and Spanish guitar flourishes present in Serbian arranger Fedor Vrtacnik's orchestration, in homage to the

Olympics' host country. As in several other songs on this album, the repetition of the **verse-chorus form** is broken by an instrumental section. Black's lyrics of love and friendship float smoothly on a pleasant melody, the words going by at a rate friendly to an international audience.

Which brings us to the crux of the debate of Lloyd Webber's undeniable worldwide success: language, obvious versus subtle in a global marketplace. The mixed to negative reviews of many of his shows are typical of the critical-popular disconnect common in long-running megamusicals. Lloyd Webber has the gift of writing a catchy tune that feels like (and in some cases actually resembles) a tune you already know from the first hearing. As to use of repetition, one man's ad nauseam is another's accessible; the same goes for the lyrics most of Lloyd Webber's collaborators set to his tunes. Lloyd Webber has tapped into a huge market, using familiar musical building blocks to reach a worldwide audience whose only common language may be musicals.

LES MISÉRABLES

When the 1980 French concept album of Alain Boublil and Claude-Michel Schönberg's *Les Misérables* landed in British producer Cameron Mackintosh's hands in 1983, Mackintosh could hear the dramatic potential of the music even without being able to understand all of Boublil's lyrics (poet Jean-Marc Natel also contributed to the original lyrics). Schönberg, the composer for this adaptation of Victor Hugo's epic novel of the same title, had gotten his start as a record producer and songwriter in France, and the music, like that of many other musicals of the era, reflects the influence of rock within its grandiose orchestral texture.

The concept album had been staged for a hundred-performance run at the Palais des Sports in Paris. For a West End commercial adaptation, Mackintosh paired with director Trevor Nunn and the Royal Shakespeare Company of which Nunn was then the artistic director. Under Nunn's direction and with Mackintosh's support, Boublil and Schönberg expanded the story. Lyricist Herbert Kretzmer's text for the English version of *Les Misérables* is not a mere translation but rather an adaptation. He also did some original work on songs that did not exist on the French album—"Stars" and "Bring Him Home," to name two well-known examples. The *Les Misérables* productions that play around the world today are all based on this West End version, which opened in 1985 and is still running, having just celebrated its thirtieth anniversary as of this writing. Similarly impressive Broadway and international success followed; the show's website boasts that it has been translated into twenty-two languages and seen by seventy million people and counting.

The musical stays close to the main plot of the Victor Hugo novel, whose title means "The Miserable Ones," and which was written in 1862 when memories of the French Revolution and subsequent political upheaval were fresh. The musical begins in 1815 when protagonist Jean Valjean seeks redemption in a new life after nineteen years of unjust imprisonment for stealing a loaf of bread. Valjean is continually pursued by a policeman, Javert, whose devotion to God and to the rule of law are equally fanatical. Javert's hypocrisy is a foil for the equally devout but less rule-bound Valjean, who years later saves young Cosette from the clutches of dishonest innkeepers Monsieur and Madame Thénardier after the death of Cosette's mother, Fantine. After Valjean rescues Cosette, the story flashes forward again to the Paris Uprising of 1832, when antimonarchist students took to barricades. A whole new generation of lead characters emerges as Cosette and the student revolutionary Marius fall in love at first sight, to the dismay of the Thénardiers' daughter Éponine, who loves Marius hopelessly. Through it all, Valjean seeks to leave his past behind. *Les Misérables'* ordinary people endure extraordinary circumstances in stories filled with love, patriotism, and secret pasts—the ingredients for a dramatic night at the theater.

LES MISÉRABLES THROUGH THE YEARS

You remembered to look at the weather forecast yesterday, so you are prepared for a blustery evening in with your favorite refreshments and an assortment of recordings of *Les Misérables* from your local library. Because of its long-lasting, continuous popularity, there are many live and recorded performances through which to experience *Les Misérables* and its web of characters, and tonight you decide to take the opportunity for comparison. You have decades of options: the original French concept album from 1980 and the 1987 original Broadway cast recording are stacked on top of the Complete Symphonic Recording, released in 1989 featuring an international cast and the Philharmonia Pit Orchestra. Lined up next to them are DVDs of the 1995 tenth anniversary recording with London's Royal Philharmonic Orchestra and the 2010 live recording of the twenty-fifth anniversary production with new pit orchestrations. This abundance of recordings provides the chance to hear how the show has evolved over the years, both in its development from a French concept album to a stage musical performed in English and translated to many other languages, and through the many revolutions in the world of music and entertainment.

One of Boublil's earliest ideas in adapting Hugo's work was how to treat the story of Fantine's descent from hope and romance into abandonment and single motherhood, and finally into poverty, prostitution, and death. Boublil wrote, *"J'avais rêvé d'une autre vie"*—"I had dreamed of another life"—which became "I Dreamed a Dream" in the English version. Only a few lines are directly translated. Herbert Kretzmer's English lyrics retain the poetic sensibility and emotion of the original, while also including more details of Fantine's backstory—an important addition when taking the show away from France, where Hugo's novel and the history around it are deeply embedded in the cultural consciousness. The use of the ensemble also evolved during the development of *Les Misérables*. On the French concept album, Fantine's fellow *misérables* hum and sing in the background, but the English "I Dreamed a Dream" is a solo with no backup vocals, painting more clearly how alone Fantine is in her hellish life. In death, she's comforted only by a hallucination of her daughter Cosette, and Valjean's promise to take Cosette into his care.

Young Cosette is staying with Monsieur and Madame Thénardier, innkeepers who force her to work long, hard hours while they pamper their own young daughter, Éponine. Boublil and Schönberg used musical theater's tradition of stereotypes to turn the Thénardiers into comedic characters, still cruel but also providing laughs, unlike their dour counterparts in the novel. In "Master of the House," it is interesting to note the different dialects chosen to connote the lower class of the Thénardiers. Cockney and American Midwest are popular choices in the English language productions, and the hard *R*s of the French on the concept album (in the equivalent song "La devise du cabaretier") also indicate a speaker of a more humble background. The humor is character driven: these unscrupulous innkeepers tell the truth as they see it, accompanied by music that Schönberg describes in a documentary on the tenth anniversary DVD as a "drinking song . . . heavy like a pint of beer." The orchestrations are also driven by the characters and story. The same musicians creating the dynamic orchestral textures for dramatic sequences of the show now sound instead like the kind of band that might be found in a seedy bar. The deliberately lazy instrumental solos, attention-grabbing trombone smears (especially at the beginning of the song on the 2010 recording), and heavy keyboard playing all enhance the tavern setting and the garish comedy of the Thénardiers.

The orchestrations for the both the French concept album and the 1985 West End production were written by John Cameron. One of the shows that inspired Boublil to write *Les Misérables* was *Jesus Christ Superstar*, and although Schönberg's melodic and harmonic writing are less rock driven than Lloyd Webber's, *Les Misérables* exists in the same contemporary aesthetic territory, aided by Cameron's orchestrations. The original orchestrations are anchored by electric bass, and feature the electronic sounds of the Yamaha DX7, one of the first popular digital synthesizers and a mainstay of pop music during the 1980s when it was manufactured. Drum fills of the type associated with arena rock of that era also make frequent appearances throughout the score to emphasize emotional moments, as you can hear near the end of "Stars" when the toms emphasize each word of Javert's declaration, "So it must be."

Recognizing that *Les Misérables* had become a long-running institution that transcended the time period in which it was created, Mackintosh tasked Christopher Jahnke, Stephen Metcalfe, and Stephen Brooker with creating "timeless" orchestrations for the 2006 Broadway revival. These new orchestrations were used in 2010 for the twenty-fifth anniversary tour, and in the subsequent Broadway, West End, and major international productions of *Les Misérables*. Much of John Cameron's excellent original work was preserved; the first obvious changes to make were to replace electronic sounds with symphonic ones. As Jahnke stated in an interview, "The second you use electric bass or electronic keyboard sounds in an orchestration, the texture runs the risk of resembling a specific decade or period within late twentieth-century or early twenty-first-century pop music." The use of sampling, or the technique of recording acoustic instruments at various pitches to create sample libraries for use in synthesizers, has greatly improved the synthesizer's ability to fool the ear into thinking it's hearing an acoustic instrument. Using up-to-date sample libraries, the distinctive and period-specific Yamaha DX7 sound becomes an out-of-tune piano in the new orchestration of "Master of the House" and a harp in "Stars." In one of the more obvious replacements, the keyboard plays a harpsichord sound in the new orchestration of the student revolutionaries' "Do You Hear the People Sing." "*A la volonté du peuple*," the concept album version of the song, uses an electric guitar to double parts of the vocal melody. In that more rock-oriented context, it is fitting to use the electric guitar's rebel image for that song, but it would be out of place in the new orchestration, where all the other sounds predate the twentieth century.

The new orchestrations were not mere replacements of bass and keyboard sounds with more symphonic-sounding equivalents. The assignment to create timeless orchestrations was an opportunity for Jahnke, who worked on the songs in which the biggest changes were made, to add his stamp on the characterization and drama in certain sections of the music, as in "Valjean's Soliloquy" ("What Have I Done"). The agitated string, brass, and timpani figures at the beginning of the music portray the depth of Valjean's self-loathing and prepare the ear for the contrasting texture of his amazement at the mercy of the bishop who comes to his aid. The new orchestrations also heighten much of Javert's music, using the sound of a French reed organ to symbolize his rigidity in his religious beliefs.

Les Misérables boasts some of the most coveted roles in the musical theater canon, with iconic solos that allow for distinctive interpretations within the framework of the composition. Each conductor and performer may interpret the story and the music a little differently, and particularly in the solos of principal characters, they work together to create an interpretation that feels authentic to that performer, rather than a carbon copy of a previous performer or a mechanical rendering of the notes on the page. In a new musical, or a production on the scale of any of these recordings, the writers are almost always involved in shaping the interpretation—an exciting opportunity for a performer.

"Bring Him Home" was written specifically for Colm Wilkinson, who originated the role of Valjean in both London and New York and returned for the tenth anniversary concert. Known as an Irish tenor (in this case accurate both for his nationality and for the light, **falsetto** vocal placement associated with the term), his voice floats with perfect control through the prayerful ballad. Wilkinson was followed on Broadway by American country singer Gary Morris, who recorded the role of Valjean on the Complete Symphonic Recording. Morris's rendering of "Bring Him Home" brings to mind the singing style of the golden age, with his full, round sound on all but the softest of notes, and vibrato throughout. On the 2010 album, John Owen Jones sings the role with more straight tone, tending to allow vibrato in long sustained notes. Vibrato, a slight, rapid wavering in the pitch, occurs naturally in good vocal technique of the kind necessary to create overtones unique to the human voice that allow it to be heard over an orchestra without amplification, as in opera. **Straight tone** is the preferred aesthetic in most rock and pop music, which relies on amplification and sound mixing to be heard over the band. Musical theater has, in the past few decades, developed a hybrid style of allowing the straight tone of a bright, forward-placed note to bloom into vibrant tone partway through the duration of the note, as can be heard throughout John Owen Jones's "Bring Him Home."

"Bring Him Home" was one of several songs that did not exist on the French concept album. "Stars," "Empty Chairs at Empty Tables," and the prologue sequence were also written for the West End production. Kretzmer created the English lyrics for those songs with Boublil's suggestions. Boublil, who speaks excellent English, has collaborated on the lyrics for his later shows, though he often begins the writing process in French. He is quoted at length on his lyric-writing and collaborative processes in Margaret Vermette's *The Musical World of Boublil and Schönberg*, speaking highly of his lyrical colleagues and making the point that "a musical should not belong to one culture. Our shows don't spring from one particular culture but they survive because they convey with music and lyrics the kinds of emotions that could be a part of any culture."

Boublil's international paradigm of musicals found its pinnacle in *Les Misérables*, and that accomplishment is proudly displayed in the encore at the end of the tenth anniversary concert. A standing ovation follows the last triumphant chords of the show, and when the star-studded cast is finished taking their bows, the full orchestra swells with the melody of "Bring Him Home" as the camera pans to seventeen Valjeans from around the world coming "home" to their *Les Misérables* family, each waving the flag of their home country. After Wilkinson sings the first stanza of "Do You Hear the People Sing," each Valjean takes a couple of lines solo in his native tongue—French, Japanese, Hungarian, and so on, demonstrating that the love stories of *Les Misérables*—romantic, patriotic, familial—are indeed universal.

GLOBALIZATION

"The sun never set on the British Empire," a phrase that captures the dominance of nineteenth-century Britain, could also be applied to the musical empires of Lloyd Webber, Boublil and Schönberg, and Cameron Mackintosh. At any given moment, somewhere in the world, professional live performances of their musicals are taking place. Bigger is the byword of the imperial world, both in terms of aesthetics and potential for profit. Bigger shows mean bigger budgets and financial risk, ruling out smaller investors, but the bigger returns and players involved can also mean a wider reach for a commercial hit. In a chicken-or-egg sort of loop, musicals originating from the West End and Broadway became international commodities during the 1980s and '90s, to the point where it is standard for a hit show to go global (as opposed to the handful of international tours with a diplomatic or political subtext before the 1980s, such as those of *Porgy and Bess* and *Hair*). Well before the end of the twentieth century, it began to take a village, or a corporation, or a village of corporations to produce a Broadway musical. To illustrate, the original 1959 production of *The Sound of Music* had four producers, and two were Richard Rodgers and Oscar Hammerstein themselves; the 1998 revival credits more than a dozen people and organizations on the producing team.

Britain in the 1980s and beyond has had the impresario Cameron Mackintosh as well as Andrew Lloyd Webber's Really Useful Group; Broadway has had Disney Theatrical Group. The live production branch of Walt Disney's entertainment juggernaut came to Broadway in 1994 with an adaptation of the animated film *Beauty and the Beast* with music and lyrics by Alan Menken, Howard Ashman, and Tim Rice. The staunchly family-friendly company led the charge in the revitalization of Times Square, and the investment paid off. Commercial hits like *The Lion King* (1997), with music by Elton John and lyrics by Tim Rice, have benefited both Disney and Broadway and spurred other theatrical productions as well as prosperity in surrounding industries. Disney teamed up with Mackintosh for the stage version of *Mary Poppins* (2006), uniting theatrical titans on either side of the Atlantic.

While Disney courted the family audience, other commercial producers banked on nostalgia, with shows that tailored the plot of a musical around a list of hit songs. A newly popular twist on the old idea of creating a musical around hit songs, these so-called **jukebox musicals** featured music of well-known pop groups. The first huge modern smash of this genre was the West End's *Mamma Mia* (2001), in which the music of Swedish pop group ABBA is structured around a book by Catherine Johnson that uses hit songs like "Dancing Queen" to tell the story of a single mother, her daughter, and three men who may be the daughter's father. Other jukebox musicals are the 1980s hit parade *Rock of Ages* (2009), and *Jersey Boys* (2005), a biographical musical about Frankie Valli and the Four Seasons, the 1960s rock group of "Sherry" and "Big Girls Don't Cry" renown.

There are those who bemoan big brand-name musicals, and it's true that answering to a corporation can confuse or dilute the authors' and creatives' intended vision of a show. However, as we will see in the final two chapters, the commodification of musicals has not quelled the creative voices of musical theater artists. If anything, it has contributed to an environment where more work can be fostered, not only on Broadway, but also in regional, developmental, and educational theater, where even more storytelling voices can find their niche.

9

MUSICALS FOR THE MTV GENERATION

Rent and *Spring Awakening*

Just after midnight on August 1, 1981, a new television channel launched its format of round-the-clock music videos with the decidedly apropos selection, "Video Killed the Radio Star," by the British New Wave duo the Buggles. That channel, of course, was MTV, then known also as Music Television. While the concept of "the best of TV, combined with the best of radio" hardly killed the latter, MTV did add a dimension to the way its target audience—teens and twenty-somethings who had been born after rock and roll took over the charts—discovered and consumed popular music.

Around the same time as MTV was gearing up for its debut, two articles were published about separate incidences of illness that were caused by what came to be known as acquired immune deficiency syndrome, or AIDS. The majority of AIDS victims were gay males, fueling homophobia and taboo around the illness, and whether through deliberate neglect or bureaucratic sluggishness, government response to the crisis was slow. The arts have always been a safe haven for those who are ostracized from mainstream society, and musical theater in particular is regarded as the domain of gay men, with a disproportionate number of artists identifying more or less openly (for their time) as gay. The epidemic devastated the Broadway community; a generation of artists lost a staggering number of their peers. With insufficient support from government and other existing organizations, individuals within the

Broadway community formed groups like Broadway Cares, Equity Fights AIDS (which merged as BC/EFA in 1992), and Gay Men's Health Crisis, to raise funds, provide care, and advocate for those suffering from AIDS.

Creating a community among like-minded individuals, finding moments of joy in the midst of illness—the 1996 musical *Rent* paints these themes in the language of MTV-era rock. It began its journey to Broadway in the late 1980s, when playwright Billy Aronson approached composer-lyricist Jonathan Larson with the idea of adapting the Puccini opera *La Bohème* to a contemporary American setting. *Rent*'s ragtag group of Bohemians live in New York's gritty East Village instead of Paris, and struggle with AIDS instead of consumption (a catchall nineteenth-century term that usually referred to tuberculosis). Larson could personally understand the characters in *La Bohème*. He lived the life of a struggling artist, and he wrote *Rent* partially as a response to the AIDS crisis that ravaged his circle of friends.

Born in 1960, Larson loved both rock and theater music. While the megamusicals that typified the 1980s showed some influence of rock, especially in styles of singing, the music sounded nothing like the music on MTV, and the fanciful stories were far removed from the grit and grunge of 1990s pop culture. Larson dreamed of creating a show that would "reclaim Broadway from stagnation and empty spectacle" and "bring musical theater to the MTV generation," as he is quoted in a March 17, 1996, *New York Times* article by Anthony Tommasini. Larson had given an interview for the *Times* after the January 24 dress rehearsal for the Off-Broadway run of *Rent* at the New York Theatre Workshop (by this point Larson was the sole author, though Aronson retained credit for the original concept and additional lyrics). The show was a hit, easily selling out the Workshop's small space, and plans were soon made for a transfer uptown to Broadway's Nederlander Theatre. Tragically, Larson did not get to taste his own long-sought success: hours after the dress rehearsal and interview, he died of an aortic aneurysm caused by an undiagnosed genetic defect. *Rent*'s success continued to grow after it opened on Broadway on April 29, 1996, winning not only the praise of the standard gatekeepers—the critics and the Tony Awards voters—but also a devoted cadre of young fans.

RENTHEADS

In an innovative sales practice that is still implemented by many Broadway shows, *Rent* offered a limited number of twenty-dollar tickets on the day of the show. Some young fans took to sleeping outside the Nederlander Theatre to ensure they were at the front of the line for those tickets. These "Rentheads," as they came to be called, were a community of their own, hanging out by the stage door to meet the actors, and going to great lengths to see the show multiple times.

Among the Rentheads were actors Rori Nogee and Guy Olivieri. Nogee wrote in an e-mail interview about being inspired by characters who reminded her of herself: "a mix of musical theater performers and rock stars. Those two things had never existed before and I didn't know it was possible." Olivieri, who went on to play the lead role of Mark in the national tour of *Rent*, described in an e-mail his experience camping out in front of the Nederlander: "We drove up from North Carolina over winter break to camp out to see it. We got in line at six p.m. for the show twenty-six hours later, just to be sure we'd get a space. I have never been so cold in my life. A homeless man peed on us. I got in a huge fight with a friend over a blanket. A very scary man wouldn't leave us alone, and we decided the best way to repel him was to sing Christmas carols at the top of our lungs to convince him we were scarier than he was. It worked. . . . It was magic. It was perfect. I sat front row center."

Nogee saw *Rent* on Broadway "sixty-nine and two halves times," and Olivieri camped out four more times while still in college in North Carolina, those times with his boyfriend. What inspired such a level of devotion? In the words of Olivieri: "I had managed to come out. It's no exaggeration to say that seeing people like me in *Rent* changed my whole worldview. It gave me a lot of courage." For some young people struggling to find acceptance, *Rent* told *their* story in *their* musical language.

RENT: FILMED LIVE ON BROADWAY

Rent ran on Broadway for over twelve years, closing on September 7, 2008. Its final cast is captured on video in *Rent: Filmed Live on Broad-*

way, which melds the best of live performance and film. Though a video can never *quite* capture the magic of being in the room with flesh-and-blood live performers, you are happy this time to trade Renthead-style overnight camping for the comforts of home video featuring first-class Broadway performers.

Opera fans will immediately notice the parallels to *La Bohème*: in the opening scene, roommates Mark (Adam Kantor) and Roger (Will Chase), like their nineteenth-century *La Bohème* counterparts Marcello and Rodolfo, try to stay warm in the unheated former industrial loft they call home. There will be other character parallels and moments of congruence with Puccini's opera throughout the show, though it is by no means a scene-for-scene adaptation. Like an opera, *Rent* has very little spoken dialogue; most of the action takes place in linear time through the lyrics, music, and elements of production. Larson borrows the operatic technique of recitative, framing the quasi-spoken sections that give the audience exposition in two clever constructs to avoid stopping the action. First, Mark, Roger, and their friends screen their phone calls, which in the *Rent*'s landline-era 1989 means the audience is privy to messages left on the answering machine. Second, Mark's actions as a filmmaker working on his film are used as a character-specific way to pinpoint the time—for example, "December 24th, 9 pm"—and narrate close-up camera shots of Roger and other characters. We learn a lot about *Rent*'s characters when people leave them messages and when Mark films them.

The accompaniment for the first minutes of the show is divided seamlessly between Roger with his onstage guitar and the guitarist in the band, which is tucked away in the upper right corner of the stage. Roger is in the middle of playing an electric guitar riff, a quotation of "Musetta's Waltz" from *La Bohème*, when the power goes out, showing their dire living situation and also hinting at Roger's inability to finish a song. *Rent*'s conductor and keyboardist (David Truskinoff) shouts a count-off to the five-piece rock band, launching us fully into the world of the show with the title song "Rent." The music has a drive seldom heard in theater music of the 1990s, while the lyrics lend themselves to action in a way that is atypical of rock, whose aesthetic is to convey feeling rather than information. The combination of the forces of rock music and dramatic lyrics makes for an opening number that both conveys rock's excitement and introduces us to the main characters. Mark and Roger's roommate relationship and mutual creative struggle is fleshed out as they wax witty about the screenplays and concert posters they burn to keep warm. The double entendre at the end of the title song refers both to their external financial difficulties and the internal conflicts tearing them apart.

"Everything is rent," indeed: by the end of the first few action-packed songs, we know that Roger is a former drug user who learned he was HIV positive from his girlfriend who then killed herself, and that Mark's girlfriend Maureen dumped him for a woman (we will meet both Maureen and her new flame Joanne initially through hearsay and phone messages). Their friend Collins (Michael McElroy) has been mugged on his way into their building, and their ex-friend-now-landlord Benny (Rodney Hicks) threatens them with eviction.

This being a musical, and a musical based on an opera at that, it's high time to introduce the element of romance that can mend things that are rent. The first love story begins in "You Okay Honey," when Angel (Justin Johnston) discovers Collins lying injured on the street. It's love at first meeting; the bouncy triplet pattern that begins when Angel introduces himself will recur in their other duets. Their immediate bond is strengthened by the discovery that they are both HIV positive. Later, in a close equivalent to a scene in *La Bohème*, Roger's neighbor Mimi (Renée Elise Goldsberry) interrupts his search for "One Song Glory," ostensibly to light her candle. "Light My Candle" has a sultry, syncopated groove that complements Mimi's flirtatiousness, but the irregular length of the musical phrases hints at Roger's ambivalence about making this new acquaintance and at Mimi's instability as a result of her drug addiction.

The immediacy of Angel and Collins's connection is further implied in "Today 4 U," Angel's drag number where Collins introduces him to Mark and Roger. Collins joins right in, playing rhythmically on a bottle of vodka to a dance beat perfectly suited to Angel's identity as a street drummer and drag performer. In "Today 4 U," Angel relates a story that happened offstage, something usually avoided in theater where the motto is "Show, don't tell"—but the real story of this moment is Angel's immediate acceptance into and, indeed, transformation of this group of dysfunctional friends. Angel's and Roger's reactions to their AIDS diagnoses couldn't be more different, as you hear in their respective solos. Angel's good luck story is interspersed with a catchy hook, in contrast to

Roger's orbiting around repeated lyrics in "One Song Glory," the repetitious "glory" less of a hook than an expression of Roger's obsession with his all-too-looming mortality.

By the time Benny returns, the main characters have been introduced and their antagonists clearly identified: Benny and the soul-destroying commercialism he represents, and the faceless but equally daunting foes of AIDS, addiction, and poverty. "You'll See" is the refrain Benny repeats to an alt-rock guitar accompaniment pattern, in an attempt to get his former roommates to come around to his point of view. He offers them a way out of paying the rent: stop the protest Maureen is planning to stage on his property. After Benny leaves, Angel continues the song, modifying the refrain to the more inviting "we'll see" as he, Mark, and Collins prepare to go out and try (still unsuccessfully) to get Roger to join them.

We finally meet Maureen's new girlfriend Joanne (Tracie Thoms) when Mark goes to help her fix Maureen's sound equipment. Maureen still exists only in voice mail and hearsay; she was onstage, but not brightly lit, when she recited her own voice mail greeting. In fact, "Tango Maureen" consists almost entirely of Maureen's erstwhile and present lovers talking about her, building an image of her for the audience before she has a chance to make an impression herself. Mark and Joanne are directly in front of the band, and you see the conductor turn during a break in the music to watch for a visual cue to begin the dance sequence. The dual connotation of the tango, seductive and combative, embodies Mark and Joanne's triangular situation and the coquettish subject of their conflict.

In the next scene, Mark and Collins join Angel at a meeting of his support group. *Rent*'s fictional Life Support is based on Friends in Deed, a nonprofit formed in 1991 to tend to the emotional and spiritual needs of people coping with AIDS or cancer. The harmonized, hymn-like affirmation of "Life Support" is punctuated by agitated piano chords. It is effectively a musicalized meditation, the agitated chords forming a musical acknowledgment of the anxious feelings that arise, returning each time to the affirmation "no day but today."

As the meeting continues, the focus switches abruptly to Mimi, who wants Roger to take her "Out Tonight." The musical change is deceptive, for Mimi, in her own way, is in the same mind-set as the Life Support group—living in the moment, no night but tonight. You marvel at the physical strength triple threat Goldsberry must have in order to belt this rock song while executing acrobatic dance moves on the railing of the set's fire escape. Mimi once again interrupts Roger's brooding with the end of "Out Tonight." He loses his temper and demands that she come back "Another Day"—a direct negation of the "no day but today" dogma of the Life Support group. These opposing themes come into **counterpoint** as Mimi tries to persuade Roger with phrases from "Life Support." The Life Support chorus, still in their meeting, joins the final choruses from across the stage in a film-like split screen effect. Roger's anxiety and that of the people at the Life Support meeting evolves in "Will I," as their fearful questions are sung to the same guitar figure as the Life Support affirmation. As the counterpoint builds to a meditative wash of sound, everyone—even ensemble members we don't know well, even Benny—joins in asking these universal questions about life and death.

The following sequence, in which the neighborhood prepares for Maureen's performance, recalls a similar street scene in *La Bohème*. The mishmash of disparate musical phrases evokes the bustle of a New York City street, while the sleigh bells, tinkly piano figure, and parodies of famous Christmas songs remind us of the holiday setting. *Rent's* structural use of holidays, and the family drama that so often surrounds them, increases the emotional impact of the story. As events in this bustling sequence build on the theme of community and intimacy, Mimi and Roger each struggle with their isolation, while Angel and Collins cement their connection. The triplet groove of both "Santa Fe" and "I'll Cover You" recalls the moment in "You Okay Honey" when Angel and Collins first met. The phrase "I'll Cover You" speaks to literal warmth at the beginning of the song as Angel gives Collins a coat to replace the one that was stolen off his back right before they met, and then captures the budding sensuality of their "sweet kisses" as they echo each other's phrases at the end of the song.

The up-tempo organ-dominated groove of "We're Okay" supports the frantic energy Joanne expends in trying to be part of two communities: the respectable upper-middle-class African American world represented by her parents and her own career as a lawyer, and the avant-garde Bohemia in which Maureen lives and breathes. Each "we're okay" has a different connotation, implied by changes in the melody or Thoms's vocal interpretation. We infer from Joanne's side of multiple phone conversations the latest developments in her relationships, most importantly with Maureen.

Finally making a grand entrance for "Over the Moon," Maureen (Eden Espinosa) is every bit of the legend that has been built up around her. "Over the Moon" is a caricature of avant-garde performance art with its mixture of spoken word, a cappella riffs, and electronic effects and samples. Maureen's over-the-top performance also functions as comic relief, as Espinosa deadpans her cowbell playing and reactions to the vagaries of her sound equipment. But Maureen's commitment to her performance piece is sincere, making it also a pointed critique of the triumph of commerce over art, represented by Benny and his development, Cyberland. The word "moon" becomes "moo" at the end, as Maureen's metaphorical cow character implores her audience to take a "leap of faith" to escape Cyberland. The mooing eventually escalates into a riot, which was precisely the reason Benny wanted the protest stopped.

The end of act 1 takes place in the Life Café, in a loose parallel of *La Bohème*'s café scene. The ebullient finale, "La Vie Bohème," moves the plot forward, as the conflict between Benny and the Bohemians escalates, and Mimi and Roger finally get together. It also shows the influence of *Rent*'s predecessor *Hair* (chapter 6), with young people celebrating their unconventional lifestyles in a list song that includes subversive references to religion and sex. The list portions of the song occur as a prolonged toast to *la vie Bohème* begun by Mark as a mock funeral, complete with synthesizer funeral organ, after Benny declares Bohemia dead. In a cheeky integration of lyrics and staging, Maureen moons Benny and his rich companions as Mark sings, "You bet your ass." Despite adversity from powerful enemies, these Bohemians end act 1 with a final toast to their chosen lifestyle while riots rage outside and Roger and Mimi share a sweet kiss.

The DVD includes a ten-minute intermission, giving you the option of fast-forwarding or getting up for refreshments. The live audience cheers wildly as the cast lines up at the front of the stage for the beginning of act 2. "Seasons of Love" also shows the influence of *Hair*, with its list lyrics and concept musical technique of suspending linear time. The song has become a staple of choir repertoire, particularly for milestone events like graduations, with lyrics general enough to be understood outside the context of the show. A simple piano figure accompanies the verses, which the cast sings in unison, searching for the measure of "a year in the life." The choruses open up into resounding harmony with the thematic one-word answer: love. The second verse features vocal solos by ensemble members Gwen Stewart and Marcus Paul James. Stewart continues to riff over the final chorus, her voice a conduit for the emotion of the song.

"Happy New Year" drops us back into linear time and action: the friends break into Mark and Roger's loft, which Benny had padlocked after Maureen's protest. The up-tempo major key shows everyone resolving to get along and work together—for now. But like most New Year's resolutions, the relationships and situations soon devolve (as they must in a show, or the audience would go home). Mark is plagued by voice mails from Alexi Darling (Andrea Goss), offering him a job at a sleazy but lucrative news show. The commercialism theme is further developed when Benny arrives, trying to engineer a public relations coup and piquing Roger's jealousy of Benny's previous relationship with Mimi. The "Happy New Year" sequence ends on an ominous note as Mimi's drug dealer (Shaun Earl) returns, along with the specter of her addiction. Maureen and Joanne give each other the ultimatum to "Take Me or Leave Me," during one of their more spectacular fights. The lyrics of Maureen's first phrases refer to "Musetta's Waltz," the same *La Bohème* aria as Roger's recurrent guitar riff. The aria's proper title is "Quando M'en Vo," referring to the first phrase in which Musetta brags about the attention she receives when she walks alone on the street. The passion in their relationship can be heard in Maureen and Joanne's vocal acrobatics, and the number ends with an abrupt "I'm gone" and a musical button that cues applause.

The theme of impermanence is further highlighted in "Without You," which begins when Roger walks away after a fight with Mimi. The continuous guitar **arpeggio** plays against the sighs of the fretless bass, a contrast that supports lyrics about a world that goes on as "I die." As the song builds, the repetitious pattern of the lyrics allows focus to fall on Mimi's voice, colored with shades of pain in every sustained note. Roger reenters and adds his voice, though he doesn't touch her. All the couples are without each other at the moment, in a manner of speaking. Angel and Collins are still together, but it is clear that Collins will soon be without his Angel: when they reappeared during a solemn reprise of "Seasons of Love," it was immediately obvious that Angel is dying.

Perhaps it is the realization of impermanence brought on by Angel's illness that brings the couples back together at the end of the song. Whatever the reason, the metaphysical power of the cycle of sex, life, death, and grief is embodied in "Contact," a dance number that once more takes *Rent* briefly into the concept musical territory of nonlinear time, abstractly representing the various characters' sex lives. Aside from the obvious vocalizations, sounds that imitate sexual intercourse dominate the first part of the number, with the titillating high-pitched synth pattern, grinding bass, and pounding rhythm of the drums and lyrics. In the middle of the song, Angel appears, and the music works together with the lighting, costumes, and staging, as he transcends his frailty to rise above the gyrating bodies. The phrases he sings are fragments we've heard before in the score, and are appropriate to his near-death state: "Take me," and a development of "Today 4 U." He also sings of love. Significantly, this is the first mention of the word since the similarly abstract "Seasons of Love," and it is the first explicit "I love you." It is unsurprising that this statement should come from determinedly positive-minded Angel. Everyone else tiptoes around the L-bomb, having been hurt by its explosions in the past. Angel's soaring vocals show that this is a quintessential death aria; even though the text is significant, it is the sound quality of his voice that matters here—a priority traditional in both opera and rock. "Contact" concludes with a mirror image of the first section, the conjugal experience having gone awry. The multifaceted portrayal of sex as a life-affirming action, source of conflict, and mode of transmission of a deadly virus lends meaning to the repetition of "It's over" at the end of the number.

The "Seasons of Love" piano figure plays as Angel's friends measure his life in loving memories, delineating a memorial service without having to change scenery in this reflective moment. Collins has more than earned his cathartic reprise of "I'll Cover You," having cared for Angel in his last days just as Angel provided warmth and healing for him in the first days of their relationship. The simple melody of "I'll Cover You" and the slow tempo of the reprise allow McElroy to express Collins's sorrow by personalizing the melody with riffs and variations. The song gradually settles into a triplet groove, though it is missing the pep of its previous iterations. With his Angel gone, so is the spring in Collins's step, and the Angel-Collins relationship has moved on to the eternal world, with the spiritual depth implied by gospel piano and organ. The rest of the cast reappears in the same positions as in "Seasons of Love," adding phrases from that song in counterpoint to Collins's lead vocal. The power of silence underscores the eternity of Collins's love for Angel, as the band and background vocals drop out under Collins's "when your heart has expired." That's how long "I'll Cover You," Collins seems to say, as his voice lingers after the band at the end of the song.

After the funeral, the friends go into a period of mourning as they stumble through their new post-Angel world. Mark introduces this "season" of grief in his solo "Halloween," supported by an arpeggiated guitar accompaniment with a syncopated bass line, reminiscent of Sondheim's ostinato patterns. Sondheim was a supporter of Larson's work, and his influence shows not only in musical gestures such as this one, but in his ability to musicalize complex emotions like the ones Mark experiences in this song. As a filmmaker, Mark naturally uses film imagery to sort through his feelings. Isolated behind the camera, he is the witness to his friends' ups and downs, and he must be thinking of Collins's, Roger's, and Mimi's HIV-positive status as the final melodic line of the song descends with him into a pit of survivor's guilt.

Several musical and dramatic themes are woven together in "Goodbye Love." Everything seems mixed up: Mark has accepted the sleazy news job, Roger is leaving for Santa Fe, and Benny and Mimi are together. The theme of community/family comes up when Collins scolds them for fighting on the day of Angel's funeral, and later when Roger and Mark throw barbs at each other for the different ways in which they disengage from relationships. The arpeggiated pattern heard in "Halloween" is developed on the keyboard throughout Mark and Roger's fight and Mimi and Roger's good-bye. Roger pushes Mimi away like he did in the beginning, reiterating a line of "One Song Glory" in counterpoint to her heartbroken good-bye. At the end of the song, Mimi bids hello to disease—a reversal of her optimistic stance in "Another Day."

The theme of commercialism is also in flux. The advantages of money are evident, as Benny, now on friendlier terms with the group, pays for Angel's funeral and Mimi's treatment. Mark, now too busy with his soul-destroying job to finish his film, comments bitterly that American identity at the end of the millennium is "What You Own." This driving rock song is the beginning of the resolution of the play. Roger adds his voice at the second verse, and the two of them work separately through their grief, finding answers to questions Mark posed in "Halloween," playing with the ideas of renting and owning, living and dying. The decision to "own" their emotions and their reality leads to artistic inspiration and the ability to connect with others, and Christmas Eve arrives with Roger back in New York and Mark ready to screen the film he had time to finish after he quit his job.

Having come full circle, the first part of the finale is peppered with themes that were introduced early in the show, as fragments of "Voice Mail," "Christmas Bells," "Tune-Up," and a reprise of "Santa Fe" highlight what has and hasn't changed over the course of the story. Mark, Roger, and Collins have made peace with the events of the preceding year, but this is not quite the end: their celebration is interrupted when Maureen and Joanne arrive carrying Mimi, who is near death.

Mimi is made as comfortable as possible, and dramatic milestones from earlier are recalled by the music that relates to them, woven together and modified to suit this moment. Mimi, shivering, begs Roger to "Light My Candle," and the fragments of the song where they first met are now set to the accompaniment of their recent "Goodbye Love." Mimi and Roger make sure they leave nothing unsaid in this moment, using the "I should tell you" motive from the end of act 1 to get it all out in the open, including the risky "I love you." Mimi manages to gasp the words, and Roger puts them in the song he finally managed to write for her, "Your Eyes." The song's lyrics show Roger leaving behind his old ways, admitting that "I have always loved you" instead of simply "I love you," because he's been holding it in for a long time. Now that he's finally learned his lesson, the electric guitar plays a cathartic longer phrase of "Musetta's Waltz." In the epitome of the rock opera aesthetic, the guitar solo underscores their passionate kiss, after which Mimi falls lifeless and Roger pours all his emotion into his cry of her name.

In one of the biggest changes from *La Bohème*, Mimi's death is only a near-death experience; Larson was adamant that his show should end with life. *Rent* ends with a repetition of the Life Support theme as Mimi revives, this time with Roger singing along with her before the others join in harmony. Two principal dramatic themes are repeated in counterpoint as the cast takes their bows: the necessity of connection to others, and living "no day but today." After the bows, original Broadway cast members and other *Rent* alumni join the closing night cast onstage for "Seasons of Love"—measuring the years in the life of a spectacularly successful and influential show.

SPRING AWAKENING

Spring Awakening, conceived in part as a concept album and developed Off-Broadway, opened on Broadway on December 10, 2006. It was the late 1990s when lyricist and playwright Steven Sater and singer-songwriter Duncan Sheik began working on the musical adaptation of German playwright Frank Wedekind's *Frühlings Erwachen: Eine Kindertragödie*. Translated as *Spring Awakening: A Children's Tragedy*, the 1891 play was frequently banned because it dealt with teenage sexuality in the repressive environment of nineteenth-century Germany, and included subjects such as sexual abuse, masturbation, homosexuality, and abortion. While seemingly unlikely material for a musical, Sater saw in the play an opportunity to give voice to the unspoken anguish of young people that he felt was all too relevant more than a century later. Rock music, as he writes in the preface to his libretto of *Spring Awakening*, "is the exact place that adolescents for the last few generations have found release from, and expression of, that same mute pain." Duncan Sheik's music lends itself to emotional expression, and his pop songs, including his most famous single, "Barely Breathing," often have a narrative arc to them. In an October 16, 2014, interview with National Public Radio, Sheik stated that when he is writing the lyrics, he starts with the music: "Usually the music will suggest some kind of emotional territory and that will suggest a theme or two." Though he didn't write the lyrics for *Spring Awakening*, Sheik's custom of creating an emotional landscape in a pop song is evident in the music he wrote for Sater's lyrics.

In recent years, there has been a parade of pop artists with Broadway ambitions, and Sheik was at the head of it. American pop icon Cyndi Lauper's upbeat adaptation of the film *Kinky Boots* opened in 2013 and is running strong on Broadway and with its national tour as of this writing. Bono and the Edge of Irish rock band U2 wrote the music for *Spider-Man: Turn Off the Dark*, whose infamously troubled run lasted from 2011 to 2014. British superstar Sting's *The Last Ship* (2014) was sunk by negative reviews, lasting only four months. As of this writing, A-list singer-songwriters like Tori Amos and Sara Bareilles have shows in development, and Duncan Sheik's next Broadway venture, a musical adaptation of the Bret Easton Ellis novel *American Psycho* (with a book by Roberto Aguirre-Sacasa, who also contributed to the book of *Spider-Man*), is slated for opening in early 2016. Not to be confused with jukebox musicals, which repurpose existing songs and create a story around them, these shows feature new music created to serve a story. Having a pop star as the composer for a show is a selling point for Broadway musicals, in a reverse from the days of Tin Pan Alley, when getting a song in a Broadway show was often the ticket to songwriter stardom.

Sater and Sheik deliberately avoided integrating scene and song in *Spring Awakening*, instead choosing to create discrete worlds for the spoken and sung word. The interpersonal action takes place in the dialogue, the formality of which is indicative of the nineteenth-century setting. By contrast, the songs comprise internal monologues, usually suspending linear time and action in the mode of a concept musical. The lyrics use colloquial language appropriate to rock and roll—a reminder that we are all the rock stars of our own lives, and that the themes of the play are as relevant in the twenty-first century as the nineteenth. The adults, all of whom are played by one actor and one actress, don't sing at all, with a couple of dramatically relevant exceptions.

Since the poetic lyrics of the songs express emotion rather than describing action, a brief synopsis will be helpful. The story focuses on three teenage characters: Wendla Bergman, Melchior Gabor, and Moritz Stiefel. Naïve Wendla begs her mother to tell her where babies come from ("Mama Who Bore Me"). Her mother tells a lie of omission that creates the conditions for her daughter's tragic end. Meanwhile, in the boys' class, freethinking Melchior defends his friend Moritz ("All That's Known"), who's struggling in school in part because of the nascent sexual fantasies that plague him ("The Bitch of Living"). Melchior promises to write for him an illustrated treatise on reproduction. Wendla and Melchior encounter each other in the woods and realize that their innocent childhood friendship has blossomed into attraction ("The Word of My Body"). It becomes clear in group numbers that the other teens are experiencing similar stirrings in the same repressive environment ("My Junk," "Touch Me," "The Mirror-Blue Night").

Wendla learns that her friend Martha's father is abusing her ("The Dark I Know Well"). Wanting to understand the pain, Wendla insists that Melchior beat her; he reluctantly accedes, then runs off in shame. The next time they meet, their attraction overcomes them, and act 1 ends just as Melchior penetrates Wendla ("I Believe"). They recognize the power of what they've done, even though Wendla doesn't know why ("The Guilty Ones").

Moritz, unjustly flunked by his teachers, and failing to find help in the one adult he trusts ("And Then There Were None"), is unable to accept the help offered him by free-spirited Ilse, and commits suicide ("Don't Do Sadness/Blue Wind"). After Moritz's funeral ("Left Behind"), Melchior's treatise on reproduction is found among Moritz's effects ("Totally Fucked"), and it is discovered that Wendla is carrying Melchior's child ("Whispering"). Melchior is sent to a reformatory, and when he finally escapes, he finds that Wendla has died of a botched abortion. He prepares to kill himself, but, visited by the ghosts of Moritz and Wendla, chooses to live instead, vowing to create a world in which the situations that brought about the deaths of his friends could not occur ("Those You've Known"). The show ends on a hopeful note, with Ilse, the girl who escaped her abusive circumstances, leading the full company, including Moritz, Wendla, and the two adults, in "The Song of Purple Summer."

SPRING AWAKENING—2006 ORIGINAL BROADWAY CAST ALBUM

You first listen to the *Spring Awakening* cast album in the background, letting Steven Sater's lyrics, the rich textures of Duncan Sheik's writing, and the voices of Wendla (Lea Michele), Melchior (Jonathan Groff), Moritz (John Gallagher Jr.), and their peers wash over you as you go about your business. As various aspects of the recording catch your ear, you pay closer attention to them and to how they relate to the story. First, the spoken text of Mrs. Gabor's letter in "And Then There Were None" stands out against the musical texture, the formality of her words to Moritz contrasting sharply with the contemporary lyrics of his reaction to them. The interpersonal action—Mrs. Gabor reaching out to Moritz in a letter—takes place in speech. No action takes place during the sung portion of the song, for he is not actually saying these things to Mrs. Gabor; it is merely what he would say if he *could* express himself. Nor are he and Ilse (Lauren Pritchard) relating to one another at the end of "Don't Do Sadness/Blue Wind"; their conversation is separate from the inner worlds they retreat to when their songs overlap.

The paradoxical wisdom and naïveté of the teenage characters is captured in the writing and interpretation of the text and music. The orchestrations, also by Duncan Sheik, use a violin, viola, and cello along with the standard rock instruments of bass, keyboard, drums/percussion, and guitars. The first sounds in the show are the sensuous sighs of the stringed instruments, joined by the contrasting textures of the harmonium (a reed organ—soft and airy) and the glockenspiel (a small percussion instrument—delicate and metallic). This introduction to "Mama Who Bore Me" accompanies Wendla's innocent exploration of her maturing body. Wendla's vocal tone throughout the show supports her portrayal as an innocent victim of a repressive society, never gaining the brassy quality of a full belt. The slightly softer tone known as the "mix" also pervades the girls' sound as they join in the second part of "Mama Who Bore Me" and describe their nascent longing in "My Junk." There is, however, a slight chesty, nasal edge to some of Martha's (Lilli Cooper) lyrics as she relives the sexual abuse she suffers from her father in the first verse of "The Dark I Know Well." Her vocal placement balances the innocence and anger of a girl who has sexual knowledge against her will.

A few of the group numbers are single sex (girls sing "Mama Who Bore Me"; boys sing "The Bitch of Living"); but many include both the boys and girls, showing the universality of the adolescent experience ("My Junk," "Totally Fucked"). As the boys imagine themselves in a woman's place in lovemaking in "Touch Me," the solo male voices build from the breathy tone of the first phrases to Georg's (Skylar Astin) soaring solo at the peak of the song, while male and female background vocals weave in and out of unison and tight harmony. The curiosity and yearning of this song are expressed in the gently rocking triplet groove, and in the gradual build of complexity in the orchestration and vocal arrangement over hypnotic four-bar chord progressions. But innocence and curiosity conflict with the shame-filled attitudes toward sex that become clear in "The Bitch of Living," whose negative personification of sexual urges (one of the aspects of "the Bitch") is dominated by insistent offbeats in the distorted guitar and the rhythm of the title lyric in the chorus. "The Bitch of Living," "And Then There Were None," and "Totally Fucked" capture the sound of teenagers full of outsize feelings trying to show they don't care, with nasal vocal placement and diction that is by turns percussive and blasé. The beginning of "Totally Fucked" also has a spark of comedic timing. The break in the vocal line in the middle of the first phrase of the lyrics ("There's a moment you know") sets up the unexpected yet matter-of-fact expletive that ends the sentence—a bit of gallows humor from Melchior before he is sent to reform school. As with all good laugh lines, there are a few beats before the next new lyric begins to allow the audience time to react without missing anything. This *kindertragödie* has surprising moments of levity that give the show a varied emotional landscape, making it both entertaining and deeply moving.

Like in Sheik's pop songs, the music creates a framework that deepens the emotion of the moment. The chord progressions and endings of many of the songs—for example, "All That's Known" and "The Guilty Ones"—leave the key ambiguous, heightening the sense of searching and irresolution experienced by the characters. Sheik is also known for incorporating electronic sounds into his musical palette. Touches of electronica can be heard in songs like "The Mirror-Blue Night," whose accompaniment is eerie and insistent, matching the lyrics.

Melodic and textual motives are developed throughout the show, making the songs cohesive as a score, and creating a bridge between the worlds of scene and song. Recurring words paint the themes of the show that are encapsulated in the title. Among the images of seasons, colors, and nature are also haunting words like whispering, ghost, and wind. The word "blind" is used in multiple contexts, including references to its purportedly being a consequence of masturbation in "The Bitch of Living" and "My Junk." *Spring Awakening* makes a clear political statement, that the source of tragedy is the unknown and unspoken. It is Melchior, with his independent thinking and determination that "one day all will know," who points the way to a brighter future. His story begins with "All That's Known," whose three rising notes of the title melody can be found elsewhere in the score. In "Whispering," Wendla borrows this motive as she sings of her hopes for Melchior's child stirring within her. At the end, "Those You've Known" reveals how the events of the play have affected Melchior, showing that his heart has been awakened along with his mind by weaving the melody and accompaniment figure of "All That's Known" together with phrases of developed lyrical and musical themes of his lost loved ones Wendla and Moritz.

While most of the songs in the show bear some concrete relation to the scenes from which they emerge, both acts end with songs whose abstract poetic imagery makes an indirect but emphatic emotional statement. At the end of act 1, the teens surround Wendla and Melchior with "I Believe," a song that imbues sexual intimacy with sacredness, symbolized by ebullient ensemble singing and words like peace and harmony (like its predecessor *Hair*). The act 1 finale retains society's shame-filled attitudes with lyrics that imply Wendla and Melchior require forgiveness for their actions. By the end of the show, all is known, and the tarnish is gone: "The Song of Purple Summer" celebrates life-affirming images, including that of a mare, stallion, and foal, borrowed from an act 1 monologue of Melchior's in which he questions the necessity of shame. The blindness, shame, and mysterious whispers that are the cause of the tragedy in this story have given way to a hopeful vision, where all, including the adult characters who join in the final choruses, are allowed to know and embrace the wonder of life.

BROADWAY AT THE END OF THE MILLENNIUM

Rent was a reaction to and a shift away from the British-dominated era of the 1980s and early '90s. It was also a beacon of hope to young performers who wanted to be rock stars as well as musical theater performers. In words from e-mail correspondence with Telly Leung, whom we saw in the ensemble of *Rent: Filmed Live on Broadway* (and who himself saw *Rent* on Broadway at least fifteen times as a teenage fan in 1996), *Rent* "changed our definition of what 'musical theater' can be. Shows like *American Idiot*, *Spring Awakening*, *Hamilton* would not exist without *Rent* as a predecessor." And so the musical that aimed to be "the *Hair* of the '90s" became the tipping point for rock and other popular genres on Broadway beyond the '90s.

Rock-influenced musicals from the 1970s and '80s such as *Grease*, *Jesus Christ Superstar*, and *Chess* notwithstanding, it was not until after *Rent* that it became the norm for universities and conservatories to include the study of belting and other contemporary vocal techniques in their programs. Versatility is important in a business whose music and performance styles have diverse influences. Classical and jazz influence are alive and well in the early twenty-first century, in the work of composers like Adam Guettel (*The Light in the Piazza*, 2005), Michael John LaChiusa, and Andrew Lippa. In the year 2000, the latter two had different versions of *The Wild Party*, based on Joseph Moncure March's 1928 narrative poem of the same title, running on Broadway and Off-Broadway, respectively. LaChiusa and Lippa each evoked the 1920s in their own way, incorporating patterns from classical music and jazz along with their own contemporary compositional voices. Mel Brooks's *The Producers* struck musical comedy gold in 2001, mining cultural stereotypes with exaggerated character voices and accents, operetta spoofs, and brassy ragtime-derived up-tempo numbers. *Ragtime* the musical, Stephen Flaherty and Lynn Ahrens's 1998 adaptation of the E. L. Doctorow novel, combines the syncopated piano rhythms of its namesake with lush vocal and orchestral writing. Composer Jeanine Tesori's contributions have ranged in style from 1920s-style jazz for *Thoroughly Modern Millie* (2002; lyrics by Dick Scanlan), blues, spirituals, and klezmer for *Caroline, or Change* (2004; lyrics by Tony Kushner), pop and musical comedy for *Shrek the Musical* (2008; lyrics by David Lindsay-Abaire). Her score for 2015's Tony-winning *Fun Home* with lyricist Lisa Kron uses everything from quasi-spoken recitative (opera) to drum fills and syncopated background vocals (rock), to convey the autobiographical story Alison Bechdel first told in comic book form.

Musical theater composers are dramatists, using not only their own unique compositional voice to tell a story, but also drawing from a palette of popular styles that have significance to a large number of people. By the turn of the twenty-first century, that palette included rock, which, clearly more than a passing fad, continues to be a meaningful outlet for theatergoers and artists of the MTV generation and beyond. Meanwhile, in the years between the *Hair*'s revolution and *Rent*'s solidification of rock on Broadway, another cultural and musical revolution began just a few miles away from Manhattan's theater district. Like rock and roll, it would come to be a source of identity and community to fans around the world, and its telling of the American Revolution would be the next big revolution in Broadway music.

10

DIVERSITY AND INTEGRATION

Hamilton

In a 2009 performance at the White House, an audience of political insiders chuckled when composer-lyricist and performer Lin-Manuel Miranda described Alexander Hamilton as someone who embodies hip-hop. Miranda performed the down-tempo rap that was an early version of the opening number to *Hamilton: An American Musical*, inspired by Ron Chernow's *Alexander Hamilton*, an exhaustively researched and engagingly told 2004 biography of the Founding Father and first U.S. secretary of the Treasury. By the time Miranda was halfway through one verse, the politicos were smiling and nodding to the beat, and six years later many of them, including the president and first lady, would be among the many celebrities attending *Hamilton* on Broadway. It opened on August 6, 2015 (after a sold-out Off-Broadway run at the Public Theater), earning healthy ticket sales and eliciting words like "game changer" and "revolutionary" from both theater and hip-hop artists. Among the accolades it has earned are a Pulitzer Prize for Miranda, a Grammy for the cast album, and the 2016 Tony Award for Best Musical.

Three decades after the Sugar Hill Gang's 1979 single "Rapper's Delight" became hip-hop's breakthrough hit, rap and hip-hop were still mostly a novelty on Broadway. It was used like rock was used in *Bye Bye Birdie*, as an occasional commentary flavor rather than as the primary mode of storytelling, in shows like *Bring In 'da Noise, Bring In 'da*

Funk (1996) and *High Fidelity* (2006). In 2014, *Holler If Ya Hear Me*, the jukebox musical of rapper Tupac Shakur's music, had a short run.

Miranda's first Broadway show, the Tony-winning *In the Heights* (2008), incorporated hip-hop into its storytelling about a predominantly Latino neighborhood in upper Manhattan. *Hamilton* went even further, illuminating subject matter that happened centuries earlier with a rapped-and-sung-through score performed by a diverse cast in which most of the principal roles of European Americans are played by African American and Latino actors. Miranda recognized a twenty-first-century hip-hop narrative in Chernow's account of the eighteenth-century orphan immigrant who through his relentless drive and talent with words wrote himself out of poverty and into history. As Miranda has said in multiple interviews, he wanted to remove every possible barrier between that story and a contemporary audience, to make it "the story of America then, told by America now."

A HIP-HOP STORY

Hip-hop has become synonymous with rap music, but the word refers to a wider culture, one that has a rich history with roots that go much deeper than the few decades since its music has emerged as a popular style. What follows is the briefest of briefs for the uninitiated, regarding hip-hop as it is relevant to *Hamilton*. Hip-hop started in the Bronx in the 1970s, with roots in the Caribbean, particularly Jamaica's sound system scene, where a vibrant street party culture developed, fostered by DJs who played records on (relatively) portable setups of turntables and loudspeakers. As hip-hop journalist Jeff Chang writes in his book *Can't Stop Won't Stop: A History of the Hip-Hop Generation*, "The blues had Mississippi, jazz had New Orleans. Hip-hop has Jamaica."

Many people leaving the political unrest of the Caribbean ended up in New York City immigrant neighborhoods like the South Bronx. In the 1950s and '60s, many residential blocks in the area had been up-ended by eminent domain during the construction of the Cross Bronx Expressway, which cut a swath through middle- and working-class neighborhoods as it connected Manhattan with the wealthy suburbs north of New York City. Those who could afford to leave for the sub-urbs did so, particularly European Americans from earlier waves of immigration, in a phenomenon known as "white flight." In the mid-1970s, in policies that barely bothered to conceal undertones of racism, classism, and xenophobia, a financially strapped New York City government severely cut back on basic services to low-income neighborhoods like the South Bronx in an effort to, in the incendiary words of housing commissioner Roger Starr, "accelerate the drainage" (of *people*) of these supposedly unsalvageable neighborhoods. Schools and fire departments were closed or severely understaffed. Many abandoned buildings were set on fire or otherwise vandalized. Much of the Bronx was divvied up by gangs formed by youths who lacked or mistrusted other sources of belonging and protection. Gangs were the de facto law of the land, sometimes also providing amenities like health clinics after city services were discontinued.

To put it in the briefest, simplest possible terms, early hip-hop culture was an alternative to gang violence. The four primary elements of hip-hop culture in its beginnings were DJ-ing, breakdancing, MC-ing, and graffiti writing—ways for an invisible generation to make themselves seen and heard and to claim their space in a creative, nonviolent (if, in the case of graffiti, often illegal) way. Three DJs popular among the seminal hip-hop parties of the early 1970s—DJ Kool Herc, Grandmaster Flash, and Afrika Bambaataa—are considered the founding fathers of hip-hop for their contributions to the culture.

Knowing that dancers at his parties clamored for the short sections of songs like James Brown's "Give It Up Turn It Loose" where the music dropped to just the rhythm, Jamaican-born DJ Kool Herc developed a technique for isolating and repeating these rhythm breaks. Using two turntables, he alternated records to create an extended loop of the break—the better for *break*dancing. Barbados-born Grandmaster Flash had always loved to tinker with machines, and he perfected Herc's looping technique. He used the mixer and turntable as musical instruments, introducing a wider audience to the unique sounds of the record scratch and "punching" (isolating very short phrases of music using the mixer).

Afrika Bambaataa was a natural leader. Originally a member of the Black Spades gang, his ability to form alliances with members of other gangs was an advantage when he formed the peace-seeking Bronx River Organization (later called simply the Organization to be less divisive), and eventually, the Zulu Nation. Various religious and other organizations tried to sell the youth of the Bronx on their dogmas, but as Chang puts it, "Zulus celebrated the instinct for survival and creation. Living young and free in the Bronx was a revolutionary act of art. To unleash on a social level these vital urges was the surest way to avoid mass death. Bambaataa's message was: *We're moving. There's room for you if you get yourself right.* Perhaps this is why, of all the utopias proffered to the teeming rabbles of outcast youth, Bambaataa's spread through the streets of the Bronx and then out into the world like a flaming wick."

The extended break beats and block party environment lent themselves to rhythmic word. The first DJs were also on the mic, keeping the crowds at their parties amped up with call-and-response phrases and introductions. As DJ-ing techniques became more involved, MC-ing also became an art of its own—rap. The rhythm break and the mic offered not only a creative outlet, but also a forum for disputes to be settled peacefully. The tradition of contests of witty repartee and verbal one-upmanship can be traced to numerous African cultures, where verbal dexterity is a currency of social status. As the popularity of its recordings grew, the genre became focused on the virtuosity of rappers and music producers. Rappers each have their own **flow**, or unique use of rhythm and language. Music producers, who replaced live DJs in the recording world, developed distinctive styles of mixing and recording techniques, sampling, and effects. Rap and hip-hop expanded and became more complex, breaking off into multiple subgenres, ultimately becoming a global language of pride, identity, and speaking truth to power.

Of course, when pride is insulted, it must be defended. In the recorded rap world, this has often taken the form of **diss tracks**, raps written to insult a rival. Such tracks are not unlike the papers and letters Alexander Hamilton wrote defending his political ideas and personal honor. In the most extreme cases, these word-driven beefs can have deadly consequences, as in the still-unsolved murders of Tupac Shakur and the Notorious B.I.G.—and in the duel between Alexander Hamilton and Aaron Burr that cost Burr his career and Hamilton his life.

LIN-MANUEL MIRANDA

The languages of hip-hop and Broadway are hardly mutually exclusive: both integrate music and dance, both largely originate from people of working-class backgrounds and have been made global phenomena by compromising with big business, and both are omnivorous in their incorporation of other styles (Jay-Z even samples *Annie* in his 1998 single "Hard Knock Life [Ghetto Anthem]"). At their best, both genres entertain while simultaneously subverting the status quo. Despite all these common traits, they are worlds apart in most people's minds. Miranda is the first to successfully fuse the two genres in a narrative musical, and he is well suited to do so. Born in New York City in 1980 to Puerto Rican parents, Miranda was raised in a predominantly Dominican neighborhood in upper Manhattan. In a podcast interview with Jon Caramanica of the *New York Times*, Miranda describes code-switching from an early age, both linguistically and musically, listening to show tunes and salsa at home, and hip-hop with his sister and friends.

He attended the academically competitive Hunter College magnet schools through the New York City public school system and earned a degree in theater at Wesleyan University, writing the first draft of *In the Heights* during his sophomore year. Playwright Quiara Alegría Hudes came on board to write the book during its several years of development, and it transferred from an Off-Broadway production to open on Broadway in 2008. Miranda's work also appeared on Broadway in Spanish translations to some of the Puerto Rican characters' lyrics for the 2009 revival of *West Side Story*, and the stage musical adaptation of the 2000 cheerleading film *Bring It On* (2012), written with Tom Kitt and Amanda Green. A sort of modern-day George M. Cohan, Miranda is a founding member of the hip-hop improv troupe Freestyle Love Supreme, and he has guest starred on television shows such as *House* and *Modern Family*. He played the lead role of Usnavi during the Off-Broadway and Broadway runs of *In the Heights*, and as of this writing is playing the title role in *Hamilton*.

Hamilton has garnered praise from hip-hop artists like Busta Rhymes and Questlove (the drummer of the Roots, who produced the *Hamilton* cast album) for being true to the ethos of hip-hop. The show is also at its core a traditional Broadway musical, containing elements of both the standard integrated book musical founded by Kern and Hammerstein, and the concept musical, bending space and time to allow us a deeper view into a character's heart and mind. The fusion of artistic languages in *Hamilton* goes beyond mere references to both Hammerstein and Grandmaster Flash, beyond even the use of a Biggie standard in the structure of the score. As Questlove writes in a September 28, 2015, article in *Rolling Stone*, "*Hamilton* isn't just a hip-hop musical or a stage presentation of hip-hop; it's organically and genuinely both things at once, in ways that are too important to be skimmed over."

So. How does a show fuse two great American art forms that seem to be diametrically opposed, and why does it matter?

HAMILTON—2015 ORIGINAL BROADWAY CAST ALBUM

It's Friday, September 25, 2015, a day you've been anticipating since you preordered the digital release of the *Hamilton* original Broadway cast recording several weeks ago. The show has generated so much hype that the entire album was streaming on National Public Radio a couple of days ahead of its official release, and it has automatically downloaded to your phone, but you are making yourself wait until you can relax and pay full attention to it. Broadway cast albums are usually recorded in a marathon session on the day off from an eight-performance-a-week show schedule. Via Miranda's social media posts, you are aware that the *Hamilton* recording process took two weeks, which, even on an album with forty-six tracks, allowed a high level of detail and perfectionism. Atlantic Records brought on Questlove and Black Thought of the hip-hop band the Roots as executive producers on the album. Orchestrator and music director Alex Lacamoire detailed in a phone interview how they contributed their expertise and sensibility to the album, making suggestions about effects like distortion, panning (the level of a sound in the left or right speaker), relative volume levels of drums, vocals, or other elements of the recording, et cetera—"condiments," as Lacamoire quoted Questlove, to what was already "a good burger." Such "ear candy" is intrinsic to a genre that grew out of live DJs using turntables and a mixer as instruments as described above.

At last, you press "Play," and are greeted by a fanfare that mixes acoustic sounds with record scratches, immediately placing you in revolutionary eighteenth-century hip-hop America. Lacamoire's genre-

melding orchestrations help establish the theatrical setting of a historical story told through a contemporary lens, as he combines a typical
pop/rock band (keyboards, guitar, bass, drums, percussion) with a string
quartet to add the unplugged, classical sound authentic to the time
period of the story, also incorporating samples and loops intrinsic to
hip-hop into the texture of the live playing that makes up the vast
majority of the score.

As with any musical, the opening sequence must also set up the
who's who of the story, and hip-hop is especially well equipped to do so.
Echoing the way a rapper will introduce himself on the mic, each character in the world of America Then played by America Now has a
distinctive way of saying his or her name. The casting is a nonissue, as
all the information about the characters can be found in their writing,
direction, and performance. The opening number "Alexander Hamilton" immediately makes the protagonist and antagonist of the story
crystal clear: Hamilton (played by Miranda) is the only person introduced by name in this song, and Aaron Burr (Leslie Odom Jr.) has the
first and last aggressive lines as "the damn fool who shot him" (in biographical musicals, there's no point in avoiding spoilers; it's about how
you get to the ending, rather than making it a surprise). Burr's narrative
check-ins throughout the story provide exposition and let us see his
mounting frustration as Hamilton seems to get in his way again and
again.

"Aaron Burr, Sir" is such a calculated, reticent individual that he
doesn't even make his own introduction. Burr's words are few and
carefully measured, his style summed up in his first advice to Hamilton:
"Talk less." He is followed by a signature chord progression throughout
the show, and often repeats text as well, indicating his obsessive thought
patterns. By contrast, Hamilton is overflowing with words, repeating
few of them except goal-oriented phrases like "Rise up" and "I'm not
throwing away my shot."

He first encounters fellow revolutionaries Hercules Mulligan (Okieriete Onaodowan), John Laurens (Anthony Ramos), and the Marquis de
Lafayette (Daveed Diggs) in the midst of a freestyle **cypher**, a group
rap in which each participant takes turns improvising. In starting the
cypher with the call-and-response announcement of "Show time!," Miranda draws a connection between eighteenth- and twenty-first-century
strivers: frequent straphangers on the New York City subway will recog-

nize it as a shout-out to the litefeet dancers who are the direct descendants of hip-hop's breakdance tradition. When Hamilton enters the cypher with a witty challenge to Burr's reticence, the pulse of the music quickens perceptibly, implying an energy shift that marks Hamilton as a natural leader. His status is cemented, musically if not yet politically, when Mulligan, Laurens, and Lafayette become the **hype** men to his lead rap in "My Shot," backing him up by spelling out his name (a reference to the Notorious B.I.G.'s "Going Back to Cali") and joining midway through the second chorus. By the end of the number, the ensemble joins the "young, scrappy, and hungry" firebrands in the mantra of revolution, and all toast the idea of freedom in "The Story of Tonight," which delightfully recalls the young revolutionaries of Les Misérables drinking together with just a bit of a French accent. The ensemble is made up of all races, and they function as a traditional Broadway chorus, completing the world in which Hamilton lives, joining in battle cries, gossip, and other actions throughout the show.

Among Alexander Hamilton's first published works were rebuttals to condemnations of the First Continental Congress written by British Loyalist Samuel Seabury (Thayne Jasperson), who used the pen name A. W. Farmer. These debates appear as "Farmer Refuted," with highly ornamented harpsichord accompaniment showing Seabury to be stuck in the past: the ornamentation and counterpoint hints at a baroque musical style, which would have been out of date even in the 1770s. Hamilton is able to battle Seabury on his own turf, his oratory skills transferable from rap to counterpoint as he gets his best insults in the spaces between Seabury's phrases.

As the revolution heats up, we also meet "The Schuyler Sisters" (Renée Elise Goldsberry, Phillipa Soo, Jasmine Cephas Jones); King George III of England (Jonathan Groff), and General George Washington (Christopher Jackson). In "You'll Be Back," the first of several times King George will drop by to comment on current events, the British monarch interrupts the hip-hop sound of his fractious colony with a Beatles-influenced pop ballad that draws parallels between the American fight for independence and a romantic breakup. Rather than introducing himself, this important leader's entrance is heralded by the ensemble at the end of "Farmer Refuted"; similarly, Washington's entrance is announced by Burr and the ensemble in "Right Hand Man." Burr fumes after Washington passes over him in favor of Hamilton for that coveted position. Like in many great dramas and hip-hop beefs, he and Hamilton start out as friends, and at this point are in the same social circle for "A Winter's Ball."

If politics is personal for the men in the story, the personal is political for the women. Angelica (Renée Elise Goldsberry), Eliza (Phillipa Soo), and Peggy (Jasmine Cephas Jones) are some of New York's most eligible bachelorettes. Weddings seem to be on Eliza's mind as she lightly sings "I do" upon entering the ball at the beginning of "Helpless," which references everything from Beyoncé to Wagner (the "Bridal Chorus" from his 1850 opera *Lohengrin*, better known in the English-speaking world as "Here Comes the Bride"). The Schuyler sisters' sound is that of a girl group such as the 1990s and early 2000s group Destiny's Child, with the sisters taking turns on lead vocal. "Helpless," which features Eliza throughout, shows the influence of Destiny's Child alumna Beyoncé's hit single, "Countdown." In a technique equivalent to "hyping" in rap, key words like "stressin'" and "blessin'" are highlighted by the other women, and the passage of "one week" and "two weeks" distills Hamilton and Eliza's courtship and marriage into a pop song.

Angelica's search for "a mind at work" in "The Schuyler Sisters" seemed to indicate she would be Hamilton's love interest, so you're a little taken aback when he ends up with Eliza. Sure enough, in "Satisfied," Angelica toasts the bride and groom with her public voice, then we "rewind" to her inner voice by prerecorded electronic effects to revisit the events of "Helpless." Goldsberry's flawless articulation illuminates both the musical sound and the meaning of the lyric. As Angelica lays out her three-point logic for directing Hamilton to her sister in a hurricane of wordplay reminiscent of Nicki Minaj's athletic verbal flow, the word "satisfied" takes on several connotations; its meaning will continue to evolve throughout the show.

Angelica and Hamilton are marked as intellectual equals by their text and music, in the sheer number of their words and the complexity of their wordplay. Their verbal dexterity includes ample use of assonance (recurring vowel sounds that don't rhyme: *Schuy*-ler, naïve, a-*side*, E-*li*-za, right); alliteration (recurring consonant sounds: key, kite), and internal or multisyllabic rhyme. Such rhyme schemes are praised in musical theater lyric writing, though usually anything other than a perfect rhyme (*cat* and *hat*, as opposed to *soon* and *gloom*, which is a near

rhyme) is frowned upon as lazy. Aside from the obvious fallacy of calling
Miranda's lyrics lazy, perfect rhyme devotees might consider this: the
genesis of rap is partly improvisational. A good MC spends a great deal
of time crafting and practicing phrases, and in the heat of a rap battle,
combines practiced phrases with newly minted improvised ones influenced by the instinct of the ear, going for both the meaning of the
words *and* for their sound in the manner of a jazz soloist, fixating on
certain vowels or consonants in a given phrase or verse, using perfect
rhyme as just one of many tools in the verbal arsenal (and as Miranda
points out in the Caramanica interview, he is perfectly capable of writing in styles that demand perfect rhyme, as in King George's songs).

Angelica's phrases vary in length, so rhymes go across punctuation
marks, as in "what it feels like to match wits" and "what the hell is the
catch? It's" in the first rapped verse of "Satisfied." Later in the verse,
"three minutes" rhymes with "agreement, it's" and "a dream and it's."
And as if it weren't enough to rhyme "dance" with the ends of the next
five lines, with multisyllabic near rhymes in most of those phrases, the
following stanza begins with the word "*hand*some." Working with an
actor at an audition for *In the Heights* (for which session your author
was the pianist), Miranda once conjured the image of a basketball
player spinning the ball on his finger: How long can you keep that
rhyme going?

As act 1 proceeds, the American Revolution reaches its bloody end
and a new nation is born, in loud, driving public scenes that alternate
with quiet interpersonal moments. The stakes of victory or loss are clear
as Miranda earns every historical fact by making the narrative personal
to each character. Hamilton and Burr's motivations are etched in ever
more detail through the rest of act 1 as their musical motives are developed and a few new sonic seeds that will bloom later in the story are
sown.

Burr repeats his mantra of hesitation, "Wait for It," on a melody that
never quite resolves, always ending the phrase on a note that implies
tension rather than release. The verse is underpinned by Burr's signature chord progression, which crept in along with him during "The
Story of Tonight (Reprise)." Burr's entrance causes a subtle shift in the
harmony of the room (but not a tempo increase like with Hamilton or
Washington) as he once again declines to take part in the revelry. Left
alone with his thoughts, he takes stock of his life and compares it to

Hamilton's, laying out the very understandable reasons for his behavior as the ensemble gradually joins the song. The ensemble members in this case are not literal characters, like they were when Hamilton inspired them to join "My Shot"; rather, they represent the universality of Burr's paralyzing fear of making mistakes.

Eliza and the women pray the men "Stay Alive," as a piano ostinato outlines the suspenseful chord progression of a protracted battle. Washington's sparse, order-barking style of rap is a counterweight to Hamilton's prolific flow. During the American Revolution, George Washington entrusted Alexander Hamilton with a great deal of high-level correspondence. Hamilton's skills of communication and persuasion were valuable as the war dragged on; still, it was a source of deep frustration to Hamilton that Washington would not give him a military command, as he viewed battlefield glory as his best chance for rising above his humble social station after the war.

These frustrations boil over when a beef with the incompetent General Charles Lee (Jon Rua) precipitates the first of three duels in the show. As Lee and Laurens prepare their weapons, "Ten Duel Commandments" deftly provides background information for those members of the audience who are rusty on their eighteenth-century dueling etiquette, while also propelling the plot and introducing the most prominent hip-hop reference in the show. The Notorious B.I.G.'s common-sense manual for would-be drug dealers, "Ten Crack Commandments," is not only referenced, but built into the structure of Hamilton's score, combined with an original melody Miranda wrote to the numbers one through ten. The "counting motive" returns several times, lurking in the score like a ticking time bomb.

"Meet Me Inside" starts as soon as Laurens's shot is fired, the sampled siren and missing half beat of the 7/8 time signature (most raps are in 4/4 time) telegraphing the urgency of Lee's injury. The title hook is a reference to DMX's "Party Up in Here," but it's no party when Washington calls Hamilton in for a reprimand. For once Hamilton's impulsiveness has set him back, as Washington orders him to go home.

Washington had a reason aside from insubordination to send Hamilton home: Eliza is pregnant. Surprise renders Hamilton (almost) speechless, and we learn a lot about Eliza in their duet "That Would Be Enough," a rare moment for her to get a word in edgewise. One of the most melodic songs in the score, her powerful feelings for Hamilton show in the **melisma** (multinote syllable) of "fraction of your *smile*" and "fragment of your *mind*." Not a fiery intellectual like her husband or sister, she uses fewer words and often doesn't rhyme them, but her repeated phrases hold the song together both lyrically and dramatically as she begs him to reconsider his priorities. Lacamoire's orchestration is stripped of all the aggressive electronica of Hamilton's public life, pared down to acoustic guitar, strings, and piano. The natural, acoustic sound will be used for family moments throughout the show, and here underscores Eliza's point that being alive and together is enough.

Miranda first conceived of *Hamilton* as a concept album, intended for repeated listening to digest the dense lyrics. Still, you notice that all the really crucial points—the dramatic gears of insults and promises, the names of key characters and events—are made clear by placing the lyric in prominent places: on a musical break, at the beginning or end of a phrase, or repeating it as a hook. Phrases that are interesting but not as important to the story go by at breakneck speed between those milestones, creating urgency and excitement, letting the listener follow the plot while leaving something to pick up on the next listen. This is especially noticeable on the next track, "Guns and Ships." Lafayette has returned with help from France that shifts the balance of the war, and persuades Washington to bring Hamilton back. This plot-forwarding information is highlighted in Burr's measured introduction, the repeated ensemble calls of "Lafayette" and "Hamilton," and Lafayette's slower rap that bridges the two call-and-response verses. In between those key points is emotional momentum from Lafayette's response raps in the verses, delivered by Diggs at a speed that is more machine gun than musket, illustrating Lafayette's command of the battlefield.

There is something prophetic about the quiet moment in which Washington calls Hamilton back to duty, in the use of the "Alexander Hamilton" theme and the richly harmonized "History Has Its Eyes on You." Washington only has a brief moment to pontificate about the future; he has a war to win in the present. Lafayette and Hamilton's easy banter before the Battle of Yorktown includes a pointed shout-out to immigrants like themselves, leaving an extra beat for audience appreciation. The huge dynamic contrasts in the orchestration of "Yorktown (The World Turned Upside Down)" describe the arc of battle, starting with the treble piano figure that captures the quiet autumn chill in the air before the siege begins. At the instrumental break during the height of battle, record scratches, vigorous pentatonic string lines, and driving electric guitar combine in a fusion of styles as epic as the raging fight (all styles, incidentally, associated with populism or revolution—hip-hop, folk, and rock). When the British surrender, chimes create an atmosphere of solemnity as the bottom drops out of the sound. From this quiet moment, the full company sings "the world turned upside down," which uses the title though not the tune of the ballad that was supposedly sung by British troops after their historic defeat, as "Yorktown" rebuilds to its final climax.

"Yorktown" feels for all the world like the act 1 finale, but this isn't the end, because this is not simply a show about the fight for independence, but rather about building a nation and a legacy. King George buys ten more minutes of act 1 with humor and the bemusedly pointed question, "What Comes Next?" This is, after all, uncharted political territory: How does America build a functional democracy, instead of ending up in "an endless cycle of vengeance?" The beautiful ballad "Dear Theodosia" draws the parallel between personal and political infancy as Burr and Hamilton each promise their firstborn they'll make a success of their newborn nation.

A beat from the infancy of hip-hop underlies the beginning of "Non-Stop" as the story whirls through the first few years after the revolution. The printed score for this song is marked "Quasi Dance Hall," referring to a sparse reggae-like beat coming out of politically tumultuous Jamaica in the late 1970s. As an orphan immigrant with no strong ties to his place of birth, Hamilton has nothing to lose and everything to gain in the success of the American experiment. Constantly confrontational, he fights for what he believes in while Burr stands by in disbelief, still "[waiting] for it." Personal matters are never far from mind even as they work to shape their new nation. All the main characters return with their motives, motivations, and conflicts, and the various themes of act 1 are woven into a sonic tapestry that is held together by a hook that marvels at Hamilton's constant writing. The first act ends with a repetition of his "my shot" motive, connecting the young, poor immigrant's verbal genius that is his "shot" with the prospects of his country.

ACT 2

There are a few new introductions to be made in act 2, the first being a pair of prominent Virginians, Thomas Jefferson (Daveed Diggs) and James Madison (Okieriete Onaodowan). Jefferson's introductory song, "What'd I Miss," is infused with the eight-to-the-bar feel and tight vocal harmonies of older pop styles boogie-woogie and jazz, implying that Jefferson was hip when he wrote the Declaration of Independence, but is out of touch after his long absence in France. He and Hamilton face off in congressional debates, framed as rap battles hosted by Washington as MC, that show the origins of some of the most persistent rifts in American politics. Jefferson's references to hip-hop greats—Grandmaster Flash's 1982 classic "The Message" in "Cabinet Battle #1," and Biggie's 1994 debut single "Juicy" in "Cabinet Battle #2"—suggest that he is gradually getting back up to speed on American politics. The counting motive makes an appearance in the track to "Cabinet Battle #1," adding to the atmosphere of this duel in the political arena. Interestingly, it is Hamilton who stoops to personal insult in the first rap battle, and Jefferson in the second: act 2 is marked by ever-evolving power plays between political rivals.

There is a Shakespearean sense of inevitability as each song in act 2 tightens the screws on the main players in our story, and in fact Hamilton alludes to the Bard in a letter to Angelica in "Take a Break." Even this sweet domestic scene shows the increasing pressures of both work and family, especially in the triangular dynamic between Hamilton, Eliza, and Angelica. Chernow writes: "Together, the two eldest sisters formed a composite portrait of Hamilton's ideal woman, each appealing to a different facet of his personality. . . . Where Eliza bowed reluctantly to the social demands of Hamilton's career, Angelica applauded his ambitions and was always famished for news of his latest political exploits." Though there was never proof that Hamilton had an affair with his sister-in-law, they certainly had an intense bond. The end of "Take a Break" is a tug-of-war between work and women, and both "Helpless" and "Satisfied" are quoted in the orchestration. When work wins, it is Angelica's theme (on the violin and harp) that melts into the languid summer scene of "Say No to This" without the relief of applause.

Burr takes delight in letting Hamilton narrate the actions that embroiled him in one of the first sex scandals in United States politics. In

"Say No to This," Hamilton and seductress Maria Reynolds betray Eliza's trust by using her word "helpless"—the lyrical equivalent of Reynolds wearing Eliza's robe. Jasmine Cephas Jones infuses Reynolds's low-range melody with vocal scoops and dark, heavy placement, in contrast to the higher tessitura and clean, bright articulation of her act 1 role, Peggy Schuyler (all four of the actors who play different named roles in each act create distinctive voices for each character). When Maria's husband (Sydney James Harcourt) arrives with a blackmail letter, accompanied by an aggressive musical figure evocative of the driving guitar and strings in "Yorktown," Hamilton pays him off.

"The Room Where It Happens" is another history lesson told through Burr's envious eyes; it is also, in musical theater parlance, an "I-want" song. Its late occurrence is significant: a protagonist's "I-want" song usually comes near the beginning of act 1, as in the case of "My Shot." But Burr the antagonist is reactive, not proactive, unable to articulate what he wants until the final chorus of his act 2 song, and even then only after Hamilton taunts him with his own mantra! As it turns out, all Burr wants is power. Even Jefferson and Madison, portrayed as enemies in this story, aspire to win a victory for their Southern constituents, whereas Burr just wants to be in the room, not necessarily to do anything constructive while he's in it.

Hamilton wants to build something that will outlive him (having moved on from simply wanting to rise up out of poverty, which he accomplished well before the end of act 1). He and Washington share this wish, one of many aspects of the father-son dynamic between the two of them. Miranda borrows George Washington's own frequent use of the biblical image of a vine and fig tree in "One Last Time," as Washington persuades Hamilton of the need for him to step down as president. Not only does Washington want to retire and enjoy some time under his own vine and fig tree, he wants the fragile new democracy to learn to function without him, that all the citizens of the country they fought so hard to form might live in safety for generations to come. Christopher Jackson's soulful rendering of these words retroactively adds another dimension to "The Story of Tonight" from act 1—even if you live to see your glory, the whole *point* is for it to outlast your life. The strings and piano play material developed from "The Story of Tonight" as Hamilton and Washington deliver a quotation from Washington's 1796 Farewell Address in "One Last Time," showing the protégé whose words Washington had trusted in a time of war come full circle in helping him draft the speech that teaches America to say good-bye to its first president.

As Washington intended, life does indeed go on without him, though perhaps with more political intrigue than he would have liked. King George's surprise and wistful envy at the idea of a leader voluntarily stepping down, and his audible quotation marks around the word "country" are a reminder what an experiment the American government was (Groff, as always, provides a side of comedy to the commentary with his colorful vocal inflections). The second U.S. president, John Adams, is dispatched in under a minute in *Hamilton*. Adams and Hamilton's hatred for one another was legendary, but the rap excoriating Adams was cut during *Hamilton*'s development. In the delicately calibrated pacing of a musical, it is necessary for the narrative to move forward after the reflective moment with Washington. The sound effect of an exploding bomb tells us everything we need to know about Hamilton's relationship with Adams, a character we hear about but never actually meet in the show.

Hamilton's ability to be a threat "as long as he can hold a pen" has already catalyzed his opponents to dig up any information they can use to destroy him. The battle music makes a return as Hamilton is cornered by Burr, Madison, and Jefferson in "We Know" with the choice between appearing to have embezzled government funds and admitting to the Reynolds affair. Though all three men join in the xenophobic aggression of taunting Hamilton with put-on Caribbean accents when they suggest he "best g'wan run back where ya come from," Jefferson and Madison relent when they learn Hamilton never broke the law, painting them as political but not personal foes. Burr, however, exits with the subtle threat that leads to "Hurricane." The beginning of this song recalls "Yorktown," but there is no Lafayette with whom to exchange witty banter in the eye of this storm, and the only weapon Hamilton has to defend himself against the growing rumors that threaten his legacy is his pen. You notice that by this time in the story, political and personal themes are so intertwined as to be inseparable. The track of "The Reynolds Pamphlet," the tell-all document in which Hamilton admitted to the Reynolds affair to clear his name of charges of financial corruption, is related to George Washington's entrance in "Right Hand Man." The music that accompanied the moment of Hamilton's first encounter with Washington (the gatekeeper to his best "shot" at a legacy) is here detuned and distorted as his reputation comes crashing down in the court of public opinion.

A sweet harp figure presages Eliza's entrance at the end of "The Reynolds Pamphlet," dissonant and out of place over the rest of the track, spelling out what a nightmarish situation Hamilton has created for his wife. The figure continues as the accompaniment of Eliza's solo "Burn," and you realize you have heard it before, albeit in a different time signature and key, in the keyboard part of the chorus of "Wait for It." As the lyrics of that song say, neither love nor death discriminates between the sinners and the saints. Neither does humiliation, and long-suffering Eliza, never at ease in the political spotlight, is now thrust into it in the worst possible way. With no control over the narrative, burning her letters to remove herself from it is the best she can do. You can hear the erosion of trust in the progression of the lyrics "I knew . . . / You said . . . / I thought you were mine." Eliza's usual even temper is shaken in her private moment, her voice starting at practically a whisper, building to an anguished cry.

Tragedy follows close on the heels of the Reynolds scandal. Philip Hamilton (Anthony Ramos) is a chip off the old block. Back in "Take a Break," he was shown to be inventive and assertive, unafraid to ask for what he wants, even at the age of nine. Someone with a keen ear or knowledge of Hamilton's biography may have intuited the significance of the counting motive's appearance in that song in his French and piano lessons with Eliza. The French version of the counting motive is a piano exercise to which Philip keeps improvising a new ending, showing his creative potential and also foreshadowing his fate. Now it comes back in "Blow Us All Away" as nineteen-year-old Philip confronts George Eacker (Ephraim Sykes) over an inflammatory speech Eacker made about Hamilton. The jaunty hi-hat beat stays as constant as Philip's family pride throughout the song, but the peppy whistle from the beginning of the song becomes detuned as the situation escalates into a duel. Philip dies with his parents by his side in a reprise of "Stay Alive"; the heartbeat of the bass drum stops in the middle of a phrase of the counting theme, and Eliza counts "*sept huit neuf*" in vain.

There are two moments in the show where Hamilton is at a loss for words, at the beginning and the end of his son's life. The only other character in our story who might be able to find words for this moment is Angelica, and it is she who sings first in "It's Quiet Uptown." The ballad shows how the tables have turned, using the piano figure from the very end of "That Would Be Enough" for the entire song. Hamilton borrows Eliza's words from their act 1 duet, which he did once before during an argument in "Non-Stop." This time, he uses her words to plead for her forgiveness. The rhythmic and melodic emphasis on the refrain's word "unimaginable" expresses just how impossible a burden it is to lose a child, and "Quiet Uptown" gives us a few minutes to grieve with the Hamiltons, finishing with a gentle button at the end of the song to let go before moving on.

It's time to move the story to its inevitable end, and Jefferson lightens the mood as he calls us back for "The Election of 1800," which reprises the music of "Washington on Your Side." In another instance of tables turning, this time it's Hamilton whose good opinion is sought. Burr finally gets his "leadership tempo bump" when he shows up at Hamilton's door to campaign, but his voice sounds strained; you can almost see the automatic smile frozen on his face. Called the father of modern political campaigning, Burr's sound bites and the ensemble reactions to it are eerily familiar: references to political parties and customs of the time (like the fact that women were not allowed to vote) are juxtaposed with phrases from election cycles more than two centuries later, completely believable in this early American narrative. When Hamilton comes out of his quiet uptown reverie to cast his surprise tie-breaking vote for his longtime nemesis Jefferson, the wheels are set in motion for Hamilton and Burr's final showdown.

Historically, the timeline and persons involved were a little more convoluted and numerous, but *Hamilton*, which employed Chernow as a historical consultant during its development, preserves the essential truth that the two men's friendship deteriorated over the years, and that Burr felt his career was impeded by Hamilton, a grudge that culminated in the exchange of several politely venomous letters and the challenge to a duel. These letters appear paraphrased as the hip-hop-infused minuet "Your Obedient Servant." The ornate formality of the closing salutation ("I have the honor to be . . . ." taken verbatim from the letters) adds levity to the deadly serious intent of the verses, a little comedy before the tragedy. "Best of Wives and Best of Women" is also a line taken from a letter, the one Hamilton wrote to Eliza shortly before the duel, which was only to be delivered to her if he was killed.

The song's familiar motives tell you they've had this quotidian conversation thousands of times before, provoking the heartbreaking realization that Eliza has no idea this is the last time they'll have it.

Of all the reasons Burr counts, it is the thought of his daughter that spurs him to fire his gun at Hamilton in "The World Was Wide Enough." Time comes almost to a standstill as the bullet makes its deadly way from Burr's pistol to Hamilton's side, and Hamilton's voice seems to be coming from far away (an effect suggested by the album's sound mixer Tim Latham) as his life flashes before his eyes. The familiar musical motives in his soliloquy are accompanied only by the sound effect of wind and the reverse record scratches that punctuate his thoughts of his legacy, the ideas he fought for, and the people he loved. Normal time and space resume, and Burr cries "Wait!" as Hamilton aims his gun in the air and the bullet reaches its fatal destination—the one time when Burr didn't wait for it, and Hamilton threw away his shot. Burr's sad conclusion that "The World Was Wide Enough" for both of them is inspired by a letter, written half-jokingly to a friend, but expressive of the reality that the duel ended both Hamilton and him. Although Burr lived another thirty-two years, his political career was essentially over, and now he's best remembered as the man who killed Alexander Hamilton in a duel.

Hamilton is remembered in part because Eliza Hamilton devoted the rest of her long life to preserving her husband's legacy. Time is a theme that comes up repeatedly throughout the show, and the thematic word is "hyped" by the full company in "Who Lives, Who Dies, Who Tells Your Story." Of all the possible morals of the story—not throwing away one's shot, the degree to which the United States is built by immigrants—the one that rings loud, clear, and universal in the finale is the question Eliza asks herself: "When my time is up, have I done enough?" The final chorale sung a cappella by the full company contains the richest, most complex vocal harmony of the show. It ends, however, on a perfect unison, the gradual distillation from many notes to one a fitting conclusion for the story of a federalist, abolitionist, uncompromising man who occasionally compromised for the good of the country. As it says on every piece of American currency minted by the banking system Hamilton initiated, *E Pluribus Unum*—out of many, one.

THE WORLD IS WIDE ENOUGH

Hamilton invites us to gather information about its characters by their words and actions rather than their appearance. This might seem an anomaly in a genre that has historically relied on stereotype—recall the strict typecasting of the romantic and comedic leads on the *Cotton Blossom* of *Show Boat* (chapter 3)—but it is actually directly in line with the aspirations of artists like Kern and Hammerstein: song flowing from story flowing from character. Certainly, a character's physical appearance influences the audience's perception of the character, but the integrated plotlines, character development, and nonlinear storytelling techniques that became indispensable to Broadway musicals over the course of the twentieth century open up avenues for illuminating character that transcend typecasting. And as shown above, it is specifically hip-hop's propensity for individualism that makes *Hamilton*'s detailed characterizations possible.

Christine Toy Johnson, an Asian American actor, playwright, and advocate for inclusive casting, whereby actors are considered for roles irrespective of race (when race is not germane to the character or story), spoke in a phone interview of how the huge commercial success of *Hamilton* completely debunks the notion that audiences will not accept non-Caucasians in lead roles except in culturally specific shows. She also spoke of her surprise as an audience member at feeling a kinship with both Hamilton and Burr, a perspective aided by inclusive casting. She highlights both points in a blog she posted immediately after seeing *Hamilton*, writing: "*No one cares* that they don't look like the guys on our money. Instead, we are able to see the story through an entirely new lens and hear it in an entirely new way which makes it possible for an Asian American female living in NYC in the 2000s to suddenly relate to white men living in NYC in the 1800s."

To listen to the stories of people who are simultaneously like and not like you, to sit with them in a darkened room, sharing your laughter, tears, and applause—this may seem a small thing, but it is an action of hope in a world filled with division and fear. Hope is the currency of the Broadway musical. Some musicals provide it in the form of comedy whose deepest meaning is a couple of hours' escape from life's problems. Many others confront those problems head-on, finding hope among the rubble of loss, illness, and oppression, and within the uncertainty of change—consider the ending of any Rodgers and Hammerstein musical. Musicals' protagonists go against the grain of society or attempt to subvert an intolerable status quo—think of Elphaba's rebellious crusade for justice, or the Tribe's desperate plea to "Let the Sun Shine In"—pointing to hope that untenable circumstances *can* change.

A snapshot of Broadway during the 2015–2016 season includes a wide array of new musicals and revivals. In addition to *Hamilton*, several other shows have diverse or non-Caucasian casts: *Allegiance*, the story of a Japanese American family in the World War II internment camps, based on the childhood of television actor George Takei; *On Your Feet*, a jukebox musical of the hits of Cuban American artists Gloria and Emilio Estefan; and revivals of African American shows *The Color Purple* and *Shuffle Along*. An acclaimed revival of *Spring Awakening* from Los Angeles theater company Deaf West transferred to Broadway for a limited run in fall 2015, with two actors in each role, one to sing and one to *sign*, a theatrical device that adds a new dimension to diversity onstage *and* sheds new light on the story's themes. The classic *Fiddler on the Roof* is slated to be revived in the 2015–2016 season, and it will be joined in the neighborhood by Broadway veterans' stage adaptations of films: *School of Rock* by Andrew Lloyd Webber, Glenn Slater, and Julian Fellowes; and *American Psycho* by Duncan Sheik and Roberto Aguirre-Sacasa. Perhaps only a true musical theater junkie would be interested in seeing every single one of these shows, but the season has something for everybody.

In his review of the jukebox musical *Beautiful: The Carole King Story* (2014), *New York Times* theater critic Ben Brantley grumpily describes the show as "modeled with sheepish but cold calculation on *Jersey Boys*," essentially dismissing it as a redundant girl edition of the popular 2005 jukebox musical about Frankie Valli and the Four Seasons. But it wasn't redundant to this female theatergoer, who had seen *Beautiful* in previews, before reviews are published, and had enjoyed the show not only because of the familiar music and actress Jessie Mueller's stellar performance as King, but also precisely because of the female perspective that makes it, while perhaps a capitalization on a successful formula, not interchangeable with *Jersey Boys*. America's great unfinished symphony is at its best when all our voices can be found within it. The world is wide enough, the way is broad enough, for both *Beautiful* and *Jersey Boys*; for both the British-tinged operetta comedy *A Gentleman's Guide to Love and Murder*, which won the Best Musical Tony Award in 2014, and *Hamilton*, whose cast album ascended to the top position of the Billboard Rap Albums chart two months after its release.

Jonathan Larson wrote in *Rent*, "The opposite of war isn't peace / It's creation!" If, as Oscar Hammerstein wrote in *South Pacific*, "you've got to be taught to hate and fear," then the Broadway musical—that deceptively frivolous, perky genre, created by the collaboration of people from multiple opposite-of-war disciplines—carefully teaches hope as a preferable alternative, much like Afrika Bambaataa promoted "Peace, Love, Unity, and Having Fun" in the early days of hip-hop. To which one can only add, in a toast to all those who venture to lend their voices (or ears!) to the hopeful chorus, a final Hammerstein reference: "Et cetera, et cetera, et cetera!"

GLOSSARY

AABA form. Song form common especially in the middle decades of the twentieth century, in which the two similar sections of music were followed by a contrasting section (the bridge), and finished by a reiteration of the first section. Often thirty-two bars in length, consisting of four eight-bar sections of music.

a cappella. Singing without instrumental accompaniment.

antagonist. The person(s) or force(s) working against the hero of the story, or protagonist.

arpeggio. A chord played one tone at a time, instead of together. Comes from "harp," as in, played in a harp-like manner.

backphrase. To sing behind the beat or behind the rhythm notated in the melody; can convey a sense of carefreeness or passion, depending on the character of the music.

bar. Measure of music containing specified number of beats (often three or four), divided on notated music by vertical lines.

bell tone. A note played on a song cue to give the singer the starting pitch. Often used for comedic effect.

belt. A loud, brassy vocal quality (there are differing views among vocal pedagogues on the exact definition of vocal colors and the proper way to produce them; this definition describes the sensation to the listener).

book musical. See first two sections of chapter 1.

book writer. See first section of chapter 1.

boom-chuck. An accompaniment pattern formed by alternating single bass notes on strong beats with middle- to high-register chords on off-beats (also called "oompah").

bridge. Sometimes also called the release, a contrasting melodic and harmonic section to the main verse and chorus of a song.

burlesque. A spoof of a serious work or performance; a parody.

button. A rhythmic "bump" on the final chord or note of a song to give it a definitive ending and cue applause.

cadence. A harmonic or melodic conclusion of a phrase or music that leads to a sense of resolution—or sometimes suspense.

chest voice. Lower part of the vocal range; typically a heavier, thicker sound than higher range (there are differing views among vocal pedagogues on the exact definition of vocal colors and the proper way to produce them; this definition describes the sensation to the listener).

chromatic. Built upon or including all twelve pitches into which most Western music divides the octave, including the notes that are not included in the primary scale or mode of the musical piece.

concept musical. See first section of chapter 7.

counterpoint. Two or more musical lines that are melodically independent, but whose interaction results in harmony.

creative team. Typically refers to the director, music director, and choreographer of a show; can also include design team and orchestrator—anyone not an author of the work, but similarly invested in the look, sound, or other creative component of a show.

cypher. A group setting descended from African forms of music and dance in which participants take turns improvising a solo to a beat laid down by musicians and/or the group itself; in hip-hop, a setting for freestyle rap jam.

diatonic. Describing harmony or melody that contains only notes from the current scale (opposite of chromatic).

diction. A performer's manner of delivering text.

diss track. A rap recorded with the intention of insulting a rival.

dynamic. The relative loudness or softness of a section of music.

eleven o'clock number. A big solo toward the end of a show. So called for the approximate time it occurred, when shows began a little later in the evening.

encore. Repetition of all or part of a popular number, as called for by the audience. Very rare in contemporary musical theater, it used to be customary for performers to do several encores of the most popular songs in a show.

exposition. Background information that is important to the audience understanding the story. It can be tricky to work into the script without feeling clunky, because it is often the type of information that would be common knowledge to the characters speaking the lines.

falsetto. A method of vocal production in the high male range, usually characterized by light tone.

fanfare. An attention-getting musical flourish, often played by brass instruments. Associated with the entrance of royalty or military personnel.

finale. The final number in each act of a musical. At the end of classic shows, often called the "finale ultimo."

flow. A rapper's individual patterns of rhythm and rhyme.

glissando. A continuous slide between two notes (as when a trombone slides between two notes) or across a wide range of notes (as on a piano or harp, rapidly traversing the low to high range of the instrument, or vice versa).

head voice. Higher part of the vocal range; typically a lighter sound than lower range (there are differing views among vocal pedagogues on the exact definition of vocal colors and the proper way to produce them; this definition describes the sensation to the listener).

hype. To join in the background on a few key words of a rap.

integration. Storytelling technique whereby the scenes, songs, dances, and other elements of a production work together to form a seamless whole.

I-want song. A solo, often occurring near the beginning of a show, in which the protagonist expresses his or her ambitions or desires (may or may not use the words "I want").

jukebox musical. A musical with a story created around the song catalog of a popular artist, group, or genre.

legato. Smooth articulation of a musical phrase.

leitmotif. Short musical ideas that are associated with a character or dramatic theme, used and developed throughout a score.

list song. A song in which the lyrics comprise a list that usually forms some kind of metaphor.

major, minor. The most common scales, or sets of pitches in an octave, in Western music. In contrast to the chromatic scale, which is made up entirely of semitone intervals between notes, major and minor scales are made up of a combination of whole tones and semitones, with two semitones per octave. The placement of semitones in a scale or mode gives it its emotional character: major scales and tonality are usually thought of as happy, bright, cheerful; minor scales and tonality are usually thought of as sad or sinister.

marcato. Forceful articulation of a musical phrase.

melisma. More than one note on one syllable of text. Can refer to a long passage of technically demanding melodies on a syllable; can also be thought of as a fancy word for "riff."

meter. The rhythmic structure of a piece or section of music, felt in the pattern of strong and weak beats in the pulse. Music is often grouped in patterns of two, three, or four beats, with the first beat (or downbeat) of each group feeling stronger in relationship to the subsequent beats. See also **offbeats.**

minstrel show. See second section of chapter 2, "Broadway's Roots in Variety."

mix. A middle ground between the heavy sound of chest voice and light sound of head voice; in the middle range (there are differing views among vocal pedagogues on the exact definition of vocal colors and the proper way to produce them; this definition describes the sensation to the listener).

motive. Short musical idea forming the building block of a piece of music.

octave. Interval between a musical pitch and the pitch that is twice or half its frequency. For example, the "A" to which many orchestras tune vibrates at 440 Hertz; the A above is 880 Hz, while the A below is 220 Hz.

offbeats. Music is organized rhythmically into a series of alternating strong and weak beats; offbeats are the weak beats.

olio. The second segment of a minstrel show, a series of unrelated performances in a variety of disciplines. Precursor to vaudeville.

opening number. The first song in a musical, often (though not always) a big group number, in which the setting, important relationships, themes of the show, and theatrical style should be established.

operetta. Light operatic entertainment; see chapter 2 section on operetta and Victor Herbert.

ostinato. An "obstinate" repetitive musical pattern.

overture. An instrumental before the show begins, often made up of prominent melodies from the show.

pastiche. A compositional technique of imitating other styles or composers, to evoke a certain time period or setting.

pentatonic scale. A scale with five tones per octave. Various pentatonic scales are common in folk music in many places in the world.

(pit) orchestra. The ensemble of musicians that provides the music for a show. They have historically often played in a "pit" below the stage, though they are sometimes above the stage, onstage, or even "remoted" in a room elsewhere in the building.

plagal cadence. A concluding chord progression in which the penultimate chord is built off the fourth note of the scale, followed by the chord built on the first, or tonic note of the scale. The word "amen" is almost always sung to this harmonic cadence.

protagonist. The hero of the story; the person the audience is meant to root for and follow throughout the story.

recitative. A passage of text, usually full of exposition, that is quasi-spoken, often on one note. A common device in opera; less so in musical theater where such text is more often executed in a spoken scene.

reprise. A song is a variation of one earlier in the show; usually shorter and with some lyrical variation, bringing back familiar musical material while showing the progression of the story.

revue. See latter half of chapter 2, "Florenz Ziegfeld and the Revue."

rubato. Ebb and flow in the pulse of a phrase of music (from Italian "robbed," as in, robbing time from one part of a phrase to feed another part of the phrase.

straight tone. Vocal tone without vibrato. Associated with purity, as in the case of a boy soprano tone; also associated with contemporary belt tone, which uses little vibrato.

syncopation. Rhythmic characteristic in which musical accents fall between the pulse of the beat.

tessitura. The vocal range in which most of a given melody occurs.

timbre. Distinctive tone of a musical instrument or voice.

time signature. Indication of the rhythmic meter of a piece or section of music (see also **meter**).

Tin Pan Alley. Nickname for the popular music and sheet music publishing industry in the late 1800s through the first few decades of the 1900s. See first section of chapter 3.

triple threat. A performer who excels at all three primary skills of musical theater: singing, dancing, and acting.

trunk song. A song that is cut from the show for which it was written; it is saved in the composer's "trunk" for potential resurrection in a later work.

underscore. Music played under dialogue, highlighting or subverting the meaning of the text, or smoothing the transition between speech and song.

unison. Two or more voices on the same pitch.

up-tempo. Fast, lively beat.

vaudeville. See second section of chapter 2, "Variety and Vaudeville."

verse-chorus form. Most common form in pop and rock music since the 1950s. Verses alternate with a chorus whose text is repeated; typically verse-chorus-verse-chorus-bridge-chorus(es).

vibrato. Regular, rapid, slight variation in pitch that, when well executed, produces a warm, rich tone.

whole tone. Musical interval of two semitones, also known as a whole step, for example, from C to D (with one note, C-sharp or D-flat, in between).

SELECTED READING

Block, Geoffrey. *Enchanted Evenings: The Broadway Musical from* Show Boat *to Sondheim and Lloyd Webber.* 2nd ed. Oxford: Oxford University Press, 2009. In-depth musical analysis of seventeen musicals from the 1920s to 1980s.

Bordman, Gerald. *American Musical Theatre: A Chronicle.* 3rd ed. Oxford: Oxford University Press, 2001. A solid reference book from origins of American musicals from origins through 1995, including season-by-season analysis and editorial by Bordman.

———. *Jerome Kern: His Life and Music.* Oxford: Oxford University Press, 1990. Mostly biographical with some musical analysis.

Buck, Gene, and Rennold Wolf. *Ziegfeld Follies of 1919*—libretto. http://www.loc.gov/resource/varsep.s53282#seq-4. Accessed November 7, 2013.

Chang, Jeff. *Can't Stop Won't Stop: A History of the Hip-Hop Generation.* New York: St. Martin's, 2005. Engaging history with lots of well-described listening examples, by acclaimed hip-hop journalist with an introduction by DJ Kool Herc.

Chernow, Ron. *Alexander Hamilton.* New York: Penguin, 2004. Hamilton biography that inspired the hip-hop musical *Hamilton.*

Cohen, Allen, and Steven L. Rosenhaus. *Writing Musical Theater.* New York: Palgrave Macmillan, 2006. Engagingly written book on what makes musicals tick, written for the prospective author in mind but of interest to enthusiasts as well.

Davis, Lee. *Bolton, Wodehouse, and Kern: The Men Who Made Musical Comedy.* New York: James H. Heineman, 1993. Reads rather like a romance novel; intricate in its detail of the Princess musical men.

Decker, Todd. *Show Boat: Performing Race in an American Musical.* Oxford: Oxford University Press, 2012. An analysis of racial themes in *Show Boat* and how those themes have been interpreted throughout the long history of the show.

de Giere, Carol. *Defying Gravity: The Creative Career of Stephen Schwartz from* Godspell *to* Wicked. Milwaukee: Applause Theatre & Cinema Books, 2008. Insight into Schwartz's creative process.

Dillingham, Charles. Unpublished memoir. New York Public Library, Charles B. Dillingham papers, Box 32. For the more fanatical devotee of early 1900s musical theater, the Dillingham papers contain not only his unpublished memoirs, but telegrams, letters, and other memorabilia from the producer's theatrical life.

Eells, George. *The Life That Late He Led: A Biography of Cole Porter.* New York: Putnam, 1967. In an interesting window into Porter's life and times, this otherwise detailed bio, written by a close acquaintance, sidesteps discussion of his homosexuality.

Ferber, Edna. *Show Boat.* New York: Grosset & Dunlap, 1926. Epic novel that is the source material for the musical.

Fordin, Hugh. *Getting to Know Him: A Biography of Oscar Hammerstein II.* Cambridge, Mass.: Da Capo, 1995.

Furia, Philip. *Irving Berlin: A Life in Song.* New York: Schirmer Trade Books, 1998. Mostly biographical; musical analysis friendly to a layperson.

Grode, Eric. *Hair: The Story of the Show That Defined a Generation.* Philadelphia: Running Press, 2010. Detailed history (not critical analysis) of the show with lots of photographs.

Hammerstein, Oscar Andrew. *Hammerstein: A Musical Theatre Family.* New York: Black Dog & Leventhal, 2010. A history of the quintessential American theatrical dynasty, written by family historian and Oscar Hammerstein II's grandson.

Kenrick, John. *Musical Theatre: A History.* New York: Continuum International, 2008. Good general Broadway history; engagingly written with a good balance of facts, analysis of styles and trends, and interesting anecdotes.

Kreuger, Miles. *Show Boat: The Story of a Classic American Musical.* New York: Oxford University Press, 1977. The definitive resource on productions of *Show Boat* through its publication date.

Lee, Baayork, Robert Viagas, and Thommie Walsh, original cast of *A Chorus Line. On the Line: The Creation of* A Chorus Line. 2nd ed. Pompton Plains, N.J.: Limelight Editions, 2006. Detailed history of the 1975 musical, with a great deal of interview material from the original cast.

Magee, Jeffrey. *Irving Berlin's Musical Theatre.* New York: Oxford University Press, 2012. In-depth musical analysis of Berlin's work, engagingly written; sections of advanced musical analysis.

Marbury, Elisabeth. *My Crystal Ball: Reminiscences.* London: Hurst & Blackett, 1924. Memoirs of prominent theatrical agent and producer of the first Princess Theatre musicals.

McBrien, William. *Cole Porter: A Biography.* New York: Knopf, 1998. A more recent biography than Eells's, which provides more insight into his life and relationships, and how they affected his writing.

McCabe, John. *George M. Cohan: The Man Who Owned Broadway.* New York: Doubleday, 1973. Mostly biographical; light on musical analysis but full of detail.

Miller, Karl Hagstrom. *Segregating Sound: Inventing Folk and Pop Music in the Age of Jim Crow.* Durham, N.C.: Duke University Press, 2010. Exploration of social and cultural forces on the formation and marketing of American pop music.

Miller, Scott. *Sex, Drugs, Rock & Roll, and Musicals.* Boston: Northeastern University Press, 2011. A look at ten rock or rock-influenced musicals and their social impact.

Mordden, Ethan. *Sing for Your Supper: The Broadway Musical in the 1930s.* New York: St. Martin's, 2005. Mordden is reliably entertaining and highly opinionated; this book is one of a decade-by-decade series of Broadway musicals.

———. *Ziegfeld: The Man Who Invented Show Business.* New York: St. Martin's, 2008. Novelistically written account of the great showman's life.

Ommen van der Merwe, Ann. *The Ziegfeld Follies: A History in Song.* Lanham, Md.: Scarecrow Press, 2009. Detailed and well-researched breakdown and analysis of the most famous series of annual revues.

Rapp, Anthony. *Without You: A Memoir of Love, Loss, and the Musical Rent.* New York: Simon & Schuster, 2006. Very personal memoir of Rapp's life while in *Rent*; interesting insight into the development of the show. Audiobook is narrated by himself.

Rimler, Walter. *George Gershwin: An Intimate Portrait.* Urbana: University of Illinois Press, 2009. As implied by the subtitle, insight into the composer's short life; little musical analysis.

Rodgers, Richard. *Musical Stages: An Autobiography.* 2nd ed. Cambridge, Mass.: Da Capo, 2002. Inside view of the composer's life and music.

Sanders, Sheri. *Rock the Audition: How to Prepare For and Get Cast in Rock Musicals.* Milwaukee, Wis.: Hal Leonard Books, 2011. Geared toward aspiring musical theater performers; contains history of different styles of rock and pop music with an angle to how they pertain to musicals.

Sater, Steven, and Duncan Sheik. *Spring Awakening.* New York: Theatre Communications Group, 2007. Libretto of the musical, including a substantial foreword by Sater.

Snelson, John. *Andrew Lloyd Webber.* New Haven, Conn.: Yale University Press, 2004. Musicological analysis of Lloyd Webber's work.

Sondheim, Stephen. *Finishing the Hat: Collected Lyrics (1954–1981) with Attendant Comments, Principles, Heresies, Grudges, Whines and Anecdotes.* New York: Knopf, 2010. The first volume of Sondheim's collected lyrics, full of all the things listed in the subtitle above (though he respects the living and saves his critiques for lyricists who are no longer around to have their feelings hurt).

———. *Look, I Made a Hat: Collected Lyrics (1981–2011) with Attendant Comments, Principles, Heresies, Grudges, Whines and Anecdotes.* New York: Knopf, 2011. Second volume of same.

Southern, Eileen. *The Music of Black Americans: A History.* 3rd ed. New York: Norton, 1997. Comprehensive history and musical analysis through of African American music and its key figures through the mid-1990s.

Starr, Larry. *George Gershwin (Yale Broadway Masters Series).* New Haven, Conn.: Yale University Press, 2010. In-depth musical analysis of Gershwin's work, engagingly written; sections of advanced musical analysis.

Stewart, Donald Travis (a.k.a. Trav S. D.). *No Applause—Just Throw Money: The Book That Made Vaudeville Famous.* New York: Faber & Faber, 2006. A fascinating account of vaudeville, key personalities, and the forces at work in its rise and fall.

Taylor, Yuval, and Jake Austen. *Darkest America: Black Minstrelsy from Slavery to Hip-Hop.* New York: Norton, 2012. An in-depth exploration of minstrelsy and related forms throughout almost two centuries of American entertainment history.

Vermette, Margaret. *The Musical World of Boublil and Schönberg: The Creators of* Les Misérables, Miss Saigon, Martin Guerre *and* The Pirate Queen. Milwaukee, Wis.: Applause Theatre & Cinema Books, 2007. Largely composed of interviews with Boublil and Schönberg and their collaborators, this book provides an insider's view of their creative process.

Waters, Edward N. *Victor Herbert: A Life in Music.* Cambridge, Mass.: Da Capo, 1978. Detailed biography with some musical analysis; many quotations from primary sources.

SELECTED LISTENING

This list mostly comprises the recordings mentioned in the chapters, with a few extras.

AUDIO

Blake, Eubie, and Noble Sissle; Jimmy McHugh and Dorothy Fields. *Songs from* Shuffle Along *and Songs from* Blackbirds. CD. Conducted by Eubie Blake and Lehman Engel. Perf. Cab Calloway, Thelma Carpenter, Avon Long. RCA Victor/Masterworks Broadway. 1952. Four selections each from hit African American musicals of the 1920s, recorded in the 1950s for RCA's "Show Time" series. *Shuffle Along* conducted by composer Eubie Blake.

Bolton, Guy, Schuyler Greene, and Jerome Kern. *Very Good Eddie: The Goodspeed Opera House Production.* CD. Musical dir. Lynn Crigler. Dir. Bill Gile. DRG Records, 1992. Excellent sound quality and performances on the 1978 recording of the Goodspeed revival of this show that transferred to Broadway.

Boublil, Alain, and Claude-Michel Schönberg. *Les Misérables (L'integrale—version originale 1980).* MP3 file, iTunes. The original French concept album, available on CD as well as streaming and download retailers.

Boublil, Alain, Herbert Kretzmer, and Claude-Michel Schönberg. *Les Misérables.* The recordings discussed in chapter 7 (also see above entry for French concept album):

- *Les Misérables (Original Broadway Cast).* Decca Broadway, 1987.

- *Les Misérables Complete Symphonic Recording.* Relativity, First Night Records, 1990. 3-disc set with entire score; recorded in 1988 with an international cast.

- *Les Misérables: In Concert at the Royal Albert Hall.* MP3, iTunes, released 1996 (10th Anniversary "Dream Cast"; also on DVD). First Night Records.

- *Les Misérables Live! (The 2010 Cast Album).* MP3, iTunes, released 2010 (25th Anniversary Production with new orchestrations; also on DVD). First Night Records.

Dante, Nicholas, Marvin Hamlisch, James Kirkwood Jr., and Edward Kleban. *A Chorus Line (Original Broadway Cast)*. CD. Musical dir. Donald Pippin. Dir. Michael Bennett. Masterworks Broadway, 1998. Original 1975 cast album rerelease; rawness and authenticity of performers who developed the show, and the original orchestrations.

———. *A Chorus Line (New Broadway Cast Recording [2006])*. Cond. Patrick Vaccariello. Dir. Bob Avian. Slicker than 1975; contains a little more dialogue for frame of reference.

Gershwin, George, and DuBose Heyward. "Summertime." Of the hundreds of professional recordings of "Summertime," here are the ones discussed in chapter 4.

- Miles Davis: *Porgy and Bess*. New York: Columbia Records, 1959.

- *Gershwin: Porgy and Bess [With Members of the Original Cast]*. CD. Broadway MCA, 1992. Early 1940s recording with Anne Brown, the original Bess; originally released on Decca.

- Billie Holiday. *Lady Day—The Best of Billie Holiday*. Sony Music Entertainment, 2001. The popular release of the Gershwin aria, originally recorded in 1935.

- Fantasia: *I Believe—EP*. MP3 file, iTunes. J Records, 2003.

Hammerstein, Oscar II, and Jerome Kern. *Show Boat: World Premiere Cast Recording*. CD. Perf. Robert Morse, Elaine Stritch, Rebecca Luker, Mark Jacoby, Lonette McKee. Cond. Jeffrey Huard. Dir. Harold Prince. Livent Music, 1994. RSPD 257. Original Toronto cast of Harold Prince 1990s revival.

Hammerstein, Oscar II, and Richard Rodgers. Recording recommendations for their five "greatest hits"—still easy to find original cast recordings, many decades after their premiere.

- *Oklahoma!* Original Broadway cast. Perf. Alfred Drake, Joan Roberts. Cond. Jay Blackton. MCA Classics, 1993. MCAD-10798.

- *Carousel*. Original Broadway cast. Perf. Jan Clayton, John Raitt. Cond. Joseph Littau. MCA Classics, 1993. MCAD-10799.

- *Rodgers and Hammerstein's Carousel*. 1994 Broadway Cast Recording. Perf. Michael Hayden, Sally Murphy, Audra Ann McDonald. Cond. Eric Stern. Angel Records, 1994. CDQ 5 55199 2 4.

- *South Pacific*. Original Broadway cast. Perf. Mary Martin, Ezio Pinza. Cond. Salvatore Dell'Isola. Book and dir. Joshua Logan. Sony Music Entertainment, 2009. 88697 49919 2.

- *The King and I*. Original Broadway cast. Perf. Yul Brynner, Gertrude Lawrence. Cond. Frederick Dvonch. MCA Classics, 1993. MCAD-10049.

- *The Sound of Music*. Original Broadway cast. Perf. Mary Martin. Cond. Frederick Dvonch. Sony Music Entertainment, 1998. SK 60583.

Lloyd Webber, Andrew, with various lyricists. *Andrew Lloyd Webber: Gold—The Definitive Hits Collection*. MP3 file, iTunes. UTV/Decca/Universal Distribution, 2002. A compilation of greatest hits, as well as a few more obscure tracks from *Whistle Down the Wind*.

Miranda, Lin-Manuel. *Hamilton (Original Broadway Cast Recording)*. Cond. Alex Lacamoire. Dir. Thomas Kail. Atlantic Records, 2015. Meticulously recorded and full of "ear candy" techniques associated with hip-hop, released on a variety of streaming services, download retailers, as well as on CD.

———. The Atlantic Records page for the *Hamilton* cast recording also contains links to Spotify playlists of music that inspired the show and its orchestrations, as well links to the booklet containing the credits and lyrics from the show. http://atlanticrecords.com/HamiltonMusic/.

Rado, James, Gerome Ragni, and Galt MacDermot. *Hair (The New Broadway Cast Recording)*. MP3 file, iTunes. Perf. Gavin Creel, Will Swenson. Cond. Nadia DiGiallonardo. Dir. Diane Paulus. Ghostlight Records, 2009. Easy to find on CD as well as streaming services and download retailers; also limited release on vinyl.

———. *Hair*. Original Broadway Cast. Perf. James Rado, Gerome Ragni, Sally Eaton, Shelley Plimpton. RCA Victor, 1968. LSO-1150. This original cast recording was hugely popular during the show's original Broadway run and is still easy to find in a variety of formats.

Sater, Steven, and Duncan Sheik. *Spring Awakening Original Broadway Cast*. CD. Musical dir. Kimberly Grigsby. Dir. Michael Mayer. Decca Broadway, 2006. B0008020-02. Excellent sound and musical direction of original Broadway production.

Schwartz, Stephen (with dialogue by Winnie Holzman). *Wicked (Original Broadway Cast Recording) [Deluxe Edition]*. Perf. Idina Menzel, Kristin Chenoweth. Cond. Stephen Oremus. Dir. Joe Mantello. Decca Broadway/Verve, 2013. B000119534-02. In addition to the original Broadway cast recording, the deluxe edition includes several bonus tracks from pop artists, German and Japanese cast albums, and the composer accompanying Broadway star Stephanie Block on piano. Easy to find on CD as well as streaming services and download retailers.

Sinatra, Frank. *Songs for Young Lovers*. Capitol Records, 1954. Sinatra's seventh studio album, his first on Capitol Records; Great American Songbook standards with arrangements by George Siravo and Nelson Riddle.

VIDEO

The Archive of American Television Presents Anything Goes. DVD. Guy Bolton, Russel Crouse, Howard Lindsay, Cole Porter, P. G. Wodehouse. Perf. Ethel Merman, Frank Sinatra, Bert Lahr. Dir. Sid Smith. Port Washington, N.Y.: Entertainment One U.S. LP, 2011. This one-hour 1954 broadcast decimates farcical plot of *Anything Goes*, but jampacks the hour with Porter's music and provides a peek of early live television and great performers of the day, including the original *Anything Goes* star Ethel Merman.

Broadway: The American Musical. DVD. Dir. Michael Kantor. Arlington, Va.: PBS Home Video, 2004. The public television miniseries hosted by Julie Andrews provides an overview of the American musical through the early 2000s.

The Great Ziegfeld. DVD. Dir. Robert Z. Leonard. Starring William Powell, Myrna Loy, Luise Rainer. Burbank, Calif.: Warner Home Video, 2004. The Oscar-winning 1936 classic captures the essence of Ziegfeld's aesthetic in one of the first big biographical films. Easy to find in multiple formats.

The King and I (50th Anniversary Edition). DVD. Oscar Hammerstein II and Richard Rodgers; screenplay by Ernest Lehman. Los Angeles, Calif.: 20th Century Fox, 2006. Yul Brynner reprises the role he originated on Broadway, opposite Deborah Kerr as Anna. The anniversary edition is full of entertaining special features.

Les Misérables. See under AUDIO: Boublil, Alain, Herbert Kretzmer, and Claude-Michel Schönberg.

Rent: Filmed Live on Broadway. DVD. Jonathan Larson. Dir. Michael John Warren. Culver City, Calif.: Sony Pictures Home Entertainment, 2009. The final cast of *Rent* on Broadway.

Show Boat (1936 film). DVD. Oscar Hammerstein II and Jerome Kern. Dir. James Whale. Perf. Paul Robeson, Irene Dunne, Helen Morgan. Burbank, Calif.: Warner Archive, 2014. Of the three film versions of *Show Boat*, this one is closest to the original stage production, including several cast members from early productions of the show. Rereleased on DVD in 2014.

Sondheim! The Birthday Concert. DVD. Stephen Sondheim and company with the New York Philharmonic. Dir. Lonny Price. Los Angeles, Calif.: Image Entertainment, 2010.

Too many Broadway stars to name in this concert retrospective on the composer's eightieth birthday.

The Sound of Music (50th Anniversary 5-Disc Edition). DVD. Oscar Hammerstein II, Richard Rodgers; Howard Lindsay and Russel Crouse; screenplay by Ernest Lehman. Dir. Robert Wise. Los Angeles, Calif.: 20th Century Fox, 2015. The 1965 classic film adaptation starring Julie Andrews as Maria von Trapp is one of the most well-known films worldwide. The 50th Anniversary Edition includes Blu-ray and DVD and contains special features.

The Sound of Music Live. DVD. Rodgers and Hammerstein; book by Lindsay and Crouse. Universal City, Calif.: Universal Pictures Home Entertainment, 2013. The NBC live broadcast of the stage version, with Carrie Underwood as Maria. The country/pop star received largely critical reviews for her efforts branching out beyond her comfort zone. Broadway talent was cast in other roles, including Laura Benanti, Christian Borle, Audra McDonald, and television star Stephen Moyer as Captain von Trapp.

The Stephen Sondheim Collection. DVD. Los Angeles, Calif.: Image Entertainment, 2003. Includes three original stage productions (*Into the Woods, Sunday in the Park with George*, and *Passion*), as well as concert productions of *Follies* and *Sweeney Todd*, and a star-studded concert at Carnegie Hall.

INDEX

42nd Street (musical), 147

a cappella, 116, 124, 174, 205
AABA form, 56, 105, 118
ABBA, 165
Adamson, Harold, 36
Afrika Bambaataa, 189, 190, 208
"After the Ball" (popular song), 33, 42, 61
Aguirre-Sacasa, Roberto, 180, 207
Ahrens, Lynn, 185
AIDS, 167–168, 171, 172
Albee, Edward Franklin, 27, 28
Allegiance, 207
Allegro, 85
Allen, Sasha, 113
American Idiot, 184
American Idol, 79, 83
American Psycho, 180, 207
Amos, Tori, 180
Andrews, Julie, 85, 103, 104
Annie, 191
Annie Get Your Gun, 85, 98
Anything Goes, 67; interpolations in, 71, 73–74; revisions and versions of, 70–71; *The Colgate Comedy Hour* live broadcast, 69–75
Aronson, Billy, 168
As Thousands Cheer, 66
Ashman, Howard, 165
Aspects of Love, 155
Astin, Skylar, 182

Babes in Arms, 67
Babes in Toyland, 31
Ball, Michael, 155
Bareilles, Sara, 180
baroque, 117, 194
Baum, L. Frank, 3
Beatles, the, 108, 118, 194
Beautiful: The Carole King Story, 207
Beauty and the Beast, 164
Bechdel, Alison, 185
Benanti, Laura, 137
Bennett, Michael, 129, 139
Berlin, Irving, 35, 36, 42, 66, 84–85, 129, 137
Bernstein, Leonard, 85, 128, 131
Beyoncé (Knowles), 195
Bill Haley and His Comets, 108
Billboard charts, 108, 111, 157, 207
Black Crook, The, 22
Black Thought (band member of the Roots), 192
Black, Don, 150, 157
Blackbirds of 1928, 49–50
blackface. *See* minstrel show
Blackton, Jay, 86
Blake, Eubie, 49, 50; biography and musical background of, 47–48; compositional style of, 51; development of *Shuffle Along*, 48
Blitzstein, Marc, 67
Bock, Jerry, 85

Bohéme, La, 168, 170, 171, 173, 174, 175, 178
Bolger, Ray, 36
Bolton, Guy, 41, 44, 70
Bond, Christopher, 136
Bono, 179
book musical, 3, 127, 129, 148, 191
Boublil, Alain, 158, 160–161, 164; lyric-writing technique of, 163; globalization and, 163–164
Boyzone, 157
Bregman, Buddy, 72
Brice, Fanny, 37
Brightman, Sarah, 150, 152, 156, 157
Bring in 'da Noise, Bring in 'da Funk, 187
Bring it On, 191
Brohn, William David, 6
Brooker, Stephen, 161
Brooks, Mel, 185
Brown, Anne, 78
Brown, Roy, 107
Bruce, Virginia, 36
Brynner, Yul, 102
Buck and Stamper, 39
Buckley, Betty, 154
Burke, Billie, 33
Burkhardt, Steel, 120
burlesque, 37
Burns, Jackie, 120
Burrows, Abe, 85
Butler, Michael, 111
Bye Bye Birdie, 108, 187

Cabaret, 127
Caesar, Irving, 75
Can't Help Lovin' Dat Man, 57–58, 60–61, 62
Caldwell, Anne, 45
Calloway, Cab, 50
Cameron, John, 161
Campbell, Alan, 156
Cantor, Eddie, 35, 46
Caramanica, Jon, 191, 196
Caroline, or Change, 185
Carousel, 85, 92–97, 104
Carpenter, Thelma, 50
Carreras, José, 157
Case, Allison, 118
Castle, Vernon and Irene, 48

Cats, ix, 147, 149, 153–154
Cavanaugh, Matt, 133
Cerveris, Michael, 135–136
Chase, Will, 170
Chenoweth, Kristin, 13
Chernow, Ron, 187–188, 200, 204
Chorus Line, A, 128, 129, 140–146; development of, 139–140; original cast of, 140–141
Church, Charlotte, 154
Clark, Victoria, 132
Close, Glenn, 156
Cohan, George M., 29, 31, 191
Colella, Jenn, 133
Color Purple, The, 207
Comden, Betty, 85
Company, 21, 128–129, 137, 139–140, 146
concept album, 148, 151, 153, 154, 157, 158, 160, 161, 162, 163, 179, 198
concept musical, 142, 191; description and examples of, 127–129; in contrast to concept album, 148; influence in *Rent*, 174, 176; influence in *Spring Awakening*, 180
Conrad, Con, 38
Cook, Donald, 54
coon song, 42–43. *See also* Tin Pan Alley
Cooper, Lilli, 182
Cort, Henry, 47
counterpoint, 51, 173, 177, 178, 194
Cradle Will Rock, The, 66–67
Craven, Frank, 45
Crawford, Michael, 152
Creel, Gavin, 114, 116
Crosby, Bing, 70
Crouse, Russel, 70, 103

Da Silva, Howard, 88
Daltrey, David, 153
Daniely, Jason, 132
Dante, Nicholas, 140
Davis, Miles, 77
de Mille, Agnes, 89
DeSylva, Buddy, 35
Diggs, Daveed, 193, 198, 200
DiGiallonardo, Nadia, 113
Disney Theatrical Group, 164–165
DJ Kool Herc, 189

Do I Hear a Waltz, 131
Doctorow, E. L., 185
Donaldson, Walter, 36
Donovan, Jason, 153
Douglas, Larry, 101
Doyle, Buddy, 35
Drake, Alfred, 87–88
Dreamgirls, 147
Du Barry Was a Lady, 73
Dunne, Irene, 55

Earl, Shaun, 175
Eaton, Sally, 115
eleven o'clock number, 137
Eliot, T. S., 149, 153–154
Elliman, Yvonne, 154
Espinosa, Eden, 174
Estefan, Emilio and Gloria, 207
Europe, James Reese, 48
Evita, 148, 149, 150, 152, 155

Fain, Sammy, 67
Fairbank, Spring, 45
Fairbanks twins, 39
Fantasia, 79
Ferber, Edna, 52, 54, 62
Fiddler on the Roof, 85, 207
Fields, Dorothy, 49, 50, 85, 138
Fields, Herbert, 85
Fifty Million Frenchmen, 50, 71
Flaherty, Stephen, 185
Flower Drum Song, 85
Follies (Sondheim musical), 50, 129, 133, 135, 137, 138, 139, 149. *See also* Ziegfeld Follies
Foster, Stephen, 24, 42
Foster, Sutton, 70
Four Seasons, The (popular band), 108, 165
Franglen, Simon, 157
Freedman, Gerald, 111
freestyle, 191, 193
Frühlings Erwachen: Eine Kindertragödie, 179
Fun Home, 185
Funny Thing Happened on the Way to the Forum, A, 128
Furth, George, 128, 134

Gallagher, John Jr., 181
Garde, Betty, 87
Gardner, Ava, 53
Garland, Judy, 3, 29
Gee, Lottie, 51
Gemignani, Alexander, 131
Gemignani, Paul, 130, 131, 135
Gentleman's Guide to Love and Murder, A, 207
Gershwin, George, 35, 67, 78, 79; biography and musical background of, 75–76; compositional style of, 66, 78, 79–80, 81; development of *Porgy and Bess*, 76–77, 80
Gilbert and Sullivan, 30
Ginsberg, Allen, 122–123
Gleason, Joanna, 134
Glee, xix, 83
Godspell, 2, 16
Goldman, James, 129
Goldsberry, Renée Elise, 171, 173, 194–195
Goss, Andrea, 175
Graham, Harry, 45
Grandmaster Flash, 189, 191
Grease, ix, 83, 125, 184
Great American Songbook, the, xxi, 15, 67, 81, 131, 137
Great Depression, the, 38, 65, 67, 84
Great Ziegfeld, The, 33–39, 42
Green Grow the Lilacs, 83, 90
Green, Adolph, 85
Green, Amanda, 191
Greene, Schuyler, 41, 45
Groff, Jonathan, 181, 194, 202
Guettel, Adam, 185
Gunn, Nathan, 132–133
Guys and Dolls, 85
gypsy (Broadway chorus member), 139
Gypsy (Broadway show), 26, 128

Hair, 107; development of, 109–111; film adaptation of, 111; hippie culture, 108–109, 110, 112, 113; legacy of, 125; musicians and orchestrations of, 112–113; revival cast album, 112–124; spirituality in music of, 116, 119, 121, 124–125; Vietnam War and, 111, 112,

119, 121–123. *See also* MacDermot,
Galt; Rado, James; Ragni, Gerome
Hall, Adelaide, 48–49
Hamilton: An American Musical, 184,
187; Broadway cast album, 192–205;
hip-hop culture and, 188, 190; hip-hop
influences and references in, 191–192,
193, 194, 195, 197, 199, 200; lyric
techniques of, 195–196, 198; motivic
development in score of, 197, 199,
201, 202, 203, 205; orchestrations of,
192–193, 197–198, 200; recording and
production techniques in, 192–193.
See also hip-hop; Miranda, Lin-
Manuel; rap
Hamlisch, Marvin, 140
Hammerstein, Oscar I, 21
Hammerstein, Oscar II, 67, 208;
biography and early career, 51–52;
innovation in form of musicals, 51, 61,
63, 86, 100, 102, 103, 128, 206; lyrics
and writing style of, 55, 59, 60, 61, 89,
91, 93, 97; mentorship of Stephen
Sondheim, 128, 132; work on *Show
Boat*, 52, 53, 56. *See also* Rodgers and
Hammerstein, *Show Boat*
Harburg, E.Y. (Yip), 133
Harcourt, Sydney James, 201
Harnick, Sheldon, 85
Harris, Charles K., 33, 42
Hart, Charles, 150
Hart, Lorenz, 67, 83–84, 132
Hart, Moss, 66
Hayden, Michael, 93
Head, Murray, 151
Hearn, George, 135–136
Helburn, Theresa, 83–84
Held, Anna, 33, 34, 36
Hellzapoppin', 67
Hendrix, Jimi, 109, 122
Herbert, Victor, 30–31, 32, 41, 129
Heyward, DuBose, 67, 76–77, 78, 80–81
Hicks, Rodney, 171
High Fidelity, 187
hip-hop, x, xix, 43, 194, 199, 200, 204;
culture of, 188–190, 193, 208;
emergence on Broadway, 187–188,
192; recording techniques of, 192, 205;
storytelling devices in, 193, 206. *See*

also freestyle; *Hamilton*; Miranda, Lin-
Manuel; rap
Hoctor, Harriet, 38
Hohl, Arthur, 55
Holiday, Billie, 78–79
Holler If Ya Hear Me, 187
Hollywood, 36, 80, 84, 107
Holm, Celeste, 90
Holzman, Winnie, 2, 8
Hoven, Blaine, 136
Hudes, Quiara Alegría, 191
Hugo, Victor, 158, 159, 160

I-want song, 8, 13, 201
In Dahomey, 25, 62
In the Heights, 188, 191, 196
integration (dramatic), 3, 39, 41, 44, 46,
52, 60, 63, 65–66, 84, 86, 89, 92, 115,
129, 144, 180, 191, 206. *See also* book
musical
interpolation, 31, 44, 45, 46, 71, 73
Into the Woods, 130, 133–134, 139

Jackson, Christopher, 194, 201
Jahnke, Christopher, 161
James, Marcus Paul, 175
Janis, Elsie, 45
Jasperson, Thayne, 194
jazz, 28, 50, 66, 75, 77, 81, 107, 110, 138,
185, 188, 196, 200
Jersey Boys, 165, 207
Jesus Christ Superstar, 125, 148, 151, 154,
161, 184
John, Elton, ix, 165
Johnson, Catherine, 165
Johnston, Justin, 171
Jolson, Al, 75
Jones, Allan, 35, 55
Jones, Jasmine Cephas, 194, 195, 200
Jones, Tom, 157
Joplin, Janis, 78, 109
Joplin, Scott, 43
*Joseph and the Amazing Technicolor
Dreamcoat*, 148, 153
Jubilee, 73
jukebox musicals, 165, 180, 187, 207

Kander and Ebb, 127
Kantor, Adam, 170

Kaufman, George S., 66
Keith, Benjamin Franklin, 27, 28, 29
Kern, Jerome, 32, 36, 37, 45, 51, 120, 133; compositional style of, 55, 56, 58, 60; innovation and influence in musical form, 44, 51, 63, 146, 191, 206; biography and musical background of, 41, 43–44; Princess Theatre musicals and, 44; work on *Show Boat*, 51–52, 53
Kerr, Deborah, 102
King and I, The, 85, 100–103, 105
King, Carole, 207
Kinky Boots, 179
Kirkwood, James Jr., 140
Kiss Me, Kate, 85
Kitt, Tom, 191
Kiyan, Kaitlin, 120
Klaw and Erlanger, 34
Kleban, Edward, 140, 142
Kober, Andrew, 120
Korbich, Eddie, 94
Kretzmer, Herbert, 158, 160, 163
Kron, Lisa, 185
Kushner, Tony, 185

Lacamoire, Alex, 192, 197
LaChiusa, Michael John, 185
Lady Be Good, 76
Lahr, Bert, 69, 71, 73, 75
Lapine, James, 133, 134, 135
Larson, Jonathan, 168, 170, 177, 178, 208
Last Ship, The, 179
Latham, Tim, 205
Lauper, Cyndi, 179
Laurents, Arthur, 85, 128, 131
Lawrence, Gertrude, 100, 101, 102
Lawrence, Megan, 120
Lawrence, Rosina, 37
Lea Michele (Sarfati), 181
Leary, Timothy, 114
Lehár, Franz, 30
Lerner and Loewe, 85
Leroux, Gaston, 150
Les Misérables, ix, 159, 194; development of, 158–159; French concept album, 158, 161, 162, 163; international reach of, 147, 163–164; orchestrations of, 161–162; vocal interpretations of roles in, 162–163. *See also* Boublil, Alain;

Schönberg, Claude-Michel

Leslie, Lew, 49
"Let the Sun Shine In", 124, 125, 206
Leung, Telly, 184
Leventon, Annabel, 117
Levy, Caissie, 115, 118
Lewis, Nicole, 120
Light in the Piazza, The, 185
Liliom, 92
Lindsay-Abaire, David, 185
Lindsay, Howard, 70, 103
Lion King, The, 165
Lippa, Andrew, 185
list song, 74, 116, 138, 174
Little Night Music, A, 129, 138
Lloyd Webber, Andrew, 150, 152, 161, 164, 207; biography and musical background of, 148–149; business acumen of, 148, 149–150, 152–153, 156, 157, 158; collaboration with lyricists, 149, 152; compositional style of, 148–149, 151, 154, 155, 156; innovations of, 149; international reach of, 147, 157–158, 164; Sondheim and, 149, 151
Loesser, Frank, 85
Logan, Joshua, 97
London, 30, 34, 53, 54, 69, 74, 147, 148, 150. *See also* West End
Long, Avon, 50
Lorraine, Lillian, 36
Loy, Myrna, 33
Lupino, Angela, 157
LuPone, Patti, 70, 136, 137, 150, 155
Lyles, Aubrey, 47–48

MacDermot, Galt, 110, 113, 118, 119, 123, 125, 141
Mackintosh, Cameron, 150, 158, 164–165
Madonna (Ciccone), 152
Maguire, Gregory, 3
Maltby, Richard Jr., 150
Mamma Mia, 165
Marbury, Elisabeth (Bessie), 44
march, 17, 18, 22, 31, 33, 38, 43, 74–75, 89, 105, 115, 122, 123
March, Joseph Moncure, 185
Martin, Mary, 98, 103, 104, 105

Mazzie, Marin, 132, 137, 138
McDaniel, Hattie, 54
McDonald, Audra, 49, 83, 93, 133, 137, 138
McElroy, Michael, 171
McGuire, William Anthony, 33
McHugh, Jimmy, 49, 50
McKechnie, Donna, 140, 143
McKee, Lonette, 63
McMartin, John, 133
Menken, Alan, 165
Menzel, Idina, 13
Merman, Ethel, 26, 69–75, 128
Merrily We Roll Along, 134, 135, 138
Merry Widow, The, 30
Metcalfe, Stephen, 161
Meyer, Joseph, 35
Michener, James, 97–98
Miller, Flournoy, 47–49
Miller, Marilyn, 37
Minaj, Nicki, 195
minstrel shows: African American
    performers and, 24–25, 26;
    development of, 23, 24; influence on
    American entertainment, 24, 26, 27,
    58; minstrel songs, 24, 42, 51, 63;
    minstrel troupes, 24; racism and, 23,
    35, 42, 55, 58, 102, 114, 121–122. See
    also musicals and race
Miranda, Lin-Manuel, 187, 188, 192, 193,
    201; biography and musical
    background of, 191; compositional
    style of, 197; lyrical style of, 195–196,
    198
Molnár, Ferenc, 92, 97
Moore, Melba, 113
Morgan, Dennis, 35
Morgan, Helen, 54, 60, 63
Morris, Gary, 163
Morrow, Doretta, 101
Motown, 120, 143
Mueller, Jessie, 207
Murphy, Donna, 137
Murphy, Sally, 93
musicals and gay culture, 68–69, 114,
    167–168
musicals and immigration, 22, 28, 37, 51
musicals and race, xxi, 22, 23–24, 25–26,
    42–43, 47, 49, 50, 51, 53, 54, 55, 57,
    62–63, 79, 80–81, 102–103, 115, 188,
    206, 207
musicals and women, xx–xxi, 23–24, 27,
    44, 95–96, 102, 108, 120–121
My Fair Lady, 85

Natel, Jean-Marc, 158
New York City, 1, 21, 41, 75, 80, 109, 110,
    113, 120, 173, 188–189, 191, 193
New York Philharmonic, 130, 133
New York Shakespeare Fesitval, 109–110,
    112
New York Theatre Workshop, 168
New York Times, The, 21, 107, 168, 191,
    207
Neway, Patricia, 104
Nichols, Darius, 114, 120
Nogee, Rori, 169
Notorious B.I.G., The, 190, 191, 194, 197,
    200
Nunn, Trevor, 154, 158

O'Horgan, Tom, 111
Odom, Leslie Jr., 193
Of Thee I Sing, 66
Offenbach, Jacques, 29
Oh, Lady! Lady!!, 44
Oklahoma!, 65, 84, 85, 86, 87–92
Old Possum's Book of Practical Cats, 149
Olivieri, Guy, 169
Olivo, Karen, 131
On the Town, 85
On Your Feet, 207
Onaodowan, Okieriete, 193, 200
opera, 13, 27, 29, 30, 31, 35, 52, 55, 75,
    77, 98, 157, 171, 178; fine line between
    musical theater and, 53, 79–81, 130,
    136, 152, 176; influence on musical
    theater, 39, 86, 154, 163, 170, 185,
    195; operetta and, 29–30; parody of in
    musical theater, 27, 37, 117. See also
    Porgy and Bess; Rent
operetta, 22, 44, 47, 52, 185, 207;
    influence on musical theater, 29–30,
    30–31, 51, 55; decline in popularity,
    31, 65; resurgence of, 146, 147
orchestration, 5, 6, 15, 19, 35, 72, 79, 80,
    120, 141, 143, 144, 152, 155, 157, 182;
    in Les Misérables, 160, 161–162; in

Hamilton, 192–193, 197–198, 200; Lloyd Webber and, 153; Sondheim and, 132–133
Osmond, Donny, 153
Osnes, Laura, 133
ostinato, 136, 177, 197
Owen-Jones, John, 163

Papp, Joseph, 110
pastiche, 129, 132–133, 137, 149
Pastor, Tony, 27, 30
Patinkin, Mandy, 134, 135, 150, 155
Paulus, Diane, 112
Peacock, Michon, 139
Pearson, Brandon, 120
pentatonic scale, 56, 101, 157, 198
Peter Pan, 83
Peters, Bernadette, 135, 137, 138
Phantom of the Opera, The, 147, 150, 152, 155, 156
Pierce, David Hyde, 130, 137
Pink Floyd, 148, 151
Pins and Needles, 67
Pinza, Ezio, 98
Pipe Dream, 85
Pippin, 2
plagal cadence, 116, 125
Plummer, Christopher, 103
Plumpton, Alfred, 34
pointillism, 135
Porgy and Bess, 67, 77; development of, 76–77; relationship to opera, 79–81. *See also* Gershwin, George; Summertime
Porter, Cole, 67, 69, 70, 85, 129; biography and musical background of, 68–69; compositional and lyrical style, 69, 71, 72, 73, 74, 75; homosexuality and, 68–69
Powell, William, 33
Presley, Elvis, 108
Pretty Girl is Like a Melody, A, 35, 137
Prince, Harold, 128–129
Princess Theatre, 43–44, 45–46, 70, 133
Pritchard, Lauren, 182
Producers, The, 185
Public Theater, The, 109–110, 111–112, 118, 140, 145, 187
Puccini, Giacomo, 98, 149, 168, 170

Pulizter Prize, 52, 66, 76, 97, 142

Questlove, 191–192

radio, x, 53, 87, 107, 167, 179, 192
Rado, James, 110, 111, 113, 114, 116, 125
Ragni, Gerome, 110, 111, 113, 114, 125
Ragtime (Flaherty and Ahrens musical), 185
ragtime (musical genre), 22, 24, 31, 41, 43, 48, 51, 61, 90, 107, 185
Rainer, Luise, 33
Ramos, Anthony, 193, 203
rap, 187, 188, 190, 193, 194, 195, 196, 197, 198, 200, 202, 207
Razaf, Andy, 49
Really Useful Group, 149, 153, 164
recitative, 80, 155, 170
Reds (Warren Beatty film), 136
reggae, 199
Reinking, Megan, 120
Rent, 208; cultural significance of, 168, 169, 184, 185; development of, 168; operatic elements of, 170, 174, 175, 176, 178; *Rent Filmed Live on Broadway*, 169–179; Rentheads, 169, 170. *See also La Bohéme*; Larson, Jonathan
Repole, Charles, 45
Requiem (Lloyd Webber piece), 150, 154
revue, 31–32, 38, 39, 44, 45, 49, 50, 65, 66, 67, 108, 127, 129
Reynolds, Herbert, 45
Rhapsody in Blue, 35, 75
rhythm & blues, 79, 107–108, 122
Riccetto, Maria, 136
Rice, Thomas "Daddy", 23
Rice, Tim, 148, 149, 152, 165
Richard, Cliff, 156
Riddle, Nelson, 72–73
Riggs, Lynn, 83
Robbins, Jerome, 128
Roberts, Joan, 89, 90
Robeson, Paul, 48–49, 54, 56, 59
rock and roll, 165, 192, 198; effect on singing of, 117–118, 141, 163; elements of in *Les Misérables*, 158, 161, 162; elements of in Lloyd Webber, 151, 152, 154, 155, 156;

elements of in *Wicked*, 2, 4, 9, 16;
emergence as a popular form,
107–108, 167; emergence on
Broadway of, 107, 111, 125, 127, 187;
rock in musicals. *See Hair*; jukebox
musicals; *Rent*; *Spring Awakening*
Rock of Ages, 165
Rodgers and Hammerstein, 97, 153, 206;
as producers, 164; first collaboration,
83–84; innovations in musical form of,
85–86, 102–103, 106; major works, 85;
writing style of, 87, 89, 91, 92, 93, 94,
96, 97, 99, 100, 101, 105
Rodgers, Mary, 132
Rodgers, Richard, 87, 97, 131;
compositional style of, 86, 88, 89, 90,
91, 93, 95, 96–98, 99, 100, 101,
105–106; influence of Jerome Kern on,
41, 120; Lorenz Hart and, 67, 83–84,
85, 132
Roots, the, 191, 192
Royal Shakespeare Company, 158
Rua, Jon, 197
rubato, 46, 96, 107, 154
Ryness, Bruce, 114
Ryskind, Morrie, 66

Sally, 37, 60
sampling (musical technique), xix, 162,
174, 190, 191, 192
Sater, Steven, 179, 180, 181
Saturday Night, 137
Scanlan, Dick, 31, 185
Schönberg, Claude-Michel, 158, 160, 161,
163, 164
School of Rock, 150, 207
Schwartz, Stephen: biography and major
works of, 2, 16; compositional style of,
4, 6, 8, 15, 16, 17, 18
Scotto, Vincent, 34
Seidel, Virginia, 45
Sengbloh, Seycon, 120, 121
sentimental ballad, 42. *See also* Tin Pan
Alley
Seurat, George, 134–135, 138
Seven Lively Arts, 67
Shakespeare, 109, 110, 112, 123, 158, 200
Shakur, Tupac, 187, 190

Sheik, Duncan, 179–180, 181, 182, 183,
207
Sheik, Kacie, 115
Show Boat, x, 38, 42, 48, 65, 84, 90, 206;
commercial success of, 53, 150;
development of, 51–53; film version,
1936, 53–62; film version, 1951, 53;
innovations in musical form of, 56–57,
59, 65–66, 80, 84; performance of race
in, 56–57, 58, 62–63. *See also*
Hammerstein, Oscar II; Kern, Jerome
Shrek, 185
Shuffle Along: 2016 Broadway production
of, 49–50; commercial success of, 47,
49; development of, 47–49;
innovations of, 49, 51; *Songs
from* Blackbirds of 1928 *and* Shuffle
Along, 50–51
Sinatra, Frank, 70, 71–74, 75, 129
Siravo, George, 73
Sissle, Noble, 47–48, 51
Slater, Glenn, 150, 207
Smash (TV show), 83
Smiles of a Summer Night, 129
Smith, Harry B., 22, 45, 47
Sondheim, Stephen, xxi, 21, 50, 81, 85,
136, 141, 155, 177; biography and
musical background of, 128;
compositional style of, 128–129, 133,
134, 135, 136–137, 138–139; concept
musicals and, 128–129; Hammerstein
and, 128, 132; Lloyd Webber and, 149,
151; lyrical style of, 128, 129–132, 133,
136; *Sondheim! The Birthday Concert*,
130–139, 150
Song and Dance (Lloyd Webber musical),
150
song plugger, 41–42, 43, 75
Soo, Phillipa, 194
sound department, 5
Sound of Music, The, 83, 85, 103–106,
153, 164
Sounds of Blackness, 157
Sousa, John Philip, 22, 33
South Pacific, 85, 97–100, 105, 106, 208
Spewack, Bella and Samuel, 85
Spider-Man: Turn Off the Dark, 179
Spring Awakening, 183, 184; concept
musical elements of, 180; development

of, 179; Original Broadway cast album, 181–184; synopsis of, 180–181. *See also* Sater, Steven; Sheik, Duncan
Starlight Express, 149, 150
Steggert, Bobby, 133
Stein, Joseph, 85
Steinman, Jim, 156, 157
Stevens, Tony, 139–140
Stewart, Gwen, 175
Stilgoe, Richard, 150
Sting, 179
Stop! Look! Listen!, 22
Stowe, Harriet Beecher, 101–102
Strauss, Johann, 30
Streisand, Barbra, 129, 151–152
Stritch, Elaine, 137–138
Styne, Jule, 128
Sugar Hill Gang, 187
"Summertime" (Gershwin/Heyward song), 81; aria from *Porgy and Bess*, 77–78; Billie Holiday recording, 78–79; Fantasia recording, 79; Miles Davis recording, 77. *See also* Brown, Anne; *Porgy and Bess*
Sunday in the Park with George, 134–135, 138–139
Sunny, 52
Sunset Boulevard, 151, 156
Survival of St. Joan, The, 16
Sweeney Todd, 130, 132, 135–136, 139
Swenson, Will, 113
Swerling, Jo, 85
Sykes, Ephraim, 203
syncopation, 24, 31, 43, 61, 62, 71, 73, 90, 106, 116, 121, 123, 145, 171, 177, 185
synthesizers, 152, 154, 161–162, 174, 176

Tales From the South Pacific, 97
television, ix, xix, xxi, 2, 69–73, 130, 152, 153, 167, 191, 207
Tesori, Jeanine, 31, 185
Theatre Guild, the, 81, 83
Thomas, Linda Lee, 68–69
Thoms, Tracie, 172, 173
Thomson, Virgil, 79, 81
Thoroughly Modern Millie, 31, 185
Times Square, 22, 139, 165
Tin Pan Alley, 41–42, 44, 45, 56, 77, 105, 129, 144, 180

Tobias, Charles, 67
Tommy, the Who's, ix, 148
Tony Award, 154, 168, 185, 188, 207
Toy Johnson, Christine, 206
Trav S. D., 25, 27
Truskinoff, David, 170
Tunick, Jonathan, 132–133, 141
Turner, Big Joe, 107–108
Twitty, Conway, 108

U2, 179
Uncle Tom's Cabin, 102
Underwood, Carrie, 83
unison, 9, 11, 14, 18, 99, 113, 175, 182, 205

Valli, Frankie, 165, 207
vaudeville, 30, 32, 34, 39, 127; Broadway performers with background in, 26, 28, 29, 47, 48, 52, 69–70; business model of, 26, 27, 28; family-friendly entertainment and, 27, 32; minstrel show and, 24, 25; technology and the rise of, 27–28, 54; types of acts in, 27, 36, 49; vaudeville circuits, 28. *See also* minstrel show; revue
Verdi, Guiseppe, 29
Verrett, Shirley, 97
verse-chorus form, 60, 158
Very Good Eddie, 41; Goodspeed cast recording, 45–47. *See also* Kern, Jerome; Princess Theatre
vocal styles and techniques,: backphrase, 73, 138; belt, 13, 14, 71, 113, 117–118, 120, 151, 154, 173, 182, 185; chest voice, 79, 105; falsetto, 163; head voice, 79, 118; mix, 79, 120, 182; straight tone, 154, 163; vibrato, 18, 35, 121, 163
Vrtacnik, Fedor, 157

Wagner, Richard, 29, 195
Walker, George, 25
Walton, Jim, 134
waltz, 7, 11, 15, 22, 30, 31, 42, 43, 51, 58, 89, 93, 99, 100, 105, 106, 129, 137, 170, 175, 178
Watch Your Step, 22
Waters, Ethel, 28, 66

Wedekind, Frank, 179

West End, 53, 74, 147–148, 149, 152, 153, 156, 157, 158, 159, 161, 163, 164, 165

West Side Story, 85, 128, 131, 137, 191

Westley, Helen, 54

Whistle Down the Wind, 156–157

Whiteman, Paul, 75

Wicked, xx, 5–20; as frame of reference for modern musicals, 1–3, 7, 20; musical style and themes of, 4, 6, 16, 20; "unlimited" theme, 6, 8, 10, 13, 15, 18, 19, 20; *The Wizard of Oz* and, 3, 6, 9, 17, 19, 20. *See also* Holzman, Winnie; Schwartz, Stephen

Wild Party, The, 185

Wilkinson, Colm, 163, 164

Williams, Bert, 25, 28, 103

Wiz, The, 3, 83, 125

Wizard of Oz, The, 3, 6, 9, 17, 19, 20, 33, 36, 69

Wodehouse, P.G., 44, 45, 60, 70, 74

Wolfe, George C., 49

Wyman, Nicholas, 45

yellowface, 102. *See also* musicals and race

Ziegfeld, Florenz, 25, 152; biography and theatrical background, 31–32; *Great Ziegfeld, The*, 33–39, 42; influence on form of musicals, 33, 38–39, 129, 141, 146, 147; *Show Boat* and, 52–53, 60, 62, 63, 150. *See also* Brice, Fanny; Held, Anna; Williams, Bert

Ziegfeld Follies, the, 32, 34–35, 46, 49, 108, 147; "A Follies Salad", 39, 44; glorifying the American girl and, 32, 33, 36–37, 38, 44, 144; *See also Follies* (Sondheim musical)

Zien, Chip, 134

ABOUT THE AUTHOR

Kat Sherrell is a conductor/pianist/writer originally from New Mexico. Her work in New York has included Broadway shows *In the Heights*, *Bring It On*, and *The Book of Mormon* and NBC's *Smash*, as well as many new musicals in various stages of development, including *Sweethearts of Swing*, for which she is the lyricist-composer. Sherrell currently resides in Seattle, where she is the associate music supervisor at the 5th Avenue Theatre.